The Revolution Will Not Be Funded

The Revolution Will Not Be Funded

beyond the non-profit industrial complex

edited by
INCITE! Women of Color Against Violence

South End Press ▷ Cambridge, Massachusetts ▷ Read. Write. Revolt.

The views expressed in the book belong to the authors and not the institutions with which they are affiliated.

cover design: Design Action Collective/Innosanto Nagara
cover photo credits: *(top)* Convention at the New Orleans Aquarium.
   Image © 1993 by Bob Sacha/Corbis; *(bottom)* Collage provided courtesy of
   Design Action Collective

page design and production: South End Press Collective/Jocelyn Burrell
This book was designed using Adobe InDesign and Adobe Illustrator CS2.

Library of Congress Cataloging-in-Publication Data
The revolution will not be funded : beyond the non-profit industrial complex /
edited by Incite! Women of Color Against Violence.
   p. cm.
 Includes bibliographical references.
  ISBN: 978-0-89608-766-8 (pbk. : alk. paper)
1. Social justice. 2. Social movements. 3. Social change. 4. Distributive justice.
5. Poverty. 6. Women's rights. 7. Non-governmental organizations. I. Incite!
Women of Color Against Violence

HM671.R48 2007
303.48'4--dc22

                                    2006037819

Printed with union labor in Canada on acid-free, recycled paper.

   12 11 10 09 08 07   2 3 4 5

South End Press
7 Brookline Street, Suite #1
Cambridge, MA 02139
http://www.southendpress.org
southend@southendpress.org

▸▸contents

The Revolution Will Not Be Funded

>>Andrea Smith

introduction

The Revolution Will Not Be Funded

IN 2004, INCITE! WOMEN OF COLOR AGAINST VIOLENCE LEARNED
the hard way that the revolution will not be funded. INCITE! began in 2000,
with the purpose of supporting a movement of feminists of color organizing
against all forms of violence—from interpersonal to state violence. When we first
organized, we were generally funded through individual donations. However,
by 2002, we found ourselves increasingly more successful in securing foundation grants to support our work. We took a stand against state funding since
we perceived that antiviolence organizations who had state funding had been
co-opted. It never occurred to us to look at foundation funding in the same way.
However, in a trip to India (funded, ironically, by the Ford Foundation), we met
with many non-funded organizations that criticized us for receiving foundation
grants. When we saw that groups with much less access to resources were able to
do amazing work without funding, we began to question our reliance on foundation grants.

Our growing suspicions about foundation grants were confirmed when, in
February 2004, INCITE! received an e-mail from the Ford Foundation with the
subject line "Congratulations!" and an offer of "a one-year or two-year grant of
$100,000" to cover our general operating expenses in response to a grant proposal
the Ford Foundation had solicited from us. Excited about the news, we committed to two major projects: the Sisterfire multimedia tour, which was organized
for 2004, and the third Color of Violence conference, to be held in New Orleans
in 2005. Then, unexpectedly on July 30, 2004, the Ford Foundation sent another
letter, explaining that it had reversed its decision because of our organization's
statement of support for the Palestinian liberation struggle. Apparently, during
the board approval process, a board member decided to investigate INCITE!
further and disapproved of what s/he found on our website. INCITE! quickly
learned from firsthand experience the deleterious effects foundations can have
on radical social justice movements. However, we also learned that social jus-

tice organizations do not always need the foundation support they think they do. Strapped with this sudden loss of funding but committed to organizing two major projects, INCITE! members started raising money through grassroots fundraising—house parties, individual calls, T-shirt sales, and so on—and we were able to quickly raise the money we lost when the Ford Foundation rescinded their grant offer.

This story is not an isolated incident of a social justice organization finding itself in a precarious state as a result of foundation funding (specifically, a lack thereof). Since the late 1970s, social justice organizations within the US have operated largely within the 501(c)(3) non-profit model, in which donations made to an organization are tax deductible, in order to avail themselves of foundation grants. Despite the legacy of grassroots, mass-movement building we have inherited from the 1960s and 70s, contemporary activists often experience difficulty developing, or even imagining, structures for organizing outside this model. At the same time, however, social justice organizations across the country are critically rethinking their investment in the 501(c)(3) system. Funding cuts from foundations affected by the current economic crisis and increased surveillance by the Department of Homeland Security have encouraged social justice organizations to assess opportunities for funding social change that do not rely so heavily upon state structures. *The Revolution Will Not Be Funded: Beyond the Non-Profit Industrial Complex* represents a collaborative effort to address these issues and envision new possibilities and models for future organizing. Several key issues are explored:

▷ *How did the 501(c)(3), or non-profit, model develop, and for what reasons? How did this model impact the direction of social justice organizing?*

▷ *How has funding from foundations impacted the course of social justice movements?*

▷ *How does 501(c)(3) status impact the relationship of social justice organizations to the state and give it opportunities to co-opt movements?*

▷ *Are there ways the non-profit model can be used to support more radical visions for social change?*

▷ *What alternatives to 501(c)(3) are there for building viable social justice movements in the US?*

▷ *What models for organizing outside the non-profit/NGO (nongovernmental organization) model exist outside the US that may help us?*

This anthology is not primarily concerned with particular types of non-profits or foundations, but the non-profit industrial complex (or the NPIC, to be defined later in the introduction) as a whole and the way in which capitalist interests and the state use non-profits to

> ▷ *monitor and control social justice movements;*
> ▷ *divert public monies into private hands through foundations;*
> ▷ *manage and control dissent in order to make the world safe for capitalism;*
> ▷ *redirect activist energies into career-based modes of organizing instead of mass-based organizing capable of actually transforming society;*
> ▷ *allow corporations to mask their exploitative and colonial work practices through "philanthropic" work;*
> ▷ *encourage social movements to model themselves after capitalist structures rather than to challenge them*

The Revolution Will Not Be Funded offers no simple answers to these questions, but hopes to continue a conversation about how to think beyond state-proctored models like the non-profit system for organizing political projects for social change. The contributors are a multigenerational assembly of organizers working inside and outside the NPIC from a variety of—even conflicting—perspectives. Before assessing these issues, however, we need to understand how the non-profit system became the predominant model within social movements today.

history of the non-profit system

Prior to the Civil War, individuals, not organizations, did most charity work. However, in the face of accelerating industrialization and accompanying social ills, such as increased poverty, community breakdown to facilitate the flow of labor, and violence, local organizations (generally headed by community elites) developed to assist those seen to be "deserving" of assistance, such as widows and children. These charities focused on individual poverty rather than poverty on the systemic level. Charities did not campaign for higher wages, for instance, but worked to ameliorate the impact of low wages on communities. As this charity movement spread, local charity organizations began to organize on the national level. In 1874, members of private charity organizations, religious agencies, and public officials from several northeastern states established the National Conference of Charities and Corrections to discuss mutual concerns (later renamed the National Conference on Social Welfare).[1]

This system of charitable giving increased exponentially during the early 1900s when the first multimillionaire robber barons, such as John D. Rockefeller, Andrew Carnegie, and Russell Sage, created new institutions that would exist in perpetuity and support charitable giving in order to shield their earnings from taxation.[2] Before the 1950s, charities were generally unregulated because few states imposed taxes on corporations; only the largest foundations with the wealthiest donors required charitable deductions. The first such foundation was organized by Margaret Olivia Slocum Sage, who, using the $70 million left to her by railroad giant Russell Sage started the Russell Sage Foundation in 1907. She was followed by Rockefeller in 1910 and Carnegie in 1911. By 1955, donations from individuals, foundations, and corporations totaled $7.7 billion, according to the American Association of Fundraising Counsel Trust for Philanthropy. By 1978, that total had grown to $39 billion. In 1998, the last year of available data, total giving had risen to $175 billion.[3]

Along with the growth in donations came a huge swell in the number of non-profit organizations. In many cases, these foundations served as tax shelters so that corporations could avoid taxes and descendants could receive their inheritance without paying estate taxes. Early on, many of these organizations employed those who had been part of the charity movement, but, unlike their charity movement predecessors, these foundations' purviews would be general, rather than specific, and their governance would rely on private, self-perpetuating boards of trustees or directors. From their inception, foundations focused on research and dissemination of information designed ostensibly to ameliorate social issues—in a manner, however, that did not challenge capitalism. For instance, in 1913, Colorado miners went on strike against Colorado Fuel and Iron, an enterprise of which 40 percent was owned by Rockefeller. Eventually, this strike erupted into open warfare, with the Colorado militia murdering several strikers during the Ludlow Massacre of April 20, 1914. During that same time, Jerome Greene, the Rockefeller Foundation secretary, identified research and information to quiet social and political unrest as a foundation priority. The rationale behind this strategy was that while individual workers deserved social relief, organized workers in the form of unions were a threat to society. So the Rockefeller Foundation heavily advertised its relief work for individual workers while at the same time promoting a pro-Rockefeller spin to the massacre. For instance, it sponsored speakers to claim that no massacre had happened and tried to block the publication of reports that were critical of Rockefeller.[4] According to Frederick Gates, who helped run the Rockefeller Foundation, the "danger is not the combination of capital, it is not the Mexican situation, it is the labor monopoly; and the danger of the labor monopoly lies in its use of armed force, its organized and deliberate war on society."[5]

Even in this earliest stage of foundation development, critics noted the potential danger of large private foundations. In 1916, the US Commission on Industrial Relations (also known as the Walsh Commission) filed a report on labor issues with Congress warning that foundations were a "grave menace"[6] because they concentrated wealth and power in the service of ideology which supported the interests of their capitalist benefactors. According to Samuel Gompers's testimony in the commission's report, "In the effort to undertake to be an all-pervading machinery for the molding of the minds of the people...in the constant industrial struggle for human betterment...[foundations] should be prohibited from exercising their functions, either by law or regulation."[7]

The Walsh report called on Congress to more strictly regulate foundations, which it did not do, given the state's historic relationship with capital. However, the resulting negative publicity encouraged foundations to fund intermediaries, such as universities, rather than doing research themselves, so that the results of such research would be more convincingly objective.[8]

During the Great Depression, the societal influence of foundations was curtailed by economic crisis. However, after World War II, particularly with the emergence of the Ford Foundation (founded in 1936), foundations regained prominence, and focused on how they could further the interests of US-style democracy domestically and abroad.[9] The Ford Foundation became particularly prominent, not only for philanthropic giving, but for its active involvement in trying to engineer social change and shape the development of social justice movements. For instance, foundations, particularly Ford, became involved in the civil rights movement, often steering it into more conservative directions, as the essay from Robert L. Allen in this collection demonstrates. At the same time, however, this civil rights involvement also aroused the ire of the Right, particularly in the South, who then called on Congress to more strictly regulate foundations. Right-wing organizations such as the Heritage Foundation claimed that tax dollars were going to subsidize left-wing causes, while on the left, progressives such as Allen were arguing that foundations were pushing social justice movements into more conservative directions.[10] Thus foundations earned critics from all sides.

Leading the Right's assault on liberal foundations was Congressman Wright Patman of Texas, who conducted a study of foundations, beginning in 1962. In reports he sent to the House of Representatives, Patman contended that economic power was consolidating in the hands of foundations; foundations were being used to escape estate taxes, compensate relatives, and pay annuities to themselves; the Internal Revenue Service (IRS) lacked proper oversight over foundations; foundations were controlling business to give them a competitive advantage over small businesses; and foundations were spending too much of their money overseas.[11] In the early 1960s, foundations were growing at a rate of 1,200 per year, and financial magazines routinely promoted foundations as tax-shelter tools.[12] In response,

Congress passed the Tax Reform Act of 1969, which reversed the previous state policy of only minimally regulating foundations. This act imposed a 4 percent excise tax on foundations' net investment income, put restrictions on the ability of foundations to engage in business operations (thus curtailing the abilities of corporations to operate tax-free as ostensible foundations), and required foundations to annually spend at least 6 percent of net investment income (reduced to 5 percent in 1988) to prevent them from growing without serving their ostensible charitable purposes. Additionally, the act required foundations to provide more comprehensive information disclosures on their operations in annual reports to be filed with the IRS and made available to citizens at foundation offices.[13]

Notwithstanding its attack on foundations, the Right also developed its own foundations. As Michael Shuman of the Institute of Policy Studies notes, while right-wing foundations actually give away *less* money than liberal foundations, the former use their funds more effectively. Progressive funders generally give money to specific issue-oriented campaigns, whereas right-wing foundations see the need to fund the intellectual projects that enable the Right to develop a comprehensive framework for presenting its issues to the public. These think tanks, research projects, journals, etcetera, may not have had an immediate short-term impact, but, in the long run, they altered the public consciousness.

> This kind of investment by the Right in public policy has paid off handsomely. Its long-term support of conservative public scholars enables them to develop and promote numerous "new Ideas."…With ample funding, they have successfully pounded their message into heads of millions, sowing confusion, apathy, and opposition to public regulation of private corporations.[14]

Right-wing foundations pour millions of dollars into funding think tanks such as the Heritage Foundation to help craft an ideological package that has fundamentally reshaped the consciousness of the public. Heritage Foundation president Edwin Feulner talks about the foresight of right-wing funders such as Richard Scaife, who saw the importance of political education. "Right-wing victories," he notes, "started more than twenty years ago when Dick Scaife had the vision to see the need for a conservative intellectual movement in America.…These organizations built the intellectual case that was necessary before political leaders like Newt Gingrich could translate their ideas into practical political alternatives."[15]

The rise of foundation support accompanied the rise of groups that organized as formal 501(c)(3) non-profit organizations, because foundations could make tax-deductible donations to non-profits, particularly after the federal government began to regulate foundation giving more strictly in 1969. According to the IRS, non-profits are "religious, charitable, scientific, or educational" organizations whose receipts are tax-exempt, and whose contributions are tax deductible for the donors. This tax-exempt status was created by Congress as part of the Revenue Act of 1913, passed after ratification of the 16th Amendment, which instituted the income tax. Generally, organizations must secure 501(c)(3) status to receive foundation grants, and they are prohibited from direct involvement in political advocacy. In 1953, the IRS estimated that about 50,000 organizations had received charity status. By 1978, that number had risen nearly sixfold. Today, charities number more than 730,000, according to the latest IRS count. As of 1998, there were 734,000 501(c)(3) organizations in the United States alone.[16] Today, foundations have assets of $500 billion and give around $33.6 billion annually,[17] and there are 837,027 non-profits, excluding religious organizations.[18]

During the late 1960s, radical movements for social change were transforming the shape of the United States while Third World liberation movements were challenging Western imperialism. Foundations began to take a role in shaping this organizing so that social protest would not challenge the capitalist status quo. Robert L. Allen, as early as 1969, warned of the co-optation of the Black Power movement by foundations. In his germinal work, *Black Awakening in Capitalist America*, reprinted in part in this anthology, Allen documents how the Ford Foundation's support of certain Black civil rights and Black Power organizations such as CORE (Congress of Racial Equality) actually helped shift the movement's emphasis—through the recruitment of key movement leaders—from liberation to Black capitalism. Similarly, Madonna Thunder Hawk describes how the offer of well-paying jobs in the non-profit sector seduced many Native activists into diverting their energy from organizing to social service delivery and program development. As Joan Roefels notes in *Foundations and Public Policy* (2003), large private foundations tended to fund racial justice organizations that focused on policy and legal reform, a strategy that effectively redirected activist efforts from radical change to social reform. It also helped to professionalize these movements, since only those with advanced degrees could do this kind of work, thus minimizing the importance of mass-based grassroots organizing. Waldemar Nielsen, in his 1972 study of the big foundations at the time, noted that funding patterns indicated that "philanthropic interest in the black [*sic*] derives from the long tradition of humanitarian concern for his [*sic*] 'plight' rather than from an ideological comment to the principle of racial equality."[19] Observing that the majority of foundation funding for racial issues went into higher education, Nielsen notes,

> Reminiscent of the ideas of Booker T. Washington, it is commonly believed that the most fruitful way to solve the problems of the blacks is to open educational opportunities to them; by climbing the rungs of the educational and occupational ladder, they will eventually achieve full economic, political, and social equality within the system. Moreover, once educational opportunities

have been opened, the primary responsibility for his advancement rests upon the black man—on his own ambition, determination, and effort.[20]

So, essentially, foundations provide a cover for white supremacy. Reminiscent of Rockefeller's strategy, people of color deserve individual relief but people of color organized to end white supremacy become a menace to society.

Another strategy developed to sublimate revolutionary movements into reformist ones was "leadership training" both domestically and internationally, whereby potential organizers were recruited to develop the skills to become policy-makers and bureaucrats instead of organizers.[21] As the essay on the NGOization of the Palestinian liberation movement in this volume shows, this strategy of "leadership development" is still being used to transform liberation struggles. As Howard Dressner, secretary of the Ford Foundation, stated in 1969,

> American society is being strained at one extreme by those who would destroy what they oppose or do not understand, and at the other by forces that would repress variety and punish dissent. We are in great need of more—not fewer— instruments *for necessary social change under law, for ready, informed response to deep-seated problems without chaos, for accommodation of a variety of views without deafening anarchy* [emphasis added]. Foundations have served as such an instrument.[22]

Meanwhile, Robert Arnove's edited volume, *Philanthropy and Cultural Imperialism,* charged that foundations

> have a corrosive influence on a democratic society; they represent relatively unregulated and unaccountable concentrations of power and wealth which buy talent, promote causes, and in effect, establish an agenda of what merits society's attention. They serve as "cooling-out" agencies, delaying and preventing more radical, structural change. They help maintain an economic and political order, international in scope, which benefits the ruling-class interests of philanthropists.[23]

As the essays in this volume will demonstrate, these critiques of foundations and non-profits still ring true today.

what is the non-profit industrial complex?

Dylan Rodríguez defines the non-profit industrial complex as "a set of symbiotic relationships that link political and financial technologies of state and owning class control with surveillance over public political ideology, including and especially emergent progressive and leftist social movements." He and Ruth Wilson Gilmore argue that the NPIC is the natural corollary to the prison industrial complex (PIC). While the PIC overtly represses dissent the NPIC manages and controls dissent by incorporating it into the state apparatus, functioning as a "shadow state" constituted by a network of institutions that do much of what government agencies are supposed to do with tax money in the areas of education and social services. The NPIC functions as an alibi that allows government to make war, expand punishment, and proliferate market economies under the veil of partnership between the public and private sectors.

Christine E. Ahn looks more closely at the role of foundations in particular. She argues that foundations are *theoretically* a correction for the ills of capitalism. However, if we look at where the actual funding goes (including who governs these institutions), we can see that most of this country's "charity"—whether individual, corporate, or foundation—is not directed toward programs, services, and institutions that benefit the poor or disenfranchised, and certainly not toward effecting social change. When wealthy people create foundations, they're exempt from paying taxes on their wealth. Thus foundations essentially rob the public of monies that should be owed to them and give back very little of what is taken in lost taxes. In addition, their funds are derived from profits resulting from the exploitation of labor. That is, corporations become rich by exploiting their workers. Corporate profits are then put into foundations in order to provide "relief" to workers that are the result of corporate practices in the first place. Rather than thinking of foundations as a source of income for which we should be grateful, Ahn suggests we reimagine them as a target for accountability, just as we might organize to hold corporations or the state accountable to the public good.

how the npic impacts movements

It is easy to critique the larger foundations, but what about smaller foundations without large endowments? Are large foundations the only problem? This question is addressed by Tiffany Lethabo King and Ewuare Osayande's work. While Ahn discusses strategies for holding foundations accountable, King and Osayande contend that this effort to reform foundations basically serves to protect elitism within social justice movements. They further argue that even self-described "alternatives" to foundation funding (such as individual giving through major donors) are still based on the same logic—that wealthy people should be the donors, and thus, inevitably, the controllers of social justice struggles. Ultimately, even these funding strategies disadvantage people-of-color organizations which do not have the same access to wealthy donors as do white-dominated organizations.

Thus, regardless of the intentions of particular foundations, the framework of funding, in which organizations expect to be funded by benefactors rather than by their constituents, negatively impacts social movements as well. Sista II Sista and Sisters in Action for Power describe how their respective initial efforts to become a non-profit ultimately shifted their focus from organizing to corporate management. When Sisters in Action for Power realized the detrimental impact the NPIC had on its work, it began to explore how its organization could reject this corporate model and instead develop structures that more closely model the vision of the society it is trying to build. This step necessitated the development of organizing strategies within an integrated mind-body-spirit framework that respects organizing processes as much as outcomes. Aware that such approaches are often antithetical to foundations' requirements that focus on short-term campaign outcomes, Sisters in Action for Power explains why it nonetheless chose to engage in campaigns to develop leadership in young women of color through a holistic framework.

Madonna Thunder Hawk reminds us that many radical movements for change are able to accomplish much—if not more—outside the non-profit system. Her essay discusses her involvement with Women of All Red Nations (formed in connection with the American Indian Movement), which did incredible work without a single foundation grant. Mindful that many contemporary activists feel they cannot do their work without starting a non-profit first, Thunder Hawk also observes that foundations only give money to more well-established NGOs who have the "expertise." But, more often than not, she warns, these purported experts are generally not part of the communities they advocate for and hence do not contribute to building grassroots leadership, particularly in indigenous communities.

In this way, the NPIC contributes to a mode of organizing that is ultimately unsustainable. To radically change society, we must build mass movements that can topple systems of domination, such as capitalism. However, the NPIC encourages us to think of social justice organizing as a career; that is, you do the work if you can get paid for it. However, a mass movement requires the involvement of millions of people, most of whom cannot get paid. By trying to do grassroots organizing through this careerist model, we are essentially asking a few people to work more than full-time to make up for the work that needs to be done by millions.

In addition, the NPIC promotes a social movement culture that is non-collaborative, narrowly focused, and competitive. To retain the support of benefactors, groups must compete with each other for funding by promoting only their own work, whether or not their organizing strategies are successful. This culture prevents activists from having collaborative dialogues where we can honestly share our failures as well as our successes. In addition, after being forced to frame everything we do as a "success," we become stuck in having to repeat the same strategies because we insisted to funders they were successful, even if they were not. Consequently, we become inflexible rather than fluid and ever changing in our strategies, which is what a movement for social transformation really requires. And as we become more concerned with attracting funders than with organizing mass-based movements, we start niche marketing the work of our organizations. Framing our organizations as working on a particular issue or a particular strategy, we lose perspective on the larger goals of our work. Thus, niche marketing encourages us to build a fractured movement rather than mass-based movements for social change.

Project South suggests that a fatal error made by many activists is presuming that one needs money to organize. While fundraising is part of organizing, fundraising is not a precondition for organizing. Project South describes how they integrate fundraising into organizing so that those who fulfill fundraising positions in Project South are trained organizers, not fundraisers.

Ana Clarissa Rojas Durazo, Alisa Bierria, and Paul Kivel trace the impact of the NPIC on the antiviolence movement. Rojas notes that the antiviolence movement became co-opted by the state through federal and state funding. Her work builds on the analysis of Suzanne Pharr, who notes that the move toward developing antiviolence organizations through the non-profit system coincided with Reaganomics. At the same time that Reagan was slashing government services, the women's movement organized itself into non-profits to provide the services the government was no longer providing. Consequently, the antiviolence movement essentially became a surrogate for the state.[24] Likewise, Bierria observes an antiviolence movement focused less on grassroots organizing and more on professionalization and social service delivery as a direct result of increased government and foundation funding. Instead of imagining domestic violence survivors who could organize on their own behalf, antiviolence organizations viewed them only as clients in need of services. Kivel argues that the NPIC assigns social service professionals a particular function within the capitalist system of managing dissent. Still, he does not suggest that there should be no social services agencies at all—rather, that social service agencies should also engage social justice organizing or must be accountable to social movements if they are to further, rather than impede, social justice.

The impact of the NPIC on the antiviolence movement has been particularly disastrous because most of the government funding it receives has been through the Department of Justice, especially with the advent of the Violence Against Women Act. As a result, antiviolence organizations have focused primarily on criminal justice solutions to ending violence that reinforce the prison industrial complex; in fact, many antiviolence organizations are now located within police departments. Women of color, who must address both gender violence within their communities and state violence against their communities, have been particularly impacted by the direction the mainstream antiviolence movement has taken. This NGOization of the antiviolence movement is also actively exported to other countries, following a model Gayatri Spivak calls "saving brown women from brown men"[25] which tends to pathologize communities in the Third World for their "backward" attitudes toward women. The goal becomes to "save" Third

World women from the extreme patriarchy in their community without look-ing at how patriarchy is connected to white supremacy and colonialism. Thus, for instance, mainstream feminist groups will support the bombing in Afghanistan to save Afghan women from the Taliban as if US empire actually liberates women. (In addition to the essays in this volume, further analysis of the co-optation of the antiviolence movement can be found in INCITE!'s previous book, *Color of Violence: The INCITE! Anthology* [2006]).

Women of color have also been particularly impacted by the role of founda-tions in the women's health and reproductive justice movements. Foundations have been active in supporting the population control movement, which blames the reproductive capabilities of women of color and Third World women for almost all social ills, including poverty, war, and environmental destruction. For instance, John D. Rockefeller III founded the Population Council in 1952 to foster international population control policies under the notion that overpopulation causes unrest, and hence, revolution.[26] The Population Council supported mass population control efforts in Latin America during the 1960s and 1970s.[27] And in the last six months of 1976, the Population Council supported the sterilization of 6.5 million people in India through the use of police raids to round up men and women, with thousands dying from infections caused by the unsanitary condi-tions under which the sterilizations were performed. In one village alone, all the young men were sterilized.[28]

Today, what Betsy Hartmann terms the "population establishment"[29] spends billions of dollars each year on population programs, policy setting, and (mis)education. Certainly, Third World/women of color want family planning services, but many of the programs foisted upon them have been implemented without concern for their health. For instance, before Norplant (a long-acting hor-monal contraceptive) was introduced in the US, the Population Council inserted it into nearly half a million women in Indonesia, often without providing coun-seling on side effects (which include menstrual irregularity, nausea, and anxiety) and without telling them that there had been no long-term studies on the drug's effects. Many were not told that it needed to be removed after five years to avoid an increased risk of ectopic pregnancy.[30] Thirty-five hundred women in India were implanted with Norplant 2 in trials that began in the 1980s, without being warned about possible side effects or screened to determine if they were suitable candidates. These programs were finally discontinued due to concerns about "ter-atogenicity and carcinogenicity." In both cases, women who wanted the implant removed had great difficulty finding doctors who could do so.[31] (Similarly, in the US, many doctors can insert Norplant, but not so many know how to remove it).

The Pew Foundation, the largest environmental grantmaker in the United States, spent over $13 million to increase public support for population control at the 1994 Cairo Conference on Population and Development.[32] Population control is one of Pew's top priorities; organized through the Global Stewardship Initiative, it targets are environmental organizations, domestic affairs and foreign policy initiatives, and religious organizations.[33] In conjunction with the Park Ridge Center, in February 1994, Pew organized a forum in Chicago on religious perspectives on population, consumption, and the environment. In May 1994, it hosted a consultation that brought together thinkers from major world religions to deliberate on population issues,[34] issuing a statement to contradict the Vatican's antichoice position.[35] As a lead-in to the Cairo conference, Pew targeted churches to support a Cairo consensus on population by organizing focus groups with different constituencies, including various religious groups. It identified the "problem" constituencies as those who "accept overpopulation as a problem in terms of unequal distribution of resources and mismanagement of resources—not numbers of people."[36] Pew then targeted the "elites" of religious communities who would understand its construction of the problems of overpopulation.[37] Its efforts met with success; in 1993, a Pew survey of 30 US denominations found that 43 percent had an official statement on population.[38] Church leaders in both evangelical and liberal denominations came out in support of the Cairo conference, lauding its steps forward on women's reproductive health issues. Through this work, Pew had, in the words of Hartmann, managed to "manufacture consensus" over the Cairo conference.[39] Through its vast financial resources, Pew has been able to change the agenda of environmental organizations and programs in order to suit its own vision for the world.[40]

non-profits and global organizing

Globally, both foundations and non-profits/NGOs have received widespread criticism for their implicit or explicit support of First World interests and free-market capitalism. Numerous foundations and non-profits have directly colluded with the Central Intelligence Agency. For instance, foundations have supported and continue to support CIA programs in educational exchanges with east Africa and Eastern Europe to maintain a US presence in these areas without the consent of Congress.[41] The CIA also employs political scientists and collaborates with professors in sponsoring university institutes. These institutes were created on the advice of foundations that assumed scholars would be more likely to cooperate with intelligence work if it were done in an academic location. These scholars also helped recruit potential allies among foreign students.[42] Additionally, the CIA directed funding through foundations to support cultural arts to recruit leftist cultural workers, and showcase US cultural achievements globally. Since the State Department could not fund such activities directly, they had to be funneled through foundations.[43] Gerald Colby and Charlotte Dennett's book *Thy Will Be Done* also charges that John D. Rockefeller III funded missionary agencies that collaborated with the CIA for several decades in Latin America. These missionaries/agents would befriend indigenous peoples in Latin America, collaborate with them to translate the Bible into indigenous languages, and then use these intermediaries to funnel intelligence information to the CIA to facilitate resource extraction and destabilize leftist regimes.[44] Critics further charge that the Ford Foundation funded programs to revitalize Indian religions in India to counter the spread of communism. This tactic has the impact of defusing opposition from a leftist framework, but also fuels religious fundamentalism and the rise of Hindu Right nationalism.[45]

Foundations have also been directly involved in squelching revolutionary movements in the Third World. The Ford Foundation was actively involved through its various programs in diverting the antiapartheid movement in South Africa from an anticapitalist to a pro-capitalist movement.[46] Cyril Ramaphosa, a secretary-general of the African National Congress who led a 1987 miners strike praised by the Ford Foundation,[47] signed a $900 million contract with Anglo American, a corporation that accounts for 25 percent of South Africa's gross domestic product and controls much of South Africa's gold and diamond mining. The goal of this collaboration is to bring "blacks into the mainstream economy" rather than to challenge the economic status quo.[48] As demonstrated in "The NGOization of the Palestine Liberation Movement," a series of interviews with four longtime activists, these same strategies are being used by NGOs to deradicalize the struggle in Palestine.

James Petras makes some similar arguments in his 1994 essay "NGOs: In the Service of Imperialism." Petras notes that despite claiming to be nongovernmental organizations, they actually support government interests. NGOs, he writes,

> receive funds from overseas governments, work as private sub-contractors of local governments and/or are subsidized by corporate funded private foundations with close working relations with the state....Their programs are not accountable to local people, but to overseas donors who "review" and "oversee" the performance of the NGOs according to their criteria and interests. The NGO officials are self-appointed and one of their key tasks is designing proposals that will secure funding. In many cases this requires that NGO leaders find out the issues the Western funding elites fund, and shape proposals accordingly.[49]

For example, he notes that NGOs direct organizing efforts away from dealing with exploitation by the World Bank to supporting micro-credit projects that place the solution to poverty on individual initiative rather than changing global economic systems. He adamantly opposes even "progressive" NGOs, arguing that they divert resources from the people, they subordinate movement leadership to NGO leadership, and they do not put their lives on the lines.

> Progressive NGOs use peasants and the poor for their research projects, they benefit from the publication—nothing comes back to the movements not even copies of the studies done in their names! Moreover, peasant leaders ask why the NGOs never risk their neck after their educational seminars? Why do they not study the rich and powerful—why us?...The NGOs should stop being NGOs and convert themselves into members of socio-political movements.... The fundamental question is whether a new generation of organic intellectuals can emerge from the burgeoning radical social movements which can avoid the NGO temptation and become integral members of the next revolutionary wave.[50]

reformulating the role of non-profits

In contrast to Petras, contributors Adjoa Florência Jones de Almeida and Paula X. Rojas suggest alternative possibilities for understanding the proper relationship between non-profits and social movements as informed by the role of non-profits in mass movements in other countries. Jones de Almeida and Rojas point out that in many countries, social movements are not necessarily dominated by non-profits. Instead, movement building is funded and determined by the constituents. These movements may make strategic alliances with non-profits or develop their own non-profits as intermediaries to fund specific aspects of their work. But a key difference is that these non-profits are accountable to social movements; they are not seen as part of the movement themselves. Furthermore, the goal is to sustain movements, not non-profits that support movements. Within the US, Ruth Wilson Gilmore suggests that many organizations can be effective even with 501(c)(3) status if they have a clear mission and purpose—and if they are funded by their constituents. She further suggests it is central to remember that our focus should not be on organizational (or career) preservation, but on furthering the movement of which an organization is a part. Eric Tang also concludes that while non-profits can have a role to support the movement, they cannot be an end unto themselves. He argues that the revolution will not be funded—we must create autonomous movements. But once we develop that mass movement, non-profits could serve as buffers that protect autonomous movements from government repression.

Most of the essays in this anthology were presented in 2004 at The Revolution Will Not Be Funded: Beyond the Non-Profit Industrial Complex, a conference organized by INCITE! Women of Color Against Violence. Co-organized by the Women of Color Collective of the University of California, Santa Barbara, this historic international gathering provided an opportunity for activists and organizers to share their struggles of organizing within the context of the non-profit system. While providing no simple answers, it did encourage a conversation on new ways to think about organizing and activism.

These essays do not necessarily represent the views of INCITE! and they do not necessarily agree with one other. Nevertheless, they provide a space for social justice organizers and activists to begin thinking of ways to build movements that either do not rely primarily on the non-profit model or position themselves differently within this system. We hope it will continue a conversation that may move us forward in developing new strategies for revolutionary work.

notes

1 Sheila Slaughter and Edward Silva, "Looking Backwards: How Foundations Formulated Ideology in the Progressive Period," in *Philanthropy and Cultural Imperialism*, ed. Robert Arnove (Boston: G. K. Hall, 1980), 55–86.

2 James Allen Smith, "The Evolving Role of American Foundations," in *Philanthropy and the Nonprofit Sector in a Changing America*, ed. Charles Clotfelter and Thomas Erlich (Bloomington: University of Indiana Press, 1999), 34–51.

3 Thomas J. Billitteri, "Donors Big and Small Propelled Philanthropy in the 20th Century," *The Chronicle of Philanthropy Gifts and Grants*, January 13, 2000, http://philanthropy.com/free/articles/v12/i06/06002901.htm.

   In 2006 the American Association of Fundraising Counsel (AAFRC) changed its name to Giving Institute: Leading Consultants to Non-Profits. See AAFRC, "AAFRC Celebrates 70 Years of Service to Philanthropic Community; Gurin Forum, Gala Set the Stage for New Name, Direction," press release, March 7, 2006, http://www.aafrc.org/press_releases/trustreleases/gala06.html.

4 Thomas Atwood, "The Road to Ludlow" (paper), http://archive.rockefeller.edu/publications/resrep/andrews.pdf.

5 Ibid.

6 Barbara Howe, "The Emergency of Scientific Philanthropy, 1900–1920: Origins, Issues and Outcomes," in *Philanthropy and Cultural Imperialism* (see note 1), 25–54.

7 Ibid.

8 Sheila Slaughter and Edward Silva, "Looking Backwards: How Foundations Formulated Ideology in the Progressive Period," in *Philanthropy and Cultural Imperialism* (see note 1), 55–86.

9 James Allen Smith, "The Evolving Role of American Foundations," in *Philanthropy and the Nonprofit Sector in a Changing America*, ed. by Charles Clotfelter and Thomas Erlich (Bloomington: University of Indiana Press, 1999), 34–51.

10 Waldemar Nielsen, *Golden Donors* (New York: Truman Talley Books, 1985), 53.

11 John Edie, "Congress and Foundations: Historical Summary," in *America's Wealthy and the Future of Foundations*, ed. Teresa Odendahl (New Haven, CT: The Foundation Center, 1987), 43–64.

12 Billitteri, "Donors Big and Small."

13 Joan Roelofs, *Foundations and Public Policy* (Albany: State University of New York Press, 2003), 15.

14 Michael Shuman, "Why Progressive Foundations Give Too Little to Too Many," *Nation*, 12/19 January 1998, 12.

15 Karen Rothmyer, "What's Conspiracy Got to Do with It?" *Nation*, 23 February 1998, 20.

16 Roelofs, *Foundations and Public Policy*, 19.

17 Steve Gunderson, "Foundations: Architects of Social Change," *eJournal USA,* May 2006, http://usinfo.state.gov/journals/itsv/0506/ijse/gunderson.htm.

18 The Nonprofit Congress, http://www.nonprofitcongress.org/sectorinfo.htm.

19 Waldemar Neilsen, *The Big Foundations* (New York: Columbia University Press, 1972), 358.

20 Ibid., 359.

21 Roelofs, *Foundations and Public Policy,* 127.

22 Ibid.

23 Robert Arnove, ed., *Philanthropy and Cultural Imperialism* (Boston: G. K. Hall, 1980), 1.

24 Suzanne Pharr, plenary address, The Revolution Will Not Be Funded conference, University of California, Santa Barbara, April 30, 2004.

25 Gayatri Chakravorty Spivak, "Can the Subaltern Speak?" in *Colonial Discourse and Post-Colonial Theory,* ed. Patrick Williams and Laura Chrisman (New York: Columbia University Press, 1994), 92–93.

26 Roelofs, *Foundations and Public Policy,* 31.

27 Reprinted in Dale Hathaway-Sunseed, "A Critical Look at the Population Crisis in Latin America" (paper, University of California, Santa Cruz, spring 1979). The efforts these men supported led to 30 percent of women being sterilized in Puerto Rico and 44 percent in Brasil, despite the fact that sterilization was illegal in Brasil. Betsy Hartmann, *Reproductive Rights and Wrongs: The Global Politics of Population Control* (Boston: South End Press, 1995), 248, 250.

28 Hartmann, *Reproductive Rights and Wrongs,* 254.

29 Ibid., 113–124. Hartmann identifies the major players as USAID, the UN Fund for Population Activities, governments of other developed countries (particularly Japan), the World Bank—which has forced Third World countries to adopt population policies contingent upon release of structural adjustment loans), the International Planned Parenthood Federation, the Population Council, various consulting firms and academic centers, foundations (particularly the Ted Turner and Pew Charitable Trusts) and various pressure groups (that is, Zero Population Growth and the Population Action International as well as environmental organizations such as the Sierra Club).

30 Ibid., 29–30.

31 Ammu Joseph, "India's Population Bomb," *Ms.* 3, no. 3 (November/December 1992): 12.

32 Hartmann, *Reproductive Rights and Wrongs,* 148.

33 Pew Global Stewardship Initiative, white paper, July 1993, 12.

34 Martin Marty, "Population and Development," *Second Opinion,* no. 20 (April 1995): 51–52. See also "Varied Religious Strands on Population," *Christian Century* 111 (July 27–August 3, 1994): 714–715.

35 "Morals and Human Numbers," *Christian Century* 111 (April 20, 1994): 409–410.

36 Pew Charitable Trust, *Report of Findings from Focus Groups on Population, Consumption and the Environment,* July 1993, 64.

37 Ibid.

38 Pew Charitable Trust, *Global Stewardship* 1, no. 3 (March 1994): 1.

39 Contrary to impressions left by the media, Carol Benson Holst points out that there are many people who were very critical of the Cairo program. For instance, her former organization, Ministry for Justice in Population Concerns, which was funded by Pew, issued a statement that was not allowed to be read at the plenary, calling the program "nothing but an insult to women, men and children of the South who will receive an ever-growing dose of population assistance, while their issues of life and death will await the Social Development Summit of 1995." Ramona Morgan Brown and Carol Benson Holst, "IPCD's Suppressed Voices May Be Our Future Hope," *Ministry for Justice in Population Concerns,* October–December 1994, 1.

Consequently, Pew (which had funded the organization knowing it was concerned primarily with the relationship between social justice and population growth) defunded the organization because it "was too accommodating to people of color." *Ministry for Justice in Population Concerns, Notice of Phase-Out,* January 1, 1995. Pew's March 1994 newsletter also dismissed the concerns women of color had about the racist implications of population control as "rumor mongering." *Global Stewardship* 1, no. 3 (March 1994): 3. For another critical view of Cairo, see Charon Asetoyer, "Whom to Target for the North's Profits," *Wicozanni Wowapi*, Fall 1994, 2–3. She writes: "Early into the conference, it became obvious that the issues facing third world countries such as development, structural adjustment, and capacity building was not high on the list of issues that the "Super Powers" wanted to address. It was clear that the issues facing world population were going to be addressed from the top down with little regard for how this may affect developing countries." While it had first seemed Pew was concerned about justice issues, it became clear that they were only interested insofar as it furthered their population agenda. Other church-based organizations have privately questioned Pew's stance on this issue, but cannot do so publicly if they do not want to jeopardize their funding. See Brown and Holst, "IPCD's Suppressed Voices."

40 Stephen Greene, "Who's Driving the Environmental Movement?" *Chronicle of Philanthropy* 6 (January 25, 1994): 6–10.

41 Barry Karl and Alice Karl, "Foundations and the Government: A Tale of Conflict and Consensus," in *Philanthropy and the Nonprofit Sector in a Changing America*, ed. Charles Clotfelter and Thomas Erlich (Bloomington: University of Indiana Press, 1999), 52–72.

42 Roelofs, *Foundations and Public Policy*, 39.

43 Ibid., 86.

44 Gerard Colby and Charlotte Dennett, *Thy Will Be Done* (New York: HarperCollins, 1995).

45 Roelofs, *Foundations and Public Policy*, 86.

46 Ibid., 141.

47 Ibid., 174.

48 Donald McNeil, "Once Bitter Enemies, Now Business Partners; South African Blacks Buy Into Industry," *New York Times*, September 24, 1996.

49 James Petras, "NGOs: In the Service of Imperialism," *Journal of Contemporary Asia* 29, no. 4 (1999): 429–440.

50 Ibid.

part i

The Rise of the Non-Profit Industrial Complex

▸▸Dylan Rodríguez

the political logic of the non-profit industrial complex

PERHAPS NEVER BEFORE HAS THE STRUGGLE TO MOUNT VIABLE movements of radical social transformation in the United States been more desperate, urgent, or difficult. In the aftermath of the 1960s mass-movement era, the edifices of state repression have themselves undergone substantive transformation, even as classical techniques of politically formed state violence—colonization and protocolonial occupation, racist policing, assassination, political and mass-based imprisonment—remain fairly constant in the US production of global order. Here, I am specifically concerned with the emergence of the US prison industrial complex (PIC) and its relationship to the non-profit industrial complex (NPIC), the industrialized incorporation of pro-state liberal and progressive campaigns and movements into a spectrum of government-proctored non-profit organizations. In my view, these overlapping developments—the rise of a racially constituted prison regime unprecedented in scale, and the almost simultaneous structural consolidation of a non-profit industrial complex—have exerted a form and content to US-based resistance struggles which enmeshes them in the social arrangement that political prisoner Mumia Abu-Jamal names an "industry of fear." In a 1998 correspondence to the 3,000-plus participants in the conference Critical Resistance: Beyond the Prison Industrial Complex, he writes,

> Americans live in a cavern of fear, a psychic, numbing force manufactured by the so-called entertainment industry, reified by the psychological industry, and buttressed by the coercion industry (i.e., the courts, police, prisons, and the like). The social psychology of America is being fed by a media that threatens all with an army of psychopathic, deviant, sadistic madmen bent on ravishing a helpless, prone citizenry. The state's coercive apparatus of "public safety" is erected as a needed protective counter-point.[1]

I wish to pay special attention to Abu-Jamal's illustration of the social fabrication of fear as a necessary political and cultural condition for the rise of the US non-profit industrial complex, which has, in turn, *enabled and complemented* the massive institutional production of the US prison industrial complex. As I understand it, the NPIC is the set of symbiotic relationships that link together political and financial technologies of state and owning-class proctorship and surveillance over public political intercourse, including and especially emergent progressive and leftist social movements, since about the mid-1970s. Abu-Jamal's "cavern of fear" illuminates the repressive and popular broadly racist common sense that both haunts and constitutes the political imagination of many contemporary progressive, radical, and even self-professed "revolutionary" social change activists. Why, in other words, does the political imagination of the US non-profit and nongovernmental organization (NGO)–enabled Left generally refuse to embrace the urgent and incomplete *historical* work of a radical counter-state, anti–white supremacist, *prison/penal/slave abolitionist* movement? I am especially concerned with how the political assimilation of the non-profit sector into the progressive dreams of a "democratic" global civil society (the broad premise of the liberal-progressive antiglobalization movement) already presumes (and therefore fortifies) existing structures of social liquidation, including biological and social death. Does Abu-Jamal's "cavern of fear" also echo the durable historical racial phobias of the US social order generally? Does the specter of an authentic *radical freedom* no longer structured by the assumptions underlying the historical "freedoms" invested in white American political identity—including the perversions and mystifications of such concepts as "democracy," "civil rights," "the vote," and even "equality"—logically suggest the *end of white civil society,* which is to say a collapsing of the very sociocultural foundations of the United States itself? Perhaps it is the fear of a radically transformed, feminist/queer/antiracist *liberation* of Black, Brown, and Red bodies, no longer *presumed to be permanently subordinated* to structures of criminalization, colonization, (state and state-ordained) bodily violence, and domestic warfare, that logically threatens the very existence of the still white-dominant US Left: perhaps it is, in part, the Left's fear of an unleashed *bodily proximity* to currently criminalized, colonized, and normatively violated peoples that compels it to retain the staunchly anti-abolitionist political limits of the NPIC. The persistence of such a racial fear—in effect, the fear of a radical freedom that obliterates the cultural and material ascendancy of "white freedom"—is neither new nor unusual in the history of the US Left. We are invoking, after all, the vision of a movement of liberation that abolishes (and transforms) the cultural, economic, and political structures of a white civil society that continues to largely define the terms, languages, and limits of US-based progressive (and even "radical") campaigns, political discourses, and local/global movements.

This polemical essay attempts to dislodge some of the theoretical and operational assumptions underlying the glut of foundation-funded "establishment Left" organizations in the United States. The Left's investment in the essential political logic of civil society—specifically, the inherent legitimacy of racist state violence in upholding a white freedom, social "peace," and "law and order" that is fundamentally designed to maintain brutal inequalities in the putative free world—is *symbiotic with (and not oppositional to)* the policing and incarceration of marginalized, racially pathologized communities, as well as the state's *ongoing absorption* of organized dissent through the non-profit structure. While this alleged Left frequently considers its array of incorporated, "legitimate" organizations and institutions as the fortified bulwark of a progressive "social justice" orientation in civil society, I am concerned with the ways in which the broad assimilation of such organizations into a non-profit industrial complex actually *enables* more vicious forms of state repression.

the velvet purse of state repression

It may be appropriate to initiate this discussion with a critical reflection on the accelerated incorporation of progressive social change struggles into a structure of state accreditation and owning-class surveillance since the 1970s. Robert L. Allen's classic book *Black Awakening in Capitalist America* was among the first works to offer a sustained political analysis of how liberal white philanthropic organizations—including the Rockefeller, Ford, and Mellon foundations—*facilitated* the violent state repression of radical and revolutionary elements within the Black liberation movements of the late 1960s and early 70s. Allen argues that it was precisely because of philanthropy's overtures toward the movement's more moderate and explicitly reformist elements—especially those advocating versions of "Black capitalism" and "political self-determination" through participation in electoral politics—that radical Black liberationists and revolutionaries were more easily criminalized and liquidated.[2] Allen's account, which appears in this collection, proves instructive for a current critique of the state-corporate alliance that keeps the lid on what is left of Black liberationist politics, along with the cohort of radical struggles encompassed by what was once called the US "Third World" Left. Perhaps as important, Allen's analysis may provide a critical analytical framework through which to understand the problem of white ascendancy and liberal white supremacy within the dominant spheres of the NPIC, which has become virtually synonymous with the broader political category of a US Left.

The massive repression of the Black, Native American, Puerto Rican, and other US-based Third World liberation movements during and beyond the 1960s and 70s was founded on a coalescence of official and illicit/illegal forms of state and state-sanctioned violence: police-led racist violence (including false imprisonment, home invasions, assassinations, and political harassment), white civilian reaction (lynchings, vigilante movements, new electoral blocs, and a complementary surge of white nationalist organizations), and the proliferation of racially formed (and racially executed) juridical measures to criminalize and imprison entire populations of poor and working class Black, Brown, and Indigenous people has been—and continues to be—a fundamental legacy of this era. Responding to the liberation-movement era's momentary disruption of a naturalized American apartheid and taken-for-granted domestic colonialism, a new coalition of prominent owning-class white philanthropists, lawmakers, state bureaucrats, local and federal police, and ordinary white civilians (from across the already delimited US political spectrum of "liberal" to "conservative") scrambled to restore the coherence and stability of white civil society in the midst of a fundamental challenge from activists and radical movement intellectuals who envisioned substantive transformation in the very foundations of US "society" itself. One outcome of this movement toward "White Reconstruction" was the invention, development, and refinement of repressive policing technologies across the local and federal scales, a labor that encompassed a wide variety of organizing and deployment strategies. The notorious Counterintelligence Program (COINTEL-PRO) of J. Edgar Hoover's Federal Bureau of Investigations (FBI) remains the most historically prominent incident of the undeclared warfare waged by the state against domestic populations, insurrections, and suspected revolutionaries. But the spectacle of Hooverite repression obscures the broader—and far more important—convergence of state and capitalist/philanthropic forces in the absorption of progressive social change struggles that defined this era and its current legacies.

During this era, US civil society—encompassing the private sector, non-profit organizations and NGOs, faith communities, the mass media and its consumers—partnered with the law-and-order state through the reactionary white populist sentimentality enlivened by the respective presidential campaigns of Republican Party presidential nominees Barry Goldwater and Richard Nixon. It was Goldwater's eloquent articulation of the meaning of "freedom," defined against a racially coded (though nonetheless transparent) imagery of oncoming "mob" rule and urban "jungle" savagery, poised to liquidate white social existence, that carried his message into popular currency. Goldwater's political and cultural conviction was to *defend* white civil society from its racially depicted aggressors—a white supremacist discourse of self-defense that remains a central facet of the US state and US political life generally. Though his bid for the presidency failed, Goldwater's message succeeded as the catalyst for the imminent movement of White Reconstruction in the aftermath of US apartheid's nominal disestablishment, and in the face of liberal reformist changes to US civil rights law. Accepting the 1964 Republican presidential nomination, Goldwater famously pronounced,

Tonight there is violence in our streets, corruption in our highest offices, aimlessness among our youth, anxiety among our elders and there is a virtual despair among the many who look beyond material success for the inner meaning of their lives....Security from domestic violence, no less than from foreign aggression, is the most elementary and fundamental purpose of any government, and a government that cannot fulfill that purpose is one that cannot long command the loyalty of its citizens. History shows us—demonstrates that nothing—nothing prepares the way for tyranny more than the failure of public officials to keep the streets from bullies and marauders.[3]

On the one hand, the subsequent exponential growth of the US policing apparatus closely followed the white populist political schema of the Goldwater-Nixon law-and-order bloc.[4] Law and order was essentially the harbinger of White Reconstruction, mobilizing an apparatus of state violence to protect *and recuperate* the vindicated white national body from the allegedly imminent aggressions and violations of its racial Others. White civil society, accustomed to generally unilateral and exclusive access to the cultural, economic, and political capital necessary for individual and collective self-determination, encountered reflections of its own undoing at this moment. The politics of law and order thus significantly encompassed white supremacist desire for surveilling, policing, caging, and (preemptively) socially liquidating those who embodied the gathering storm of dissidence—organized and disarticulated, radical and protopolitical.

In this historical context, COINTELPRO's illegal and unconstitutional abuses of state power, unabashed use of strategic and deadly violence, and development of invasive, terrorizing surveillance technologies might be seen as *paradigmatic of* the contemporary era's revivified white supremacist hegemony.[5] Contrary to the widespread assumption that COINTELPRO was somehow excessive, episodic, and extraordinary in its deployment of (formally illegal and unconstitutional) state violence, J. Edgar Hoover's venerated racist-state strategy simply reflected the imperative of white civil society's impulse toward *self-preservation* in this moment.[6] Elaborating the white populist vision of Goldwater and his political descendants, the consolidation of this white nationalist bloc—which eventually incorporated "liberals" as well as reactionaries and conservatives—was simply the *political* reconsolidation of a white civil society that had momentarily strolled with the specter of its own incoherence.

Goldwater's epoch-shaping presidential campaign in 1964 set up the political premises and popular *racial* vernacular for much of what followed in the restoration of white civil society in the 1970s and later. In significant part through the reorganization of a US state that strategically mobilized around an internally complex, substantively dynamic white supremacist conception of "security from domestic violence," the "law and order" state has materialized on the ground and has generated a *popular consensus* around its modes of dominance: puni-tive racist criminal justice, paramilitary policing, and strategically deployed domestic warfare regimes have become an American way of life. This popular-ized and institutionalized "law and order" state has built this popular consensus in part through a symbiosis with the non-profit liberal foundation structure, which, in turn, has helped *collapse* various sites of potential political radical-ism into nonantagonistic social service and pro-state reformist initiatives. Vast expenditures of state capacity, from police expansion to school militarization, and the multiplication of state-formed popular cultural productions (from the virtual universalization of the "tough on crime" electoral campaign message to the explosion of pro-police discourses in Hollywood film, television dramas, and popular "reality" shows) have conveyed several overlapping political mes-sages, which have accomplished several mutually reinforcing tasks of the White Reconstructionist agenda that are relevant to our discussion here: (1) the staunch criminalization of particular political practices embodied by radical and other-wise critically "dissenting" activists, intellectuals, and ordinary people of color; this is to say, when *racially pathologized bodies* take on political activities criti-cal of US state violence (say, normalized police brutality/homicide, militarized misogyny, or colonialist occupation) or attempt to dislodge the presumed sta-bility and "peace" of white civil society (through militant antiracist organizing or progressive anti–(state) racial violence campaigns), they are subjected to the enormous weight of a *state and cultural* apparatus that defines them as "criminals" (e.g., terrorists, rioters, gang members) and, therefore, as essentially *opportunis-tic, misled, apolitical,* or even *amoral* social actors; (2) the fundamental political constriction—through everything from restrictive tax laws on community-based organizations to the arbitrary enforcement of repressive laws banning certain forms of public congregation (for example, the California "antigang" statutes that have effectively criminalized Black and Brown public existence on a massive scale)—of the appropriate avenues and protocols of agitation for social change, which drastically delimits the form and substance that socially transformative and liberationist activisms can assume in both the short and long terms; and (3) the state-facilitated and fundamentally *punitive* bureaucratization of social change and dissent, which tends to create an *institutionalized* inside/outside to aspiring social movements by funneling activists into the hierarchical rituals and restrictive professionalism of discrete campaigns, think tanks, and organi-zations, outside of which it is usually profoundly difficult to organize a critical mass of political movement (due in significant part to the two aforementioned developments).

In this context, the structural and political limitations of current grassroots and progressive organizing in the United States has become stunningly evident in light of the veritable explosion of private foundations as primary institutions through which to harness and restrict the potentials of US-based progressive activisms. Heavily dependent on the funding of such ostensibly liberal and progressive financial bodies as the Mellon, Ford, and Soros foundations, the very existence of many social justice organizations has often come to rest more on the effectiveness of professional (and amateur) grant writers than on skilled—much less "radical"—political educators and organizers. A 1997 *Atlantic Monthly* article entitled "Citizen 501(c)(3)" states, for example, that the net worth of such foundations was over $200 billion as of 1996, a growth of more than 400 percent since 1981. The article's author, Nicholas Lemann, goes on to write that in the United States, the raw size of private foundations, "along with their desire to affect the course of events in the United States and the world, has made foundations one of the handful of major [political] actors in our society—but they are the one that draws the least public attention."[7] As the foundation lifeline has sustained the NPIC's emergence into a primary component of US political life, the assimilation of political resistance projects into quasi-entrepreneurial, corporate-style ventures occurs under the threat of unruliness and antisocial "deviance" that rules Abu-Jamal's US "cavern of fear": arguably, forms of sustained grassroots social movement that *do not* rely on the material assets and institutionalized legitimacy of the NPIC have become largely *unimaginable* within the political culture of the current US Left. If anything, this culture is generally disciplined and ruled by the fundamental imperative to preserve the integrity and coherence of US white civil society, and the "ruling class" of philanthropic organizations and foundations may, at times, almost unilaterally determine whether certain activist commitments and practices are appropriate to their consensus vision of American "democracy."

The self-narrative of multibillionaire philanthropist George Soros—whom the PBS program *NOW* described as "the only American citizen with his own foreign policy"[8] brings candor and clarity to the societal mission of one well-known liberal philanthropic funder-patron:

> When I had made more money than I needed, I decided to set up a foundation. I reflected on what it was I really cared about. Having lived through both Nazi persecution and Communist oppression, I came to the conclusion that what was paramount for me was an open society. So I called the foundation the Open Society Fund, and I defined its objectives as opening up closed societies, making open societies more viable, and promoting a critical mode of thinking. That was in 1979....By now I have established a network of foundations that extends across more than twenty-five countries (not including China, where we shut down in 1989).[9]

Soros's conception of the "Open Society," fueled by his avowed disdain for laissez-faire capitalism, communism, and Nazism, privileges political dissent that works firmly within the constraints of bourgeois liberal democracy. The imperative to protect—and, in Soros's case, to selectively enable with funding—dissenting political projects emerges from the presumption that existing social, cultural, political, and economic institutions are in some way perfectible, and that such dissenting projects must not deviate from the unnamed "values" which serve as the ideological glue of civil society. Perhaps most important, the Open Society is premised on the idea that clashing political projects can and must be brought (forced?) into a vague state of reconciliation with one another.

> Instead of there being a dichotomy between open and closed, I see the open society as occupying a middle ground, where the rights of the individual are safeguarded *but where there are some shared values that hold society together* [emphasis added]. I envisage the open society as a society open to improvement. We start with the recognition of our own fallibility, which extends not only to our mental constructs but also to our institutions. What is imperfect can be improved, by a process of trial and error. The open society not only allows this process but actually encourages it, by insisting on freedom of expression and protecting dissent. The open society offers a vista of limitless progress....
>
> The Open Society merely provides a framework within which different views about social and political issues can be reconciled; it does not offer a firm view on social goals. If it did, it would not be an open society.[10]

Crucially, the formulaic, naïve vision of Soros's Open Society finds its condition of possibility in untied foundation purse strings, as "dissent" flowers into viability on the strength of a generous grant or two. The essential conservatism of Soros's manifesto obtains "common-sense" status within the liberal/progressive foundation industry by virtue of financial force, as his patronage reigns hegemonic among numerous organizations and emergent social movements.

Most important, the Open Society's narrative of reconciliation and societal perfection marginalizes radical forms of dissent which voice an *irreconcilable* antagonism to white supremacist patriarchy, neoliberalism, racialized state violence, and other structures of domination. Antonio Gramsci's prescient reflection on the formation of the hegemonic state as simultaneously an organizational, repressive, and *pedagogical* apparatus is instructive: "The State does have and request consent, but it also 'educates' this consent, by means of the political and syndical associations; these, however, are private organisms, left to the private initiative of the ruling class."[11]

Certainly, the historical record demonstrates that Soros and other foundation grants have enabled a breathtaking number of "left-of-center" campaigns and projects in the last 20 years. The question I wish to introduce here, however, is whether this enabling also exerts a disciplinary or repressive force on contemporary social movement organizations while nurturing a particular ideological and structural *allegiance* to state authority that preempts political radicalisms.

Social movement theorists John McCarthy, David Britt, and Mark Wolfson argue that the "channeling mechanisms" embodied by the non-profit industry "may now far outweigh the effect of direct social control by states in explaining the structural isomorphism, orthodox tactics, and moderate goals of much collective action in modern America."[12] That is, the overall bureaucratic formality and hierarchical (frequently elitist) structuring of the NPIC has institutionalized more than just a series of hoops through which aspiring social change activists must jump—these institutional characteristics, in fact, *dictate the political vistas of NPIC organizations themselves.* The form of the US Left is inseparable from its political content. The most obvious element of this kinder, gentler, industrialized repression is its bureaucratic incorporation of social change organizations into a "tangle of incentives"—such as postal privileges, tax-exempt status, and quick access to philanthropic funding apparatuses—made possible by state bestowal of "not-for-profit" status. Increasingly, avowedly progressive, radical, leftist, and even some self-declared "revolutionary" groups have found assimilation into this state-sanctioned organizational paradigm a practical route to institutionalization. Incorporation facilitates the establishment of a relatively stable financial and operational infrastructure while avoiding the transience, messiness, and possible legal complications of working under decentralized, informal, or "underground" auspices. The emergence of this state-proctored social movement industry "suggests an historical movement away from direct, cruder forms [of state repression], toward more subtle forms of state social control of social movements."[13]

Indeed, the US state learned from its encounters with the crest of radical and revolutionary liberationist movements of the 1960s and early 70s that endless, spectacular exercises of military and police repression against activists of color on the domestic front could potentially provoke broader local and global support for such struggles—it was in part because they were so dramatically subjected to violent and racist US state repression that Black, Native American, Puerto Rican, and other domestic liberationists were seen by significant sectors of the US and international public as legitimate freedom fighters, whose survival of the racist state pivoted on the mobilization of a global political solidarity. On the other hand, the US state has found in its coalition with the NPIC a far less spectacular, generally demilitarized, and still highly effective apparatus of political discipline and repression that (to this point) has not provoked a significant critical mass of opposition or political outrage.

Central to this sublimated state discipline and surveillance are the myriad regulatory mechanisms that serve to both accredit and disqualify non-profit social change groups. The Internal Revenue Service, tax laws of individual states, the US Postal Service, and independent auditors help keep bureaucratic order within—and the political lid on—what many theorists refer to as the post-1960s emergence of "new social movements." McCarthy, Britt, and Wolfson conclude that this historical development has rather sweeping consequences for the entirety of civil society:

> Another consequence of the growth of this system is a blurring of the boundaries between the state and society, between the civil and the political. Our analysis suggests that a decreasing proportion of local groups remain unpenetrated by the laws and regulations of the central state....Some analysts see civil space declining as the result of a fusion of the private and political by the activists of the "new" social movements who politicize more and more civil structures in the pursuit of more comprehensive moral and political goals. Our analysis views the construction as more the consequence of state penetration of the civil, and the consequences in more traditional terms—a narrowing and taming of the potential for broad dissent.[14]

The NPIC thus serves as the medium through which the state continues to exert a fundamental dominance over the political intercourse of the US Left, as well as US civil society more generally. Even and especially as organizations linked to the NPIC assert their relative autonomy from, and independence of, state influence, they remain fundamentally tethered to the state through extended structures of financial and political accountability. Jennifer Wolch's notion of a "shadow state" crystallizes this symbiosis between the state and social change organizations, gesturing toward a broader conception of the state's disciplinary power and surveillance capacities. According to Wolch, the structural and political interaction between the state and the non-profit industrial complex manifests as more than a relation of patronage, ideological repression, or institutional subordination. In excess of the expected organizational deference to state rules and regulations, social change groups are *constituted by* the operational paradigms of conventional state institutions, generating a reflection of state power in the same organizations that originally emerged to resist the very same state.

> In the United States, voluntary groups have gained resources and political clout by becoming a shadow state apparatus, but are increasingly subject to state-imposed regulation of their behavior....To the extent that the shadow state is emerging in particular places, there are implications for how voluntary organizations operate. The increasing importance of state funding for many voluntary organizations has been accompanied by deepening penetration by the state into voluntary group organization, management, and goals. We argue that the transformation of the voluntary sector into a shadow state apparatus could ultimately shackle its potential to create progressive social change.[15]

the npic as political "epistemology": the cooptation of political imagination

More insidious than the raw structural constraints exerted by the foundation/state/non-profit nexus is the way in which this new industry grounds an epistemology—literally, a *way of knowing* social change and resistance praxis—that is difficult to escape or rupture. To revisit Abu-Jamal's conception of the US "cavern of fear," the non-profit industrial complex has facilitated a bureaucratized *management of fear* that mitigates against the radical break with owning-class capital (read: foundation support) and hegemonic common sense (read: law and order) that might otherwise be posited as the necessary precondition for generating counter-hegemonic struggles. The racial and white supremacist fears of American civil society, in other words, *tend to be respected and institutionally assimilated* by a Left that fundamentally operates through the bureaucratic structure of the NPIC. As the distance between state authority and civil society collapses, the civic spaces for resistance and radical political experimentation disappear and disperse into places unheard, unseen, and untouched by the presumed audiences of the non-profit industry: arguably, the most vibrant sites of radical and proto-radical activity and organizing against racist US state violence and white supremacist civil society are condensing among populations that the NPIC cannot easily or fully incorporate. Organized, under-organized, and ad hoc movements of imprisoned, homeless, and undocumented people, as well as activists committed to working beneath and relatively autonomous of the NPIC's political apparatus, may well embody the beginnings of an alternative US-based praxis that displaces the NPIC's apparent domination of political discourse and possibility. Such a revitalization of radical political vision is both urgent and necessary in the current moment, especially when the US state's constant global displays of violence and impunity seem to imply that authentically radical challenges to its realms of domination are all but doomed.

Even a brief historical assessment of the social movement history reveals the devastating impact of state violence on the political imagination and organizing practices of progressive and radical political workers in the United States. Noam Chomsky, for example, argues that the watershed year of 1968 signified a turn in the institutional and discursive trajectory of state violence and repression, departing from the spectacular, peculiar imagery of more traditionally brutal repressive techniques. Framing the state's partial movement away from technologies of violent public spectacle (assassinations, militarized police raids and "riot control," and so forth) to a more complex, surreptitious, multidimensional apparatus of coercion, Chomsky's elaboration of a new "culture of terrorism" echoes Abu-Jamal's "cavern of fear." While Chomsky's critique focuses on an analysis of the Iran-contra scandal in the mid-1980s, one also finds resonance with the state's attempts to preemptively contain and liquidate political disorder through the white supremacist criminalization and mass-based incarceration fostered by the Reagan administration's simultaneous initiation of a "War on Drugs." As the prison and policing apparatuses began to flower at the pinnacle of the Reagan-Bush bloc, so the culture of terrorism provided a context for their reproduction and expansion:

> As the Vietnam war escalated through the stages of subversion, state terrorism, and outright US aggression, disaffection and protest among the public became a significant force, preventing the government from declaring the national mobilization that would have been required to win what was becoming a major war....The general dissidence, particularly among the youth, was perceived in elite circles as a serious problem by itself in 1968, while within the Pentagon, there was concern that sufficient military force be held in reserve to control domestic disorder if the US aggression visibly increased. The key phrase is "visibly"; it was fear of the public that led to the expansion of clandestine operations in those years, on the usual principle that in our form of democracy, if the public escapes from passivity, it must be deceived—for its own good.[16]

The key terms here are *clandestinity* and *deception*: the lessons of 1968 demonstrated that state and owning-class elites needed to maintain a delicate balance between two parallel, interdependent projects. On the one hand, repressive state violence had to be sustained under shrouds of secrecy to prevent the potential coagulation and crisis of a domestic dissent bloc. On the other hand, the state also acknowledged that within the discursive structure of a bourgeois liberal democracy, people had to be *convinced* that a "free" way of life pivoted on the state's ability to violently enforce it: that is, the state required a *pedagogy of "common sense"* that could effectively "teach" people to consent to its profoundly expansive and historically unprecedented methodologies of domestic and global warfare/militarization. The subtle change in the production of a hegemonic state—its absorption of social change movements and simultaneous construction of new strategies for the production of a popular consent—now manifests deeply and widely in the terrains of civil society. Civil institutions that once housed what Aldon Morris calls the "indigenous centers" of social movement and resistance organizing (e.g., schools, churches, families, friendship networks)[17] are now far more likely to exhibit the penetration of the state through a popular epistemology that considers the violent policing of order to be a necessary condition of social life generally.

The rearticulation of state coercion into the massive institutional and discursive formation of the post-Goldwater "law and order" society goes hand in hand with the slow, steady, and voluntary entry of establishment Left organizations into a dependent relation (albeit uneasy and at times conflicted) with the neo-liberal state and philanthropic foundations. This is not to suggest that a "pure" autonomy from state authority and discipline is attainable, but rather to argue that resistance and counter-hegemonic organizations dismantle the possibility of radical antagonism as they move into closer proximity to—and dependence on—the centers of state power and (philanthropic) capital. Wolch suggests several critical dimensions to this "dynamic of reduced autonomy":

1. The state will force voluntary groups to plan reactively, in response to new state policies and practices. This is in contrast to enabling groups to plan proactively, to decide on their own goals and objectives, and how to achieve them.
2. Contracts and grants will increasingly come with requirements for stringent, rigid, and quantitatively oriented approaches to planning, evaluation, and monitoring.
3. Those organizations unable to meet the expanding demands for planning will become increasingly marginalized and may not be able to secure state funding. Such standards for organizational practice will have structural effects, controlling the rise of antiestablishment social movements and pushing marginal groups to produce direct services instead of advocacy outputs.
4. Newly formed groups may be jeopardized by new government funding programs.
5. There may be little room for voluntary sector development and new initiatives. As more statutory agencies seek to use voluntary groups to provide basic community services, the ability of the voluntary sector to develop innovative approaches to social problems may be severely inhibited. Group activities may become aligned to funding agency needs and expectations for types of services to be delivered. In the process, the type of group output is likely to change toward direct services administered by professionals and away from advocacy and participation.[18]

Under current circumstances, organized dissent movements and organizations in the United States are often compelled to replicate the bureaucratic structures of the small business, large corporation, and state—creating centralized national offices, gathering political (and, at times, Hollywood) celebrities and luminaries onto boards of directors, and hiring "professional activists" whose salaries depend largely on the effectiveness of professional grant writers. It is worth repeating the tacit though no less far-reaching *political* implication of this historical development, insofar as social change campaigns, organizations, and aspiring movements increasingly articulate their reason for existence through the imperatives of *obtaining the financial support and civil sanction of liberal philanthropy and the state*. While it is beyond my intent to adequately address the multiple pragmatic and theoretical problems accompanying this political development, it is worth asking several interrelated questions that reflect on our current condition as activists, scholars, writers, and intellectuals who are enmeshed in the disciplinary restrictions imposed by the NPIC: What are the inherent limits to the vistas of "social change" or transformation *mandated* by the US Left's incorporation into the NPIC and its emphasis on career/organizational security? Should the NPIC *itself* be conceptualized as a fundamental target of radical social transformation (whether it is to be seized, abolished, or some combination of both)? Can people struggling for survival, radical transformation, and liberation (including and beyond those who identify themselves as "activists") outside the tentacles of the NPIC generate new grassroots, community-based, or even "underground" structures and institutions capable of sustaining movements against the US racist state and white supremacist civil society?

beyond the npic: the lessons of anti-colonialism and "decolonization"

As this anthology attempts a critical and material intervention on the political stasis generated by the non-profit industrial complex, we can and should recall the recent history of socially disenfranchised and oppressed Black and Third World peoples whose demands for liberation and radical freedom (which I am distinguishing from the white bourgeois freedom that is hegemonic in the United States) have represented, for white civil society, the specter of its own undoing. I want to emphasize the importance of this contemporary liberationist lineage because I have observed a peculiar dynamic in the current political landscape that makes political fodder of this liberationist legacy. With increasing frequency, we are party (or participant) to a white liberal and "multicultural"/"people of color" liberal imagination that venerates and even fetishizes the iconography and rhetoric of contemporary Black and Third World liberation movements, and then proceeds to *incorporate* these images and vernaculars into the public presentation of foundation-funded liberal or progressive organizations. I have also observed and experienced how these organizations, in order to protect their non-profit status and marketability to liberal foundations, actively self-police against members' deviations from their essentially reformist agendas, while continuing to appropriate the language and imagery of historical revolutionaries. Having lived in the San Francisco Bay Area from 1995 to 2001, which is in many ways the national hub of the progressive "wing" of the NPIC, I would name some of those organizations (many of which are defunct) here, but the list would be too long. Suffice it to say that these non-profit groups often exhibit(ed) a political practice that is, to appropriate and corrupt a phrase from fellow contributor Ruth Wilson Gilmore, *radical in form, but liberal in content.*[19]

In this vein, Robert Allen surmises that the emergence of a white liberal hegemony over the non-profit industry during the 1970s was an explicit attempt—in fact, an authentic conspiracy of collaboration among philanthropists and state officials, including local police and federal administrators—to dissipate the incisive and radical critique of US white supremacist capitalism, the white suprem-acist state, and white civil society that was spreading in the wake of domestic Black and Third World liberation movements. What Allen does not explicitly state, although he does imply, is that the rise of the white liberal philanthropic establishment had lasting political effects that ultimately equaled (and in some ways surpassed) the most immediate repressive outcomes of COINTELPRO and its offspring. It is the *paradigm-shaping political influence* of the post-1970s white philanthropic renaissance that remains the durable and generally underanalyzed legacy of late 20th-century White Reconstruction.

My point, at the risk of stating the historically obvious, is that the produc-tion of the white liberal—and now ostensibly "multicultural" though still white liberal hegemonic—non-profit industrial complex has actually facilitated, and continues to facilitate, the *violent* state-organized repression of radical and revo-lutionary elements within the Black and Third World liberation movements of the late 1960s and early 70s, as well as what remains of such liberation strug-gles today. In other words, the symbiosis between the racist state and white civil society that I discuss above is not simply a relationship of convenience—it is a *creative relation of power* that forms a restricted institutional space in which "dis-sent" movements may take place, *under penalty of militarized state repression* (a political violence that has, through the pedagogical work of the state, won a broad approval from US civil society more generally). I should be clear in what/ whom I am implicating here: I am *not* speaking narrowly of the openly conserva-tive and right-wing foundations, such as the Heritage Foundation, that so many on the establishment Left unanimously agree are fundamentally reactionary or politically retrograde. Rather, I am speaking to the putatively kind, benevolent, humanist and humanitarian liberal-progressive foundations that this very same establishment Left relies on, that is, the same foundations that often fund this Left's political work, scholarship, and activism—like Ford, Soros, and Mellon, for example. It seems that when one attempts to engage a critical discussion regard-ing the political problems of working with these and other foundations, and especially when one is interested in naming them as the gently repressive "evil" cousins of the more prototypically evil right-wing foundations, the establishment Left becomes profoundly defensive of its financial patrons. I would argue that this is a liberal-progressive vision that marginalizes the radical, revolutionary, and proto-revolutionary forms of activism, insurrection, and resistance that refuse to participate in the Soros charade of "shared values," and are uninterested in trying to "improve the imperfect." The social truth of the existing society is that it is *based on* the production of massive, unequal, and hierarchically organized disenfranchisement, suffering, and death of those populations who are targeted for containment and political/social liquidation—a violent social order produced under the dictates of "democracy," "peace," "security," and "justice" that form the *historical and political foundations* of the very same white civil society on which the NPIC Left is based.

If we take seriously, for the sake of argument, the political analysis articulated by Palestinians struggling against the Israeli occupation, or that of imprisoned radical intellectuals/activists and their free-world allies desperately fighting to dismantle and abolish the prison industrial complex, or that of Indigenous peoples worldwide who, to paraphrase Haunani-Kay Trask, are literally fighting against their own planned obsolescence,[20] then it should become clear that the Soros philosophy of the Open Society, along with other liberal foundation social imaginaries, are at best philanthropic vanities. At worst, we can accuse the Soros, Ford, Mellon, and Rockefeller foundations, and their ilk of NGOs and non-profit organizations, of accompanying and facilitating these massive structures of human domination, which simply cannot be reformed or "reconciled" in a manner that legitimates anything approaching a vision of liberation or radical freedom.

While many professional intellectuals (academics, lawyers, teachers, progressive policy think tank members, journalists), community-based social change organizations, non-profit progressive groups, student activists, and others in the establishment Left pay some attention to the unmediated violence waged by state formations (whether official agents of state military power or its unofficial liaisons) on targeted individuals and communities, the implicit *theoretical* assumptions guiding much of this political-intellectual work have tended to *pathologize* state violence, rendering it as the scary illegitimate offspring of a right-wing hegemony. The logical extension of this political analysis is the notion that the periodic, spectacular materialization of direct relations of force are the *symptomatic* and extreme evidence of some deeper set of societal flaws. In fact, the treatment of state violence as a *nonessential facet* of the US social formation is the discursive requirement for the establishment Left's strained attempts at political dialogue with its more hegemonic political antagonists: whether they are police, wardens, judges, legislators, or foundations. In this way, a principled and *radical* opposition to both the material actuality and political legitimacy of racist US state violence—which is inescapably a principled and radical opposition to the existence and legitimacy of the US state itself—is constantly deferred in favor of more "practical" or "winnable" campaigns and demands.

There is thus a particular historical urgency in the current struggle for new vernaculars that *disarticulate* the multilayered, taken-for-granted state practices of punishment, repression, and retribution from common notions of justice, peace, and the good society. Arguably, it is this difficult and dangerous task of disarticulation, specifically the displacement of a powerful, socially determinant "law and order" common sense,[21] that remains the most undertheorized dimension of contemporary struggles for social transformation. A generalized climate of (moral) defensiveness, political retreat, and pragmatic antiradicalism permeates the current critical discourse, such that the political and historical ground ceded to the punitive state and its defender-advocates mitigates against the flowering of new and creative knowledge productions. Antagonistic, radical, and proto-radical political practices—spurred by the desire to resist and abolish the normalized violence and undeclared domestic warfare of the American state—remain politically latent and deeply criminalized in the current social formation.

While the establishment Left conceptualizes its array of incorporated, entrepreneurial, non-profit 501(c)(3) organizations and NGOs as the fortified command center of progressive social justice movements within civil society, I remain constantly disturbed by the manner in which this political apparatus, the NPIC, perversely reproduces a dialectic of death. That is, the NPIC's (and by extension the establishment Left's) commitment to *maintaining* the essential social and political structures of civil society (meaning institutions, as well as ways of thinking) reproduces and enables the most vicious and insidious forms of state and state-sanctioned oppression and repression—by way of my previous examples, Israeli occupation, mass-based imprisonment, and the ongoing genocide of indigenous peoples. I will conclude this essay with a historical allegory of sorts.

Albert Memmi, in his anticolonialist meditation *The Colonizer and the Colonized* (1965), centrally addressed the *problem of presence* that marked the typological white supremacist domination of the colony. The colonizer—historically and prototypically, the categorical white man to whom many such theorists refer—ultimately found the Native indispensable, and not just because he could siphon and steal the Native's labor and other "natural" resources. The Native's indispensability was found, rather, in his/her bodily presence, which was nothing less than the affirmation of life's materiality for the settler. Memmi contends that it was through this very presence that whiteness found its form of articulation, its passage from the realm of the imaginary to the grittiness of material relation. Of the settler white man, Memmi writes,

> He knew, of course, that the colony was not peopled exclusively by colonists or colonizers. He even had some idea of the colonized from his childhood books; he has seen a documentary movie on some of their customs, preferably chosen to show their peculiarity. But the fact remained that those men belonged to the realms of the imagination....He had been a little worried about them when he too had decided to move to a colony, but no more so than he was about the climate, which might be unfavorable, or the water, which was said to contain too much limestone. Suddenly these men [sic] were no longer a simple component of geographical or historical décor. They assumed a place in his life.

> *He cannot even resolve to avoid them. He must constantly live in relation*
> *to them, for it is this very alliance which enables him to lead the life which he*
> *decided to look for in the colonies; it is this relationship which is lucrative, which*
> *creates privilege* [emphasis added].[22]

The white colonizer was consistently unsettled by the movement between the two primary requirements of the white colony and its underlying processes of conquest: the extermination of indigenous human societies, and the political-cultural naturalization of that very same (deeply unnatural) process. Memmi expounds on the dynamic and durable relationship between these forms of domination, ultimately arguing that the containment and strategic (social and physical) elimination of targeted populations is inseparable from the global ideology of Euro-American colonial domination that posits its sites of conquest as infinitely, "naturally" available for white settlement. Here, we might think about the connectedness between Memmi's definition of the colonial power relation and the current conditions of possibility for white civil society in the alleged aftermath of the colonial epoch.

The forced proximity between settlers and natives, or white civil society and its resident aliens, entails a historically persistent engagement between categories of humans generally defined by the colonizer as existential opposites. This intimacy defines the core antisociality of colonial conquest and the living history it has constructed: that is, contrary to more vulgar theorizations, the colonizer is not *simply* interested in ridding of the colonized, breaking them from indigenous attachments (to land, culture, community), or exploiting their bodies for industrial, domestic, or sexual labor. Memmi's colonizer (and liberation theorist Frantz Fanon's "settler") also desires an antisocial "human" relation, a structured dialogue with the colonized that performs a kind of autoerotic drama for the colonizer, a production of pleasure that both draws upon and maintains a distinct power structure.

Such is the partial premise for Fanon's contemporaneous meditation on the *war of social truths* that rages beneath the normalized violence of any such condition of domesticated domination and structured political dialogue. For Fanon, it is the Manichaean relation between colonized and colonizer, "native" and "settler," that conditions the subaltern truths of both imminent and manifest insurgencies. Speaking to the anticolonialist nationalism of the Algerian revolution, Fanon writes,

> The problem of truth ought also to be considered. In every age, among the peo-
> ple truth is the property of the national cause. No absolute verity, no discourse
> on the purity of the soul, can shake this position. The native replies to the living
> lie of the colonial situation by an equal falsehood. His dealings with his fellow-
> nationals are open; they are strained and incomprehensible with regard to the

settlers. Truth is that which hurries on the break-up of the colonialist regime; it is that which promotes the emergence of the nation; it is all that protects the natives, and ruins the foreigners. In this colonialist context there is no truthful behavior: and the good is quite simply that which is evil for "them."[23]

Truth, for Fanon, is precisely that which generates and multiplies the historical possibility of disruptive, subversive movement against colonial oppression. The evident rhetoric of oppositionality, of the subaltern "good" that *necessarily* materializes "evil" (or criminal) in the eyes of domination, offers a stunning departure from the language of negotiation, dialogue, progress, moderation, and peace that has become hegemonic in discourses of social change and social justice, inside and outside the United States. Perhaps most important, the political language of opposition is premised on its open-endedness and contingency, a particular refusal to soothe the anxiety generated in the attempt to displace a condition of violent peace for the sake of something else, a world beyond agendas, platforms, funding structures, and practical proposals. There are no guarantees, or arrogant expectations, of an ultimate state of liberation awaiting on the other side of the politically immediate struggle against the settler colony.

We might, for a fleeting moment, conceptualize the emergence of the NPIC as an institutionalization and industrialization of a banal, liberal political dialogue that constantly disciplines us into conceding the urgent challenges of a political radicalism that fundamentally challenges the existence of the US as a white settler society. The NPIC is not wholly unlike the institutional apparatus of neocolonialism, in which former and potential anticolonial revolutionaries are "professionalized" and granted opportunities within a labyrinthine state-proctored bureaucracy that ultimately reproduces the essential coherence of the neocolonial relation of power itself. The NPIC's well-funded litany of "social justice" agendas, platforms, mission statements, and campaigns offers a veritable smorgasbord of political guarantees that feeds on our cynicism and encourages a misled political faith that stridently bypasses the fundamental relations of dominance that structure our everyday existence in the United States: perhaps it is time that we formulate critical strategies that fully comprehend the NPIC *as the institutionalization of a relation of dominance* and attempt to disrupt and transform the fundamental structures and principles *of a white supremacist US civil society*, as well as the US racist state.

notes

1 Mumia Abu-Jamal, "The Industry of Fear," open correspondence to Critical Resistance: Beyond the Prison Industrial Complex, July 1998.
2 Robert L. Allen, *Black Awakening in Capitalist America: An Analytic History* (1969; repr., Trenton, NJ: Africa World Press, 1990). An excerpt from *Black Awakening* is reprinted in this volume.

3 Barry Goldwater, acceptance speech, 28th Republican National Convention, San Francisco, CA, July 16, 1964.

4 Some useful background texts include: Jael Silliman and Anannya Bhattacharjee, eds., *Policing the National Body: Race, Gender and Criminalization in the United States* (Cambridge, MA: South End Press, 2002); Christian Parenti, *Lockdown America: Police and Prisons in the Age of Crisis* (New York: Verso Press, 2000); Ted Gest, *Crime and Politics: Big Government's Erratic Campaign for Law and Order* (New York: Oxford University Press, 2001); Jill Nelson, ed., *Police Brutality: An Anthology* (New York: W. W. Norton, 2000); Stuart Hall, et. al., *Policing the Crisis: Mugging, the State, and Law and Order* (New York: Holmes & Meier, 1978).

5 See Ward Churchill and Jim Vander Wall, *Agents of Repression: The FBI's Secret Wars Against the Black Panther Party and the American Indian Movement* (Boston: South End Press, 1988), 1–62.

6 See generally Curt Gentry, *J. Edgar Hoover: The Man and the Secrets* (New York: W. W. Norton, 1992).

7 Nicholas Lemann, "Citizen 501(c)(3)," *The Atlantic Monthly* 279, no. 2 (February 1997), http://www.theatlantic.com/issues/97feb/5013c/5013c.htm.

8 George Soros, interview by David Brancaccio, *Now,* PBS, September 12, 2003, transcript, http://www.pbs.org/now/transcript/transcript_soros.html.

9 George Soros, "The Capitalist Threat," *The Atlantic Monthly* 279, no. 2 (February 1997), http://www.theatlantic.com/issues/97feb/capital/capital.htm.

10 Ibid.

11 Antonio Gramsci, *Selections From the Prison Notebooks,* ed. Quintin Hoare and Geoffrey Nowell Smith (New York: International Publishers, 1995), 259.

12 John McCarthy, David Britt, and Mark Wolfson, "The Institutional Channeling of Social Movements by the State in the United States," *Research in Social Movements, Conflicts and Change* 13 (1991): 48.

13 Ibid.

14 Ibid.

15 Jennifer R. Wolch, *The Shadow State: Government and Voluntary Sector in Transition* (New York: The Foundation Center, 1990), 15.

16 Noam Chomsky, *The Culture of Terrorism* (Boston: South End Press, 1988), 6.

17 See Aldon Morris, *The Origins of the Civil Rights Movement: Black Communities Organizing for Change* (New York: Free Press, 1986).

18 Wolch, *The Shadow State,* 206–207.

19 Ruth Wilson Gilmore has often spoken of the generally underexplored and undertheorized political possibilities in engaging organizing strategies that are "conservative in form, but radical in content." She speaks of such strategies manifesting in historically conservative spaces, such as the church or mosque, while articulating a political critique and praxis that envisions radical social transformation.

20 See Haunani-Kay Trask, "The New World Order," in *From a Native Daughter: Colonialism and Sovereignty in Hawaii* (Honolulu: University of Hawaii Press, 1999), 58–63.

21 My use of the term *common sense* derives from Antonio Gramsci's conception of the assumptions, truths, and general faiths that predominate in a given social formation or hegemony.

22 Albert Memmi, *The Colonizer and the Colonized* (New York: Orion Press, 1965), 7–8.

23 Frantz Fanon, *The Wretched of the Earth* (New York: Grove Weidenfeld, 1963), 50.

▸▸Ruth Wilson Gilmore

in the shadow of the shadow state

Organized philanthropy is playing a significant role in this age of tottering social standards, crumbling religious sanctions, perverse race attitudes, and selfish and ulterior motives.—Ira De A. Reid, 1944 [1]

EVEN IN TODAY'S WORLD, IRA REID'S WORDS STILL RING TRUE, descriptive of a scenario many contemporary social justice activists think is unique to our times. Yet, more than 60 years ago the dimensions of organized philanthropy's "significant role" in the African American community prompted Reid to write an incisive analysis in which he noted two things. First, during a period of about 20 years, both reformist and radical Black groups had become increasingly dependent on foundation gifts over membership dues. Second, both donors and recipients acted on assumptions about each other *and* about the possibility for social change which, regardless of intent, reinforced the very structures groups had self-organized to dismantle.[2] These two obstacles—dependency and accommodation—did not destroy the US mid-century freedom movement; activists took down US apartheid in its legal form. Freedom was not a gift, even if donations advanced the work for freedom. Our challenge is to understand these paradoxes in the early 21st century, at a time when the US-led forces of empire, imprisonment, and inequality have even seized the word "freedom," using the term's lively resonance to obscure the murderous effects of their global military, political, and economic crusade.

Is there a non-profit industrial complex (NPIC)? How did it come into being? How is it powerful? In this essay I will work through these questions rather generally (one might say theoretically) and then illustrate how the mid-20th-century history is complicated in ways we can emulate, if not duplicate. And finally, I will offer a few suggestions about how organizations might think about funders, and about themselves. Other contributors to this volume will amplify specific instances and opportunities that current grassroots activists can use to strengthen and liberate our work, such that we are able to achieve non-reformist reforms on the road to liberation.

the non-profit industrial complex

During the past decade or so, radical thinkers have done a few turns on the term "military industrial complex." Mike Davis's "prison industrial complex"[3] was the first to gain wide use, in part because of the groundbreaking 1998 conference and strategy session Critical Resistance: Beyond the Prison Industrial Complex. It is useful to briefly consider what these "~ industrial complexes" consist of, and why they matter, by going back to President Dwight D. Eisenhower's 1961 farewell address to the nation, in which he introduced the concept "military industrial complex." He warned that the wide-scale and intricate connection between the military and the warfare industry would determine the course of economic development and political decision-making for the country, to the detriment of all other sectors and ideas. His critique seems radical when we remember he was a retired general, an anticommunist (speaking at the height of the Cold War), and an unabashed advocate of capitalism. But he spoke against many powerful tides. As a matter of fact, the United States has never had an industrial policy divorced from its military adventures (from the Revolutionary War forward), and the technical ability to mass-produce many consumer products, from guns to shoes, was initially worked out under lucrative contracts to the US military. However, in the buildup to World War II, and the establishment of the Pentagon in its aftermath, the production, delivery, and training for the use of weapons of mass destruction reconfigured the US intellectual and material landscape through the establishment of military bases, secure weapons research facilities, standing armed forces, military contractors, elected and appointed personnel, academic researchers (in science, languages, and area studies especially), pundits, massive infrastructural development (for example interstate highways), and so forth. Many taken-for-granted technologies, from the internet to Tang-brand powdered citrus drink, were developed under the aegis of national security. The electoral and economic rise of the southern and western states (the "Sunbelt") ascended via the movement of people and money to those regions to carry out the permanent expansion and perfection of killing people on an industrial scale. In other words, without the military industrial complex, presidents Nixon, Carter, Reagan, Bush I, Clinton, and Bush II would never have achieved the White House.

When activists started to use the term "prison industrial complex" they intended to say as much about the intricate connections reshaping the US landscape as were suggested by the term "military industrial complex." From "tough on communism" to "tough on crime," the consistency between the two complexes lies in how broadly their reach has compromised all sorts of alternative futures. The main point here is not that a few corporations call the shots—they don't—rather an entire realm of social policy and social investment is hostage to the development and perfection of means of mass punishment—from prison to post-release conditions implicating a wide range of people and places. Some critics of this analytic framework find it weak because the dollar amount that circulates through the prison industrial complex is not "big" enough to set a broader economic agenda. The criticism is wrong in two different ways: first, the point of the term "prison industrial complex" is to highlight the devastating effect of industrialized punishment that has hidden, noneconomic as well as measurable dollar costs to governments and households; and second, the term's purpose is to show how a social policy based in coercion and endless punishment destroys communities where prisoners come from and communities where prisons are built. The connection between prisons and the military is both a not-surprising material one (some military firms have become vendors to prison systems, though most beneficiaries of prison and jail spending are individual wage earners—including retired military) and a not-surprising ideological or cultural one—the broad normalization of the belief that the key to safety is aggression.[4]

How does "non-profit industrial complex" fit into the picture? Both the military and the prison industrial complex have reshaped the national landscape and consequently shifted people's understanding of themselves in the world—because norms change along with forms. Both the military and prison industrial complexes have led *and* followed other changes. Let's look at the state's role in these complexes. Importantly, part of the work the aggression agencies do is serve as the principal form of legitimacy for the intrigues of people who want to gain or keep state power these days. Why would they even need such cover? They and their ideologues have triumphed in promoting and imposing a view that certain capacities of the state are obstacles to development, and thus should be shrunken or otherwise debilitated from playing a central role in everyday economic and social life. But their actions are contrary to their rhetoric. Strangely, then, we are faced with the ascendance of antistate state actors: people and parties who gain state power by denouncing state power. Once they have achieved an elected or appointed position in government they have to make what they do seem transparently legitimate, and if budgets are any indication, they spend a lot of money even as they claim they're "shrinking government." Prison, policing, courts, and the military enjoy such legitimacy, and nowadays it seems to many observers as though there was never a time things were different. Thus normalization slips into naturalization, and people imagine that locking folks in cages or bombing civilians or sending generation after generation off to kill somebody else's children is all part of "human nature." But, like human nature, everything has a history, and the antistate state actors have followed a peculiar trajectory to their current locations.

During the past 40 years or so, as the Sunbelt secured political domination over the rest of the US, capitalists of all kinds successfully gained relief from paying heavily into the New Deal/Great Society social wage via taxes on prof-its. (The "social wage" is another name for tax receipts.) At the same time, they have squeezed workers' pay packets, keeping individual wages for all US workers pretty much flat since 1973, excluding a blip in the late 1990s that did not trickle down to the lowest wage workers but raised higher level salaries. These capitalists and their apologists hid the double squeeze behind their effective rhetorical use of issues such as civil rights and affirmative action to invoke in the late 1960s and after the "wages of whiteness"—which any attentive person should have figured wouldn't pay any better than they did at the close of Reconstruction a hundred years earlier.[5] While even white workers did not gain wage increases, the gen-eral southern strategy paid off, bringing Nixon to the White House, and bringing "the government"—the weak social welfare state—under suspicion. From then until now, the agenda for capitalists and relatively autonomous state actors has been to restructure state agencies that had been designed under the enormous emergency of the Great Depression (the New Deal) and its aftermath (loosely, the Great Society) to promote the general welfare.

While neoconservatives and neoliberals diverge in their political ideals, they share certain convictions about the narrow legitimacy of the public sector in the conduct of everyday life, despite the US constitutional admonition that the gov-ernment *should* "promote the general welfare." For them, wide-scale protections from calamity and opportunities for advancement should not be a public good centrally organized to benefit everyone who is eligible. Antistate state actors come from both camps, and insist that the withdrawal of the state from certain areas of social welfare provision will enhance rather than destroy the lives of those aban-doned. Lapsed New Deal Democrat Patrick Moynihan called it "benign neglect," while Reagan heir George H. W. Bush called it "a thousand points of light." In this view, the first line of defense is the market, which solves most problems efficiently, and because the market is unfettered, fairness results from universal access to the same ("perfect") information individuals, households, and firms use to make self-interested decisions. And where the market fails, the voluntary, non-profit sector can pick up any stray pieces because the extent to which extra economic values (such as kindness or generosity or decency) come into play is the extent to which abandonment produces its own socially strengthening rewards. That's their ideal: a frightening willingness to engage in human sacrifice while calling it something else.

In fact, for so large and varied a society as the United States, abandonment is far too complicated for any single ideologue, party, or election cycle to achieve; experience shows abandonment takes a long time and produces new agencies and structures that replace, supplement, or even duplicate old institutions. Many factors contribute to this complexity. One is that large-scale public bureaucracies are hard to take down completely, due to a combination of their' initiative and inertia; another is the fear that a sudden and complete suspension of certain kinds of social goods will provoke uprisings and other responses that, while ultimately controllable, come at a political cost. Here's where non-profits enter the current political economy.

As a "third sector" (neither state nor business), non-profits have existed in what's now the US since the mid-17th century, when colonial Harvard College was incorporated. Today there are nearly 2 million non-profits in the US, including, along with educational institutions, hospitals, schools, museums, operas, think tanks, foundations, and, at the bottom, some grassroots organizations. While the role of some of these organizations has not changed significantly, we *have* seen increased responsibility on the part of non-profits to deliver direct services to those in need of them. What also distinguishes the expansion of social-service non-profits is that increasingly their role is to take responsibility for persons who are in the throes of abandonment rather than responsibility for persons progressing toward full incorporation into the body politic.

Jennifer Wolch developed the term "shadow state" to describe the contemporary rise of the voluntary sector that is involved in direct social services previously provided by wholly public New Deal/Great Society agencies.[6] Legislatures and executive branches transformed bureaucracies basically into policing bodies, whose role became to oversee service provision rather than to provide it themselves. This abandonment provoked a response among organizations that advocated on behalf of certain categories of state clients: the elderly, mothers, children, and so forth.[7] It also encouraged the formation of new groups that, lacking an advocacy past, were designed solely to get contracts and the jobs that came with them. To do business with the state, the organizations had to be formally incorporated, so they became non-profits. Thus, for different reasons, non-profits stepped up to fill a service void.

The expansion of non-profit activities structurally linked to public social services was not new, nor could it be said that when public services were on the rise the voluntary sector stayed home. To the contrary, for more than 100 years the relationship between public and voluntary had been a fairly tight one.[8] But for Wolch, the shadow state's specific provenance is the resolution of two historical waves: the unprecedented expansion of government agencies and services (1933–1973), followed by an equally wide-scale attempt to undo many of those programs at all levels—federal, state, county, local.[9]

Antistate state actors welcomed non-profits under the rhetoric of efficiency (read: meager budgets) and accountability (read: contracts could be pulled if anybody stepped out of line). As a result of these and other pressures, non-profits providing direct services have become highly professionalized by their relationship with the state. They have had to conform to public rules governing public money, and have found that being fiduciary agents in some ways trumps their principal desire to comfort and assist those abandoned to their care. They do not want to lose the contracts to provide services because they truly care about clients who otherwise would have nowhere to go; thus they have been sucked into the world of non-profit providers, which, like all worlds, has its own jargon, limits (determined by bid and budget cycles, and legislative trends), and both formal as well as informal hierarchies. And, generally, the issues they are paid to address have been narrowed to program-specific categories and remedies which make staff—who often have a great understanding of the scale and scope of both individual clients' and the needs of society at large—become in their everyday practice technocrats through imposed specialization.[10] The shadow state, then, is real but without significant political clout, forbidden by law to advocate for systemic change, and bound by public rules and non-profit charters to stick to its mission or get out of business and suffer legal consequences if it strays along the way.

The dramatic proliferation of non-profits in the 1980s and after also produced a flurry of experts to advise on the creation and management of non-profits and the relationship of public agencies to non-profits, further professionalizing the sector. High-profile professors of management, such as Peter F. Drucker, wrote books on the topic, and business schools developed entire curricula devoted to training the non-profit manager.[11] As had long been the case, every kind of non-profit from the largest (hospitals and higher-education establishments) to the smallest sought out income sources other than public grants and contracts, and "organized philanthropy" provided the promise of some independence from the rule-laden and politically erratic public-funding stream for those involved in social welfare activity.

While we bear in mind that foundations are repositories of twice-stolen wealth—(a) profit sheltered from (b) taxes—that can be retrieved by those who stole it at the opera or the museum, at Harvard or a fine medical facility,[12] it is also true that major foundations have put some resources into different kinds of community projects, and some program officers have brought to their portfolios profound critiques of the status quo and a sense of their own dollar-driven, though board-limited, creative potential. At the same time, the transfer to the baby boomer generation (those born between 1946 and 1964) of what by the year 2035 will be trillions of dollars of inherited wealth began to open the possibility for more varied types of funding schemes that non-profits might turn to good use as some boomer heirs seek specifically to remedy the stark changes described in these pages.[13] Such initiatives and events encouraged grassroots social justice organizations that otherwise might have continued their work below the Internal Revenue Service and formal-funding radar to incorporate as non-profits to make what they have consistently hoped to be great leaps forward in social justice.[14] In other cases, unincorporated grassroots groups receiving money under the shelter of existing non-profits have been compelled to formalize their status because auditors have decided that the non-profits who sponsor them have strayed outside the limits defined by their mission statements.

The grassroots groups that have formally joined the third sector are in the shadow of the shadow state. They are not direct service providers but often work with the clients of such organizations as well as with the providers themselves. They generally are not recipients of public funds although occasionally they get government contracts to do work in jails or shelters or other institutions. They have detailed political programs and deep social and economic critiques. Their leadership is well educated in the ways of the world, whatever their level of formal schooling, and they try to pay some staff to promote and proliferate the organization's analysis and activity even if most participants in the group are unpaid volunteers. The government is often the object of their advocacy and their antagonisms—whether because the antistate state is the source of trouble or the locus for remedy. But the real focus of their energies is ordinary people whom they wish fervently to organize against their own abandonment.

The "non-profit industrial complex" describes all of the dense and intricate connections enumerated in the last few paragraphs, and suggests, as is the case with the military industrial complex and the prison industrial complex, that something is amiss. What's wrong is not simply the economic dependencies fostered by this peculiar set of relationships and interests. More important, if forms do indeed shape norms, then what's wrong is that the work people set out to accomplish is vulnerable to becoming mission impossible under the sternly specific funding rubrics and structural prohibitions that situate grassroots groups both in the third sector's entanglements and in the shadow of the shadow state. In particular, the modest amount of money that goes to grassroots groups is mostly restricted to projects rather than core operations.[15] And while the activist right (which has non-profits and foundations up the wazoo) regularly attacks the few dollars that go to anti-abandonment organizations, it has loads of funds for core operations; as of the end of the last century, the Right had raised more than $1 billion to fund *ideas*.[16] How core can you get? In other words, although we live in revolutionary times, in which the entire landscape of social justice is, or will shortly become, like post-Katrina New Orleans because it has been subject to the same long-term abandonment of infrastructure and other public goods, funders require grassroots organizations to act like secure suburbanites who have one last corner of the yard to plant.

what is to be done?

Let's go back to the mid-20th-century to think about what kinds of options people employed to make best use of the resources they had at hand. We saw that "organized philanthropy" caused problems even as it also produced opportunities. The dual obstacles to liberation occasioned by the vexed relationship between funders and "minority" organizations—dependency and accommodation—did not destroy the antiapartheid movement. I suggest that part of what helped secure a better outcome was that Reid[17] and other critics pointed out what kinds of problems had materialized over the course of several decades, and people put their minds and hands to solving the problems without abandoning themselves. Thus the problems were not absolute impediments, especially insofar as the recognition of them produced the possibility for some organizations—and their funders—to see each other differently and more usefully. More to the point, along the broadly interlocked social justice front that swept across the country in the mid-century, the committed people took the money and ran. I don't mean they lied or they stole, but rather that they figured out how to foster their general activism from all kinds of resources, and they were too afraid of the consequences of stopping to cease what they'd started. They combined flexibility with opportunity in the best sense, working the ever-changing combination toward radical goals. And they did not fool themselves or others into pretending that winning a loss—sticking a plant on a mound of putrid earth in a poisoned and flooded field—was the moral or material equivalent to winning a win. Here are snapshots of four cases that illustrate what I mean. These are not complete histories; those stories have been well written by many and should be read by activists who want to learn from the past in order to remake the future. If people living under the most severe constraints, such as prisoners, can form study groups to learn about the world, then free-world activists have no excuse for ignorance, nor should they rely on funder-designed workshops and training sessions to do what revolutionaries in all times have done on their own.

1949—pacifist/anarcho-feminist organizing in the san francisco bay area. Pacifica Radio formed when a small group of white activists tried to figure out how to use radio for radical ends. They were inspired by radio's potential rather than daunted by its limitations. Their challenge was to make broadcast possible without advertising, because, in their view, commercial sponsorship would always compromise independent expression. To evade capitalist control they became a subscription, or listener-sponsored, organization that also, over time, combined foundation support with the dollars sent in each year from ordinary households. Without a single advertisement from that day until now, they have largely funded themselves from the bottom up.[18] Pacifica became a foundation that developed a small national network, and as it grew from the first station, its complexity made the straightforward goals of the founders a challenge to secure. In the late 1990s, the national board tried to sell off the network's main asset—the 50,000-watt KPFA station—using the then-prevalent logic of non-profit management to veil their effort to limit independent expressive art and journalism. The fact that such a board came to direct the foundation was an outcome of the pressures to professionalize that all non-profits have encountered during the period under review. The gargantuan efforts needed to fight back against the board and re-democratize Pacifica's governance forced the organization to confront its internal racial and gendered hierarchies.[19] Thus, a formidable means to amplify radical voices during the mid-century freedom movement developed from the grassroots, and success made it vulnerable to the structural constraints that squeeze even relatively mighty organizations that work today in the shadow of the shadow state.

1955—urban antiracist activism in the jim crow south. In the folktale version, the Montgomery Bus Boycott started when Rosa Parks was too tired to move to the back of the bus. But, of course, we know the boycott was not a spontaneous event. Parks acted as part of a larger organization, and also as one of a series of refuseniks who sat in the front of the segregated public from 1943 forward. How did a group of people concentrated in but not exclusively located in Montgomery, Alabama, manage to assault and scale apartheid's wall? The people who organized themselves had short-, medium-, and long-term goals to raise awareness, to involve the masses, and to desegregate the buses as a means to undo other aspects of apartheid. Three key political formations were involved: the Dexter Avenue Baptist Church, the Women's Political Council, and the Montgomery Improvement Association. Each filled a different role, and all three were funded from the bottom up. The Women's Political Council—which comprised grassroots thinkers, including activist-scholars—crafted the plans and maintained a low profile during their execution. The Montgomery Improvement Association organized carpools that ensured boycott participants would be able to get to and from work and not lose their jobs or neglect their households. The Dexter Avenue Church served as a staging ground, and the place from which the principal rhetoric of equality as fairness emerged, in the form of thrilling speeches by the young Martin Luther King, Jr. The collaboration by these groups evaded the obstacle of accommodation and worked relatively independently of the major African American organizations that were fighting for the same goal. And while the Dexter Avenue Church had no intention of disappearing, the other two organizations were flexible in their design and in their intended longevity, with the outcome rather than the organization the purpose for their existence.[20]

1956—agricultural labor/antiracist activism. A third example is from the Agricultural Workers Organizing Committee (AWOC), a largely Filipino American and

Japanese American grouping associated with the Congress of Industrial Organizations. The group began to organize in 1956 with the goal of reviving the type of radical agricultural organizing that had shut down harvests in California's Central Valley in 1933 and nearly succeeded a second time in 1938. They fought a hard battle; both state and federal law forbade farmworkers from organizing, and the *bracero* (or guest worker) program had undermined even illegal field organizing from 1942 onward. One of the techniques used by AWOC to get "buy in" from workers was to require a large chunk of their meager wages to fund the organization's activities. In this view, when one owns something one cannot sell—such as membership in an organization—one is more likely to participate in it. While AWOC did not succeed, its funding structure was adopted by César Chávez and Dolores Huerta when they started the United Farm Workers (UFW). Their work began as the *bracero* program ended, and while they still confronted legal sanctions against their work, they had the advantage of workers who, though migrant, were increasingly based in the region permanently.[21] Their campaigns powerfully combined the language of civil rights with that of labor rights,[22] and when the UFW reached beyond the fields for support they fashioned a variety of ways that people throughout the US and beyond could demonstrate solidarity, be it through writing checks, lobbying for wage and safety laws, forming coalitions in support of farmworkers, or refusing to eat grapes and other fruits of exploited labor.[23]

1962—coffee-table politics. Many are looking for an organizational structure and a resource capability that will somehow be impervious to cooptation. But it is impossible to create a model that the other side cannot figure out. For example, imagine neighborhoods in which women come to have a political understanding of themselves and the world. They go to their neighbors and say, "Hey read this, it changed my life. I'll babysit your kids while you do." In this appealing model, the written works circulate while women care for each other's children and form a cooperative system, which does not have paid staff. Because of what they have learned, they go on to run for school board and lobby legislators, and ultimately exercise huge impacts on local, state and national elections. Sounds like a great model, right? Yes, it does. It's also the origin of the New Right in California.[24] This is the movement that attempted to put Barry Goldwater in the White House, that put Ronald Reagan in the governor's mansion, Richard Nixon in the White House, and Ronald Reagan in the White House. This is the movement that has done the grassroots work that created the need for the shadow state to rise.

If contemporary grassroots activists are looking for a pure form of doing things, they should stop. There is no organizational structure that the Right cannot use for its own purposes. And further, the example of the New Right points out a weakness in contemporary social theory that suggests the realm of "civil society"—which is neither "market" nor "state"—is the place where liberatory politics necessarily unfold. Michael Mann shows how quite the opposite happened in the Nazi takeover of Germany, arguing that a dense civil society formed crucial infrastructure for the party.[25] I argued earlier that "forms create norms," and it might appear that this last section is contradictory. Yes and no. Form does not mean blueprint, but rather the lived relations and imaginative possibilities emanating from those relationships. In a sense, form is a resolutely geographical concept, because it is about making pathways and places rather than searching endlessly for the perfect method and mode.

Grassroots non-profits should uniformly encourage funders to move away from project-driven portfolios; if the results enjoyed by the activist Right are any indication, $1 billion for ideas would go a long way toward regenerating the devastated landscape of social justice. Funders who want to return their inherited wealth to the communities who produced it should reflect on whether they are building glorious edifices that in the end perpetuate inequality. Reid pointed out the mismatch between the gleaming physical plant segregated colleges and universities built with foundation support and the weak curricula designed to produce a professional managerial class whose lifework would be to keep their people in check.[26]

Finally, grassroots organizations that labor in the shadow of the shadow state should consider this: that the purpose of the work is to gain liberation, not to guarantee the organization's longevity. In the short run, it seems the work and the organizations are an identity: the staff and pamphlets and projects and ideas gain some traction on this slippery ground because they have a bit of weight. That's true. But it is also the case that when it comes to building social movements, organizations are only as good as the united fronts they bring into being. Lately funders have been very excited by the possibility of groups aligning with unlikely allies. But to create a powerful front, a front with the capacity to change the landscape, it seems that connecting with *likely* allies would be a better use of time and trouble. Remembering that likely allies have all become constricted by mission statements and hostile laws to think in silos rather than expansively, grassroots organizations can be the voices of history and the future to assemble the disparate and sometimes desperate non-profits who labor in the shadow of the shadow state.

notes

1 Ira De A. Reid, "Philanthropy and Minorities," *Phylon*5, no. 3 (1944): 266.
2 Ibid.
3 Mike Davis, "Hell's Factories in the Fields," *Nation*, January 1995, 32–37.

4 See Ruth Wilson Gilmore, "Fatal Couplings of Power and Difference: Notes on Racism and Geography," *The Professional Geographer* 54, no. 1 (2002): 15–24; Omer Bartov, *Murder in Our Midst: The Holocaust, Industrial Killing, and Representation* (New York and Oxford: Oxford University Press, 1996).

5 W. E. B. Du Bois, *Black Reconstruction in America, 1860–1880* (1935; repr., New York: Atheneum, 1992); David Roediger, *The Wages of Whiteness* (New York: Verso, 1991).

6 Jennifer Wolch, *The Shadow State: Government and the Voluntary Sector in Transition* (New York: The Foundation Center, 1990).

7 For a thorough analysis of the politics of health see Jenna M. Loyd, "Freedom's Body: Radical Health Activism in Los Angeles, 1963-1978" (Ph.D. dissertation, University of California, Berkeley, 2005).

8 See Reid, "Philanthropy and Minorities." See also Jennifer Klein, *For All These Rights: Business, Labor, and the Shaping of America's Public-Private Welfare State* (Princeton, NJ: Princeton University Press, 2003).

9 For a sense of the global dimension of this growth see Lester M. Salamon, "The Rise of the Nonprofit Sector," *Foreign Affairs* 73, no. 4 (1994): 109–122.

10 Robert W. Lake, "Structural Constraints and Pluralist Contradictions in Hazardous Waste Regulation," *Environment and Planning A* 24 (2002): 663–681; Robert W. Lake, "Negotiating Local Autonomy" *Professional Geographer* 13, no. 5 (1994): 423–442.

11 Peter F. Drucker, *Managing the Nonprofit Organization: Principles and Practice* (New York: HarperCollins, 1990).

12 Teresa Odenthal, *America's Wealthy and the Future of Foundations* (New York: The Foundation Center, 1987).

13 Lester M. Salamon, "The Nonprofit Sector at a Crossroads: The Case of America," *Voluntas: International Journal of Voluntary and Nonprofit Organizations* 10, no.1 (1999): 5–23.

14 Robin Garr, *Reinvesting in America: The Grassroots Movements That Are Feeding the Hungry, Housing the Homeless, and Putting Americans Back to Work* (Reading, MA: Addison-Wesley Press, 1995). See also Ruth Wilson Gilmore, *Golden Gulag: Prisons, Crisis, Surplus, and Opposition in Globalizing California* (Berkeley: University of California Press, 2007).

15 Robert O. Bothwell, "Philanthropic Funding of Social Change and the Diminution of Progressive Policymaking," in *Non-profit Advocacy and the Policy Process: A Seminar Series* 2 (Washington, DC: The Urban Institute, 2001): 67–81.

16 David Callahan, *$1 Billion for Ideas: Conservative Think Tanks in the 1990s* (Washington, DC: National Committee for Responsive Philanthropy, 1999).

17 Reid, "Philanthropy and Minorities."

18 Lewis Hill, "The Theory of Listener-Sponsored Radio," *The Quarterly of Film, Radio and Television* 7, no. 2. (winter 1952): 163–169.

19 Iain A. Boal, draft statement of purpose, Coalition for a Democratic Pacifica, Berkeley, CA, December 29, 1999.

20 Robin D. G. Kelley, *Race Rebels* (New York: The Free Press, 1996) and Robin D. G. Kelley, *Freedom Dreams* (Boston: Beacon Press, 2003).

21 Gilmore, *Golden Gulag*; Laura Pulido, *Environmentalism and Economic Justice* (Tucson: University of Arizona Press, 1996).

22 Marshall Ganz, "Resources and Resourcefulness: Strategic Capacity in the Unionization of California Agriculture, 1959–1966," *American Journal of Sociology* 105, no. 4 (2000): 1003–1062.

23 Pulido, *Environmentalism and Economic Justice*; Ganz, "Resources and Resourcefulness."

24 Lisa McGirr, *Suburban Warriors: The Origins of the New American Right* (Princeton, NJ: Princeton University Press, 2002).

25 Michael Mann, *Fascists* (Cambridge: Cambridge University Press, 2004).

26 Cathy Cohen, *Boundaries of Blackness: AIDS and the Breakdown of Black Politics* (Chicago: University of Chicago Press, 1999).

>>Robert L. Allen

from Black Awakening in Capitalist America

Editor's Note: This is an excerpt from Robert L. Allen's classic Black Awakening in Capitalist America. *Readers will note that it assumes knowledge of events from the Black Power era. Also, most of his sources are not cited. Nevertheless, nearly four decades later Allen's analysis of the Ford Foundation's impact on the Black Power movement is prophetic and sufficiently clear to audiences today that we are including this excerpt as it appeared in 1969; departures from the original are indicated in brackets.*

"THE YEAR 1967," WROTE JAMES FORMAN OF THE STUDENT NON-violent Coordinating Committee (SNCC), "marked a historic milestone in the struggle for the liberation of black people in the United States and [was] the year that revolutionaries throughout the world began to understand more fully the impact of the black movement. Our liberation will only come when there is final destruction of this mad octopus—the capitalistic system of the United States with all its life-sucking tentacles of exploitation and racism that choke the people of Africa, Asia, and Latin America."[1]

There can be little doubt that Forman was right in pointing to 1967 as an important turning point in the history of black America. It was a year of unprecedented massive and widespread urban revolts. It was the year that so-called riots became an institutionalized form of black protest. Attempts to build black united fronts were taking place around the country. There was the Black United Front of Washington, DC, the North City Congress in Philadelphia, the United Front in Boston, the Black United Conference in Denver, and the Black Congress in Los Angeles. These were coalitions which sought to alter power relations in the cities where they existed [and] to establish some measure of black control or influence in those cities. They also faced the…same dangers of manipulation and co-optation. They had to come to grips with the threat of gradual takeover by more conservative blacks who have little desire to serve the community.

The simple but unfortunate fact is that the militants are usually less well organized than the Urban League, the NAACP, [the Southern Christian Leadership

Council], preachers, teachers, and social workers who are invited to participate in the [struggle for black liberation]. Consequently, it is relatively easy for these representatives of the privileged black bourgeoisie to take control of organizations ostensibly dedicated to militant reform, to enabling black people to assume control over their own lives. If this process of takeover goes unchecked, the united front is transformed into an instrumentality serving the interests of the black middle class alone. The needs of the popular black masses go by the board, and a new oppressive elite assumes power. It is only to the extent that the united fronts serve the needs and aspirations of the great bulk of black people that they can be regarded as progressive organizations. To the extent that they fall in the hands of a privileged and opportunistic elite, they become simply an added burden strapped to the back of black America....

The ouster of Harlem Congressman Adam Clayton Powell from the House of Representatives prompted the Congress for Racial Equality (CORE) to concretize its interest in electoral politics. On January 16, 1967, [the organization's national director] Floyd McKissick issued a call for a conference to create a national black political structure. "No political machinery now in existence," he said, "is available to us through which our just hopes and aspirations can be achieved." He told reporters that the proposed structure would be "an apparatus, not a [political] party." This apparatus would assist CORE in deciding whether to support the Democratic or Republican parties or "develop an independent platform which it will attempt to sell to the Democrats or Republicans." McKissick added that black people were moving toward bloc voting throughout the United States. He said that both national political parties had failed blacks, and he sought to "elevate the black man to a state of equality in the decision-making processes of government." He expressed the hope that the proposed political structure would become a "formidable bloc" by the time of the 1968 national elections.

Thus CORE was in the contradictory position of espousing greater black involvement in electoral politics even though it was precisely in this sphere—with the humiliating ouster of Powell—that black people had just suffered a significant political defeat. But the temptations of electoral politics were too great to be denied. The proposed conference never took place, but CORE and its tacit ally, the Black Power Conference, moved progressively closer to becoming little more than political lobbies advocating reforms, taking whatever political crumbs they could garner for themselves.

CORE was to take other curious turns, and eventually ally itself with an arm of the very power structure which it claimed to be fighting. Early in 1967 the Ford Foundation made grants of several hundred thousand dollars to the NAACP and the Urban League. A few months later the Foundation gave $1 million to the NAACP Legal Defense Fund's new National Office for the Rights of Indigents.

But for the purpose of urban pacification these groups were less than satisfactory, since there was serious doubt as to how much control they exercised over the young militants and frustrated ghetto blacks who were likely to be heaving Molotov cocktails during the summer. If its efforts to keep the lids on the cities were to succeed, the Foundation had to find some way to penetrate militant organizations which were believed to wield some influence over the angry young blacks who are trapped in the urban chaos.

The first move in this direction occurred in May 1967, when the Foundation granted $500,000 to the Metropolitan Applied Research Center (MARC), a newly created organization in New York with a militant-sounding program headed by Dr. Kenneth B. Clark, a psychology professor who at one time was associated with Harlem's anti-poverty program. When it was organized the previous March, MARC announced that its purpose was to "pioneer in research and action on behalf of the powerless urban poor in northern metropolitan areas." Clark's strategy was to get the large corporations involved in the ghetto. "Business and industry are our last hope," he once remarked. "They are the most realistic elements of our society." Interestingly, in a brochure MARC compared itself with the semi-governmental RAND Corporation, which does research for the Air Force. The difference between the two, according to the brochure, is that MARC is not associated with the government, nor is it limited to research. It is also an action organization.

One of MARC's first actions was to name Roy Innis, then chairman of CORE's militant Harlem chapter, as its first civil rights "fellow-in-residence." The May 11 announcement also stated that the Reverend Martin Luther King, Jr., president of the Southern Christian Leadership Conference, and the Reverent Andrew Young, one of King's chief aides, had "agreed to take part in the fellowship program."

Innis received a six-month fellowship. "The civil rights fellowships," wrote the *New York Times* on May 12, "are designed to give the leaders an opportunity to evaluate their programs and tactics and undertake long-range planning." MARC's staff was to aid the leaders in their studies, and the fellows were to draw salaries equal to those they received from their organizations or from private employment.

Clark said he had also discussed fellowships with Floyd McKissick, national director of CORE; Stokely Carmichael, then chairman of SNCC; Whitney Young of the Urban League; and Roy Wilkins of the NAACP.

MARC's next move was to call a secret meeting [at the home of Dr. Clark] of civil rights leaders for May 27. Subsequently, another such meeting was held June 13 at a Suffern, New York, motel among Clark and leaders of nine major civil rights groups. At the conclusion of that meeting, Clark announced a joint effort to calm Cleveland's racial tension. He said the "underlying causes of unrest and despair among urban ghetto Negroes, as well as clear indications of their grim, sobering and costly consequences, are found in classic form in Cleveland."

What Clark did not mention was that the Ford Foundation had been trying to "calm" Cleveland since 1961 by financing various local research and action projects. But despite this joint effort, Cleveland blew up in 1966, and further serious rumblings were heard in the early spring of 1967.

Clearly, a new approach was needed in Cleveland, and the stage was set for the Ford Foundation's first direct grant to a militant group—the Cleveland chapter of CORE. The Foundation announced on July 14 that it was giving $175,000 to the Special Purposes Fund of CORE to be used for "training of Cleveland youth and adult community workers, voter registration efforts, exploration of economic-development programs, and attempts to improve program planning among civil rights groups." In explaining the grant, [Ford Foundation president] McGeorge Bundy said that Foundation staff and consultants had been investigating Cleveland "for some months." In fact, he said, "it was predictions of new violence in the city that led to our first staff visits in March."

Apparently realizing that the grant might give the impression of a close relationship developing between the Foundation and CORE, Bundy added: "The national officers of CORE have dealt with us on this matter in a businesslike way, and neither Mr. Floyd McKissick nor I supposes that this grant requires the two of us—or our organizations—to agree on all public questions. It does require us both to work together in support of the peaceful and constructive efforts of CORE's Cleveland leadership, and that is what we plan to do."

It must be said that CORE was vulnerable to such corporate penetration. In the first place, they needed money. Floyd McKissick in 1966 had become national director of an organization which was several hundred thousand dollars in debt, and espousal of black power scared away potential financial supporters.

Second, CORE's militant rhetoric but ambiguous and reformist definition of black power as simply black control of black communities appealed to Foundation officials who were seeking just those qualities in a black organization which hopefully could tame the ghettos. From the Foundation's point of view, old-style moderate leaders no longer exercised any real control, while genuine black radicals were too dangerous. CORE [fit] the bill because its talk about black revolution was believed to appeal to discontented blacks, while its program of achieving black power through massive injections of governmental, business, and Foundation aid seemingly opened the way for continued corporate domination of black communities by means of a new black elite.

Surprisingly, to some, CORE's program as elaborated by Floyd McKissick in July 1967, was quite similar to [MARC's] approach. Both organizations see themselves as intermediaries whose role was to negotiate with the power structure on behalf of blacks and the poor generally. Both suggested that more government and private aid was necessary, and both sought to gain admission for poor blacks and whites into the present economic and political structure of US society. McKissick, who became the second CORE official to accept a MARC fellowship, criticized capitalism, but only because black people were not allowed to participate fully in it.

Within a few months the Ford Foundation could apparently view its grant to Cleveland CORE as a qualified success. There was no rebellion in Cleveland in the summer of 1967, and in November, Carl Stokes became the first Negro mayor of a major American city—a fact which temporarily eased tensions in the ghettos. "We are not satisfied with the speed with which the program has moved," said James Cunningham, a consultant retained by the Foundation to monitor the project, "but it has shown real potential. I see it as a flowering of what black power could be."

The first phase of the project was an intensive voter registration drive in three slum wards in August. This was followed by a voter education program to instruct black people on voting procedures and to get them to the polls. This program included mailings and meetings with candidates. The net result of this phase of the program was to aid in the election of Carl Stokes, a fact of which Cleveland CORE boasted in its report on the project.

Another part of the program, designated as a "youth leadership training program," began in November. In all, some 62 youths, ranging in age from seventeen to twenty-one, were involved in this project. The project was designed, according to the CORE report, to "identify and train urban ghetto youth in those [...] skills which can serve as an alternative to frustration and violence...." To this end the youngsters attended classes on black history, African history, and social science. They were taught skills in canvassing, interviewing, and recording community opinions. There was apparently little discussion of who would ever read (not to mention act upon) their interviews and reports of community sentiment. Some of the [project] staff...were taken on visits to black-owned businesses in Chicago. In short, youths who had no faith in the "system" were taught that if only they could resocialize themselves, they might fit in after all.

The director of the youth training program, Philip Carter, said his project hoped to show that "the legitimate hostilities and aggressions of black youth" could be "programmed" into socially acceptable channels. He expressed the hope that the youths being trained would become "young black urban renewal specialists, young black sociologists, and young black political scientists." He did not say—and did not need to say—in whose interest these young black experts would be put to work. The mere fact that there aren't any genuinely black-controlled educational institutions guarantees that if they are to work, they must work in the interest of continued white domination of every facet of black life.

Militant rhetoric was used to cover up the cooptative nature of this project. "Our job as an organization," said Arthur Evans, a member of Cleveland CORE and national first vice chairman of the organization, "is to prepare people to make a decision on revolution or not. The choice is whether to take land and resources and redistribute them." The evidence of the [Cleveland project] suggests that CORE decided against revolution.

This militant rhetoric deceived no one, least of all those who financed the project. In his annual report for 1967, McGeorge Bundy dismissed "the preachers of hate" as so much "spume on the wave of the past," but he concluded that "no one who has dealt honestly with legitimately militant black leaders will confuse their properly angry words with any conspiracy to commit general violence...." So much for Mr. Evans's cagey talk about revolution.

Unfortunately for Bundy, "legitimately militant black leaders" do not necessarily speak for or represent anyone but themselves. The violence which hit Cleveland the next year should have amply demonstrated this fact.

Developments at CORE's convention in Oakland, California, early in the month of July 1967, provide further insight into that organization's strategy. One of the most important events at that meeting was the presentation of an impressive twelve-page report by Roy Innis's Harlem chapter. The report gave a summary of Harlem CORE's "program for the gaining of control or the creation of institutions in our community...." "We call this," the report stated, "a program of separate but not segregated institutions." In the area of economics, the report announced that Innis, as chapter chairman, had joined with a group of young black men in Harlem in organizing a "small business investment corporation that will have a broad-based stockholding membership." The organization was to be known as the Harlem Commonwealth Council, Inc. (HCC), and Innis became a member of its board of directors. Referring to HCC, the report continued: "Money will be raised in the black community that will be matched 2 to 1 by small business loans, and this money will be used to invest in or to create businesses in Harlem, or possibly light industry." Thus Harlem CORE was pioneering in formulating a strategy for the rise of black capitalism.

In the field of education, Harlem CORE reported that in March it has launched its demand for black control of the schools in Harlem by proposing the creation of an independent board of education for Harlem selected and completely controlled by and responsible to the black people of Harlem. According to the proposal, integration had failed, and the only way to achieve quality education for Harlem's youngsters was through community control of its schools. Harlem CORE set up a Committee for Autonomous Harlem School District and began organizing support for the proposal.

Interestingly, the following November, McGeorge Bundy recommended that New York City's school system be decentralized into thirty to sixty semiautonomous local districts. Bundy had been named head of a special committee on decentralization at the end of April after the state legislature directed Mayor Lindsay to submit a decentralization plan by December 1 if the city were to qualify for more state aid. Lindsay, an astute political liberal, insisted that decentralization was "not merely an administrative or budgetary device, but a means to advance the quality of education for all our children and a method of insuring community participation and achieving that goal." Bundy's proposal would allow for not one but possibly several school boards for Harlem. Harlem CORE's school board committee therefore found itself in the position of being on the same side as the *New York Times* in giving critical support to the Bundy plan, while both the New York City Board of Education and the United Federation of Teachers (UFT) opposed it. Bundy and the *Times* saw that decentralization could be modified and applied in a manner that would not seriously change the overall functioning of the educational system, while the UFT was so blindly engrossed in immediate problems that it failed to realize that its long-term interests lay neither with the school board nor in the course proposed by Bundy.

Tension between teachers and black parents had risen as a result of a three-week teachers' strike that fall. The teachers thought parents were attempting to usurp their professional rights and privileges. The parents, on the other hand, attacked the teachers as racists and the destroyers of their children. Bundy was well aware of this escalating tension while writing his report *Reconnection for Learning*. But he also knew that the teachers had in their union an established mechanism for channeling their discontent. The parents had no such channel, and there was always the danger that their anger, having no institutionalized outlet, might escalate into violence. Hence it was an urgent necessity for the parents in some way to be "reconnected" to the schools if disruptive conflict were to be avoided. The mechanism for accomplishing this end appeared to be limited school decentralization, which would allow some parent participation—thereby mitigating dangerous clashes—while at the same time precluding genuine community control of the schools by masking control under a new facade.

CORE's Oakland meeting was shaken briefly by a rebellion of dissident nationalists who thought that the strategy of separate community institutions was too limited in scope. The nationalists wanted CORE to endorse complete separation of blacks from white America. They sought to have the organization approve the idea of a separate black state. They also wanted CORE to exclude white members. On this latter point a compromise was reached and the convention agreed to strike the word "multiracial" from the section of the organization's constitution that describes its membership. White liberals loudly decried this compromise. The *New York Times,* for example, lamented editorially that "white co-strugglers have been given a clear message that they will be relegated to second-class citizenship within the organization. To put it bluntly, CORE membership now stands for racial inequality." CORE, however, was no longer attuned to this traditional white liberal view of the meaning of racial equality. In the second half of the sixties, having a quota of white members was no longer required to legitimatize a black freedom organization. (And neither was white membership necessary to insure that a black organization conformed to the desires of white society. Indirect control and manipulation of the black liberation movement was the hallmark of the new liberalism, which even went so far as to endorse black power and black separatism—not to mention black capitalism—as a means of sidetracking black revolution.)

The programmatic thrust of the CORE convention was outlined a few weeks later by McKissick. [On] the occasion of his remarks, McKissick denounced the statement condemning riots issued by Martin Luther King, A. Philip Randolph, Roy Wilkins, and Whitney Young. Their statement approved violent repression of riots and said in part: "Killing, arson, looting are criminal acts and should be dealt with as such. Equally guilty are those who incite, provoke and call specifically for such actions. There is no injustice which justifies the present destruction (by "rioters" or retaliating troopers?) of the Negro community." McKissick replied that history would record the ghetto explosions that summer as the beginning of the "black revolution" and as "rebellions against repression and exploitation." In a tactfully worded statement, McKissick accused the four civil rights leaders of opportunism: "We believe that it is unfortunate that our brothers felt it necessary to condemn Black men for rebelling against that which oppresses—that they found it opportune to decry the violence of the victim. It is fruitless to condemn without offering solutions and it can only force Black people to question those who condemn."

"We wouldn't have the violence if someone hadn't made some mistakes," said the CORE leader. He then went on to outline CORE's program for correcting these "mistakes." Some of his specific proposals sounded remarkably like what Harlem CORE had recommended:

> Black people seek to control the educational system, the political-economic system and the administration of their own communities. . . .
> Ownership of the land area in places such as Harlem must be transferred to the residents of Harlem—individually or collectively. Existing governmental programs such as the Demonstration Cities Program, the Federal Housing Authority, the Commerce Department Programs, along with the contributions from private industry, must be coordinated to accomplish this end.
> Ownership of businesses in the ghetto must be transferred to Black People—either individually or collectively. . . .

These paragraphs suggest certain economic changes, but they leave unanswered the critical question of in whose interest is economic power to be exercised? Simple transference of business ownership into black hands, either individually or collectively, is in itself no guarantee that this will benefit the total community. Blacks are capable of exploiting one another just as easily as whites.

It was this ambiguity, however, that opened the way for CORE to move toward black capitalism. What had begun as a Harlem CORE project was now shaping up as the over-all strategy of national CORE. Black power was slowly but relentlessly coming to be equated with the power of black business. This despite the fact that black business had never been a powerful social entity. Most ghetto businesses tend to be marginal operations such as beauty salons, barbershops, small grocery stores, and other retail and service businesses. In 1967, one-quarter of all businesses in Harlem, for example, were black-owned, but in all of New York City only a dozen or so black-owned or -managed enterprises employed more than ten people.

The history of black business in the US fails to disclose any significant venture in steel, automobiles, telephone, railroads, and most other industrial fields. The white corporate oligopoly has excluded blacks from the mainstream of American corporate endeavor, except in certain areas of banking, insurance, and publishing. But in at least two of these areas, the black businessman is largely fighting a rearguard action.

In 1948, the National Negro Insurance Association could claim to have sixty-two member companies with assets of over $108 million. As of 1963, *The Negro Handbook* listed eighty-nine black insurance firms, with total assets of only $26 million. The top ten white firms alone claimed assets of over $100 billion in 1967.

As for banks, in February 1969, Dempsey J. Travis, president of an association of Negro mortgage bankers, told a conference that the number of black-owned commercial banks, for instance, had declined to 20 in 19 cities from 49 in 38 cities in 1929. [In 1969,] there is very little that would suggest any reversal of these over-all trends. Moreover, in cities where a significant black business class exists, it usually is a conservative force rather than a militant one advocating for the massive restructuring of the US economic system.

The proposed CORE program tried to reverse the general downward trend and create new and expanded black businesses by demanding that existing white-controlled economic enterprises be transferred to black ownership. However, such a transfer could alter economic realities in the ghetto only if ownership and control of business activities became collective and community-wide. Individual ownership or limited-stock corporations restrict effective control (and resulting benefits) to a narrowly circumscribed class of persons within the black community. If the community as a whole is to benefit, then the *community as a whole must be organized to manage collectively* its internal economy and its business relations with white America. Black business firms must be treated and operated as *social property,* belonging to the general black community, not as the private property of individuals or limited groups of individuals. This necessitates the dismantling of capitalist property relations in the black community and their replacement with a planned communal economy. But CORE had no intention of tampering with the "free enterprise" system.

McKissick chose to ignore the ramifications of these considerations in his anxiety to project CORE as *the* most prominent and serious organization in the militant black movement. CORE, he concluded his statement, stands ready "to serve as a coordinating agent to assist all Black People, of any philosophy." Subtly addressing himself to those with money to spend and who want to put out the flames in the cities, he contended that if CORE's programs were "adequately funded and fully implemented" then it just might be possible to "alter the future of America from its present self-destructive course...."

In summary, CORE and the cultural nationalists draped themselves in the mantle of nationalism, but upon examination it is seen that their programs, far from aiding in the achievement of black liberation and freedom from exploitation, would instead weld the black communities more firmly into the structure of American corporate capitalism. The reformist or bourgeois nationalism—through its chosen vehicle of black capitalism—may line the pockets and boost the social status of the black middle class and black intelligentsia, but it will not ease the oppression of the ordinary ghetto dweller. What CORE and the cultural nationalists seek is not an end to oppression, but the transfer of the oppressive apparatus into their own hands. They call themselves nationalists and exploit the legitimate nationalist feelings of black people in order to advance their own interests as a class. And chief among those interests is their desire to become brokers between the white rulers and the black ruled.

note

1 James Forman, *1967: High Tide of Black Resistance* (New York: SNCC International Affairs Commission, 1968), 1.

>>Christine E. Ahn

democratizing american philanthropy

NOT SINCE THE GILDED AGE—THE SAME ERA THAT WITNESSED
the rise of so many major American foundations—has the United States faced a
wider divide between the wealthy and the poor. According to the Internal Revenue Service, from 1992 to 2000, the average income of the 400 richest Americans
grew from $46.8 million to $174 million.[1] Meanwhile the poor are becoming
poorer: the 2000 US Census reports that 12 percent of the American population
lives below the federal poverty level (around $18,000 for a family of four; in 1990,
it was $12,700). While government spending on military expenditures reaches
record highs and the tax base continues to shrink, a permanent and expanding
class of Americans lives in extreme poverty.[2] Middle-class families are also feeling the pinch of mounting debt and lessening economic and social security.
According to the Center for Budget and Policy Priorities, the middle class—sta-
tistically characterized as those in the middle-fifth income bracket—had an
average after-tax income of $41,900 in 2000, a 15 percent rise. In 1979 (the first
year the Congressional Budget Office started to gather these statistics), the
wealthiest 1 percent of Americans had just under half the after-tax income of the
poorest 40 percent of Americans. In 2000, the richest 1 percent of Americans had
more money to spend after taxes than the bottom 40 percent.[3]

Yet even as this crisis escalates, at every level of government we see harsh cuts
in education, health care, and other essential human services. As federal, state,
and local funds dry up, the public turns to philanthropy and charities to pick up
where government has left off.[4] Conservatives, for example, slash federal welfare
benefits to fund marriage promotion as a poverty-prevention policy targeting
poor women, then call on churches, non-profits, and volunteers to help people
without food, homes, jobs, or health care under the mantle of "compassionate
conservatism."[5] Many Americans are seduced by the idea that piecemeal voluntary efforts can somehow replace a systematic public approach to eliminating
poverty. But this reasoning is based on the inherent falsehood that scarcity—
rather than inequality—is at the root of these persisting social and economic
problems.[6] This worldview nurtures a culture of noblesse oblige, the belief that

the wealthy and privileged are obliged to help those less fortunate, without examining how that wealth was created or the dangerous implications of conceding such power to the wealthy. But that same reliance on the generosity of the wealthy poses grave threats to democracy because it assumes that foundation grants, rather than organizing and political power, will lead to social change. Here I do not argue that social justice organizations should not take foundation grants—in fact, they should, particularly to fund think tanks and other rigorous intellectual engagement with political issues and policy debates. But it is critical that social justice organizations abandon any notion that foundations are *not* established for a donor's private gain.[7] In recent years, for example, the media has reported on several instances of egregious abuse and mismanagement by our nation's private foundations: improper spending, lavish travel, self-dealing,[8] and excessive compensation of foundation trustees and executives. In response, leaders of the philanthropic community have ignored or dismissed these wrongful acts as the occasional bad apple in the otherwise pristine philanthropic barrel. Whether because they regard their assets as private or because very few standards—either governmental regulation or market forces—govern their behavior, America's 65,000 private foundations are, for the most part, institutions that are undemocratic and unaccountable to the public. Unlike the government, which is accountable to the public through various channels (slow as they might be and unrealistic as they may seem under the junior Bush administration's tyrannical regime), most private foundations are governed by a handful of very wealthy people who are affiliated with the foundation by family or business ties.

This essay provides a critical perspective on philanthropy and its relationship to democracy. It explores how foundations divert money away from the collective tax base and ways foundations have been undemocratic in their governing practice and in advancing an elitist agenda. While not exhaustive, with this discussion I hope to challenge all of us as participants of a democracy to think critically about the role foundations play in these times of declining government responsibility and growing concentrations of power among the wealthiest corporations and individuals in the United States and in the world.

an inequitable system

A common feature of every level of government, from city to state to federal, is the struggle with debilitating deficits. One glaring reason why every level of government is facing a major budget deficit is because the very rich are paying far less in taxes, thanks to successive tax cuts for the wealthiest enacted by President George W. Bush and a Republican-dominated Congress. While the average income of the wealthiest Americans nearly quadrupled between 1992 and 2000, the percentage of taxes they paid did not keep pace. The richest 400 paid an average of 22.3 percent of their income in federal income tax in 2000, compared with 26.4 percent in 1992. According to *New York Times* reporter David Cay Johnston, "Two factors explain most of this decline, according to the IRS: reduced tax rates on long-term capital gains and bigger gifts to charity." Naturally, cuts in capital gains taxes from the sale of an investment such as a home, art, or corporate stock will reduce the taxes paid by the super wealthy, but little is known or understood about the role that charitable giving plays on the declining tax base.

Charitable giving, by foundations, corporations, and individuals (both living and through bequests), has been growing steadily over the decades. According to Giving USA, the yearbook of philanthropy written and researched by the Center of Philanthropy at Indiana University, total charitable giving in 2005 rose 6 percent from the previous year to more than $260 billion. Although individual contributions accounted for the lion's share (76.5 percent), foundation grantmaking accounted for 11.5 percent of the total giving. (In the same year, foundation giving rose 5.6 percent to $30 billion. The Gates Foundation, which I discuss in more detail later, is responsible for a significant portion of this increase.) The Foundation Center, which reported this information, attributed the increase to the growth in the number of foundations and to the steady growth of the stock market in 2004 and 2005.[9] One could hardly dispute the fact that foundation giving largely benefits the wealthy since the bulk of the money is given to their trustees' alma maters, the opera, and to museums; more, foundation giving represents an alternative to paying high estate taxes, which now surpass 50 percent on large estates.[10] When public funds are so desperately needed today, why should foundations use public money to forward their own private agendas and protect their own financial and political interests? The very existence of the tax incentive means that charitable expenditures are not purely private. Foundations are made partly with dollars which, were it not for charitable deductions allowed by tax laws, would have become public funds to be allocated through the governmental process under the controlling power of the electorate as a whole. In fact, it is estimated that at least 45 percent of the $500 billion foundations hold in their coffers belong to the American public.[11] As Harvard University professors Akash Deep and Peter Frumkin note, "When a foundation is created today, the burden of lost tax revenue is borne by citizens today in the form of a tax expenditure"[12] with the promise that it will be paid out in future. Here is a hypothetical (and simplified) example of how the creation of foundations diverts money away from our collective tax pool.

Our tax laws require that after a person dies, 50 percent of her or his worth (only, in most cases, if it exceeds $2 million) be paid in taxes to the Treasury Department. However, John Doe Millionaire has an option that most ordinary

Americans lack: he can avoid taxation by creating the John and Jane Doe Millionaire Foundation. Suppose John Doe Millionaire possesses, for practical purposes, an estate worth $200 million. Upon his death, he would have to pay 50 percent estate tax, or $100 million, to the US Treasury. Instead, we, the American public, agree to forego the $100 million and, in return, allow him to create the John and Jane Doe Millionaire Foundation to give to charities according to how he sees fit. Due to current tax law, which requires foundations to spend a minimum of 5 percent of their taxable assets each year on grants *and* related administrative expenses, the John and Jane Doe Millionaire Foundation must give only $5 million each year.

a lack of public accountability

The board and staff of today's foundations are predominantly white, middle-aged, and upper class. According to a 1982 survey from the Council on Foundations, the foundation trade group, 77 percent of all foundation board members surveyed were men and 96 percent were white. In 2000, 66 percent of foundation board members were men and 90 percent were white.[13] Although a handful of liberal foundations may employ some program officers that are people of color or progressive, it is ultimately foundation trustees who have the final say in the grantmaking process. And with few exceptions, foundation trustees are extensions of America's banks, brokerage houses, law firms, universities and businesses—hardly a broad representation of the American population. Rarely, if ever, will you find a teacher or a working-class person on the board of a foundation.

Not only are foundation trustees entrusted with billions of dollars to make grants to advance their agendas, a substantial majority of these elite, who already earn handsome salaries from their professions, actually get paid to serve as trustees on the boards of foundations. It is unheard of to be compensated to serve on the board of a non-profit organization. Yet this is standard practice in the majority of America's private foundations. In a 2003 Georgetown University study on trustee fees conducted by Pablo Eisenberg, Channapha Khamvongsa, and myself, we found that 64 percent of the 176 largest foundations and 79 percent of smaller foundations we studied paid trustee fees. While compensation varied, the worst cases were the Kimball Art Foundation in Texas, which paid each of its two trustees $750,000, and the Annenberg Foundation, which paid its trustee, Walter Annenberg, $500,000 in 1998. The total amount paid to trustee members by the 238 foundations we studied was almost $45 million in 1998. It is ironic that the burden of our nation's social problems increasingly falls into the laps of foundations, the most elitist institutions in our country, whose boards are almost entirely composed of wealthy people and highly paid professionals, and who—as study after study shows—benefit personally and ideologically from the current social and economic order.

foundation "payout"

Not only have the bulk of foundations' funds gone to establishment institutions, including their very own trustees—the actual dollars that have gone to social change work, particularly in relation to overall investments and funds, can be characterized as stingy. Another controversial side of philanthropy is the tax policy that governs foundation "payout," the term used to describe the annual qualifying distribution of financial assets. Although foundations must pay out 5 percent of their assets annually, this does not mean they give out 5 percent of their assets as grants. This 5 percent includes administrative expenses such as rent and salaries, program-related investments, amounts set aside for future charitable projects, and trustee fees. The payout rate was actually reduced to 5 percent in 1981 by Congress. As a result, the ratio of grant payouts to assets dropped from 8 percent in 1981 to 6 percent by the end of the 1980s and to below 5 percent in 1997. Given current enormous public needs, courageous leaders from progressive foundations and non-profits have demanded an increase in the private foundation payout rate to at least 6 percent, excluding administrative and operating expenses. Yet the majority of foundations have insisted that they cannot afford to pay out more if they hope to conserve their resources for the future, particularly with the emergence of new and unforeseeable social problems due to uncertainty in financial markets.[14]

Even if foundations want to preserve their assets, study after study tells us foundations can afford to pay more. A 1999 study commissioned by the Council on Foundations found that from 1950 to 1998, foundations could have paid 6.5 percent annually and still would have grown their assets by 24 percent.[15] A 2001 Harvard University study showed that from 1972 to 1996, the 200 largest foundations yielded an average return of 7.62 percent annually on their investment returns while paying out an average of 4.97 percent. At a 2003 meeting of the Northern California Grantmakers, US Bancorp's Piper Jaffrey presented findings which showed that an investment portfolio comprising 70 percent equity stocks and 30 percent government bonds earned an inflation-adjusted return of nearly 8 percent from January 1980 through December 2002.[16] In other words, foundations are *making* money.

Why would there be so much resistance to paying out more when the assets of private foundations are actually growing? One theory is that foundations with higher assets generally have more prestige and privilege, and "because assets are closely correlated to power, trustees admit a tendency to wanting to grow their foundations."[17] It is also precisely because the investment committees of foundation boards are almost entirely composed of businessmen, whose aims are to steer the foundation's assets toward growth for its own sake and to support the capitalist system that the board members and their fellow elites benefit from.[18] The fact that most private foundations are governed by wealthy white men may partially explain why only 1.9 percent of all grant dollars in 2002 were designated for Black/African Americans; 1.1 percent for Latina/os; 2.9 percent for the disabled; 1 percent for the homeless; 0.1 percent for single parents; and 0.1 percent for gays and lesbians.[19] The majority of grants go to universities, hospitals, research, and the arts, while barely 1.7 percent goes to fund civil rights and social action. According to a new National Committee for Responsive Philanthropy (NCRP) report, "Obviously, many of these board members—who often set general programmatic goals for foundations and give final approval of grants—do not reflect the constituencies that would most benefit from progressive social and political changes."[20] It's about time the American public takes a hard look at who governs foundations and where the money does and does not go. This has led Pablo Eisenberg, the nation's leading critic of philanthropy to assert, "It is as though philanthropy exists for its own sake, rather than for the communities it is intended to serve."[21]

advancing an elite agenda through philanthropy

The following three examples reflect both the potential and the limits of philanthropy to create large-scale social change. The first story focuses on conservative foundations and how they strategically directed funds toward shaping ideology to protect the wealthy. The second story outlines the disastrous results of efforts by liberal foundations to advance their elitist agenda to solve global hunger. The final story is about the world's richest man using philanthropy to address both serious global problems and to improve his public image.

▷ *the success of conservative philanthropy*

The well-heeled and strategic philanthropy of conservative foundations have successfully moved national ideology, and, hence, policy, toward the Right. As a result, conservative issues, such as downsizing federal government and increasing states' rights, free-market capitalism and deregulation, individual property rights, and "traditional values" like opposing gay civil rights have become central to national policy debates. In a groundbreaking 1997 NCRP study of 12 prominent conservative foundations, Sally Covington documented the impact these foundations had on politics and society. She found that they controlled over $1.1 billion in assets and awarded $300 million in grants from 1992 to 1994. Of that, they directed $210 million to the following:

▷ *$88.9 million to support conservative scholarships and programs by training the next generation of conservative thinkers and activists in universities, and law and business schools;*

▷ *$79.2 million to build and strengthen a national infrastructure of think tanks and advocacy groups, like the Heritage Foundation and the American Enterprise Institute;*

▷ *$16.3 million to finance alternative media outlets, media watchdog groups, and public television and radio;*

▷ *$10.5 million to assist conservative pro-market law firms and law clinics;*

▷ *$9.3 million to support a network of regional and state-based think tanks and advocacy institutions; and*

▷ *$5.4 million to groups transforming the views and practices of religious and philanthropic leaders.*[22]

The strategic funding by conservative foundations to build a political infrastructure testifies to the enormous power held by foundations. As Covington observes:

> It is not simply the volume of money being invested that merits serious attention, but the way in which these investments have helped to build the power and influence of the conservative policy movement. These 12 funders directed a majority of their grants to organizations and programs that pursue an overtly ideological agenda based on industrial and environmental deregulation, the privatization of government services, deep reductions in federal anti-poverty spending and the transfer of authority and responsibility for social welfare from the national government to the charitable sector and state and local government.[23]

These foundations were effective because they focused their grantmaking programs on shaping ideas by building strong institutions and granting general operating support, as opposed to project-specific grants. They also funded state and local-level advocacy, institutions and intellectuals that generated conservative ideas, and a broad array of institutions employing diverse strategies to advance a conservative agenda. But, perhaps most important, these foundations have been funding their grantees' work for the long haul, some for even two decades or more.[24] According to Jeff Krehely, "They also had a national political party that was crafting a strong identity, as well as a clear statement of values." In contrast to their liberal counterparts, these foundations were not afraid to take risks or face potential government retribution.

In contrast, their liberal counterparts have received only one fourth as much support to build a political infrastructure to challenge the prevailing conservative ideology. For example, Covington found that in 1995, conservative multi-issue policy institutions such as the Heritage Foundation, the American Enterprise Institute, the Free Congress Research and Education Foundation, the Cato Institute, and Citizens for a Sound Economy collectively had a revenue base of over $77 million. In contrast, groups that might be considered their progressive counterparts—the Institute for Policy Studies, the Economic Policy Institute, Citizens for Tax Justice, the Center on Budget and Policy Priorities, the Twentieth Century Fund, the Center for the Study of Social Policy, OMB Watch, and the Center for Community Change—had only $18.6 million at their disposal.[25] Without long-term, financial support, it is almost impossible to be an aggressive, bold institution that is positioned to realize ideas into action.

Furthermore, although large liberal foundations have far more assets than conservative foundations, the latter have been so successful because they have been strategic. As social programs are defunded, "many mainstream and progressive organizations consider providing direct services to disadvantaged and disenfranchised populations and communities as their priority, not advocating policy change."[26]

Clearly, conservative foundations have been successful. Their ideological platform now shapes public policy and debate today. Their agenda includes less government, lower taxes for the wealthy, restrictions on the right to sue, and a free market unfettered by regulations or public interest concerns. They have led the assault against affirmative action and abortion, and have aggresively mobilized for the privatization of Medicare and Social Security. As a new NCRP report, "Axis of Ideology: Conservative Foundations and Public Policy," warns, "Bush has also worked to permanently repeal the estate tax by 2009, which would be devastating to the public interest, since the tax generates $45 billion in revenue for public and charitable needs, and its repeal would only benefit the few wealthiest Americans."[27] The report also finds that conservative foundations already have an infrastructure in place, now more wealth, and a successful two-pronged approach of "funding policy ideas at both the state and national levels."[28]

For example, the leading right-wing think tank, the Heritage Foundation, reaped $28,569,700 in grants from conservative foundations from 1999 to 2001. With this support, it launched the Center for Legal and Judicial Studies, which has produced publications such as *Support and Defend: How Congress Can Save the Constitution from the Supreme Court* and *In Defense of Marriage*. The Heritage Foundation, in its 2002 annual report, boasts that its experts were seen on national television more in that year than in the entire 1990s. It has also invested in training the next generation of conservative leaders through formalizing congressional internships and building a 200-seat auditorium, conference facilities, and office space and housing for interns.[29]

▷ *unintended consequences*

Right-wing foundations are not alone in strategically directing funds to achieve their goals. Liberal foundations are just as culpable as their right-wing counterparts in advancing a seemingly pragmatic agenda with tremendous effects on societies and the environment. In what is perceived as the single largest and longest-lasting initiative of American philanthropy, the Rockefeller Foundation, and later the Ford Foundation, bankrolled the massive global restructuring of agriculture known as the Green Revolution. The ostensible goal was to end world hunger by transferring Western scientific agricultural techniques to less-developed countries to increase crop yields. In just 50 years, the Green Revolution increased food production substantially, but it also permanently transformed agriculture and destroyed the livelihoods of millions of farmers and villages that had been in existence for hundreds of years.

Although the stated intention of the officers, trustees, and scientists of the Rockefeller Foundation was to solve the seemingly intractable problem of global hunger, investigative journalist Mark Dowie presents a parallel story of elites that were just as motivated to curb population growth in the Global South and stave off radical communist insurgency.

The Green Revolution was seeded in 1941 in Mexico, which was a fertile place and time for a Rockefeller-funded agricultural science project. Mexico had a new president, Avilo Camacho, who was pro-US and favored private property rights. Although private land ownership and free-market principles replaced former president Lázaro Cárdenas's socialist policies (including large-scale land reform), the political instability in Mexico and the region caused by massive food shortages continued to concern the Rockefeller Foundation. Dowie writes, "Throughout the region, the Rockefeller family's massive investments made them vulnerable to the kind of instability that results from a hungry populace."[30] In other words, a program to end hunger was wielded as a tool to suppress a communist revolt. By 1943, researchers in the Rockefeller Foundation's Mexican Agriculture Program were teaching Mexican and other Latin American agronomists techniques to grow massive quantities of food by employing the tools of the Green Revolution: pesticides, fertilizers, and other ecologically damaging techniques.[31]

While the funders promoted their agenda as a humanitarian effort, the Rockefeller Foundation archives show that cold war geopolitics and the fear of population growth motivated the trustees at least as much as feeding the masses. Mexico and India, which were enduring political instability and burgeoning populations, were primed for a mass communist insurgency. The Malthusian[32] philosophy that overpopulation caused hunger was the prevailing belief among elites at that time and was the underlying ideology that drove foundations to promote the Green Revolution. The International Development Advisory Board (IDAB), chaired by Nelson Rockefeller, recommended that the IDAB cooperate with countries like Mexico and India in "a vigorous food production drive that would break the back of famine and hunger"—and thereby stabilize their governments.[33] This ignored the fact that poverty was often the result of tightly concentrated economic power that limited people's access to land and purchasing power.[34]

The Green Revolution did produce record-breaking amounts of food, but with tremendous ecological and social consequences such as the depletion of soils around the world with the application of pesticides and fertilizers and the massive displacement of subsistence farmers that accompanied the industrialization of agriculture. As Dowie notes, 30 years ago, when the Green Revolution was still germinating, there were fewer than 1 million hungry people on the planet. The Green Revolution may have yielded "extremely productive"[35] quantities of food, but the fact that over 800 million people around the world face hunger daily amid overabundant food supplies can hardly be considered a victory. Although the Green Revolution was largely promoted and financed by governments, private foundations like the Rockefeller Foundation played a pivotal role in advancing technological solutions to problems that threatened elite control: political insurgency and population growth.

▷ doing-good and good PR

Foundations have also used their money to improve their public image and deflect scrutiny from the people and corporations that created them. Take, for example, founder of Microsoft and software giant Bill Gates, who is combining doing-good with smart public relations. Gates and his wife, Melinda, are co-trustees of the Bill and Melinda Gates Foundation. Through the Gates Foundation—which has more assets than any other foundation in the world—the chairman of the world's largest corporation[36] spends almost $6 billion each year vaccinating Africans from disease.[37] It is estimated that through his philanthropy, the Gates Foundation has saved more than 100,000 lives.

But let's think about this for a minute. What do vaccines (and the drug companies that manufacture them) have in common with Microsoft and its software and hardware products? One thing they share in common is that their patents are protected by the Trade Related Intellectual Property Rights (TRIPS) rules of the World Trade Organization.[38] According to investigative reporter Greg Palast, "TRIPS gives Gates a hammerlock on computer operating systems worldwide, legally granting him the kind of monopoly the Robber Barons of yore could only dream of. But TRIPS, the rule which helps Gates rule, also bars African governments from buying AIDS, malaria, and tuberculosis medicine at cheap market prices."[39]

In other words, with his left hand, Bill Gates spends billions of dollars through the Gates Foundation to vaccinate the millions of Africans dying of AIDS. Meanwhile, with his right hand, "his Foundation has invested $200 million in the very drug companies stopping the shipment of low-cost AIDS drugs to Africa."[40]

conclusion: holding foundations accountable

Historically, foundations have financed civil society organizations that have challenged the excesses of government and corporate power. But they have also been a means for the elite to preserve their wealth and power. In our organizing for better government and cleaner corporations, we must also press for more democracy in philanthropy. Since foundations and the demand for their funds are not about to magically disappear, I think we need to start somewhere, with an eye toward a long-term plan. I am not about to offer any magical solutions nor specific policy proscriptions.[41] However, I do want to close this essay with some thoughts to hopefully initiate some action.

First, foundations can and should pay out more of their assets to charities. In 2003, a bipartisan bill in Congress introduced by Roy Blunt, Republican from Missouri, and Harold Ford, Jr., Democrat from Tennessee, would have required foundations to distribute 5 percent of their assets annually—all in grants. The legislation would have prohibited foundations from counting administrative costs like rent and staff salaries against the 5 percent. This amount is still highway robbery, and, as Pablo Eisenberg has so eloquently put it, "Foundations should accept a slight payout increase as a good deal. It's a better deal than they deserve."

Unfortunately, the nation's largest foundations mounted an extensive lobbying campaign to defeat this provision of the legislation. The hundreds of thousands of dollars that they spent on this "self-defense" lobbying could be counted—ironically—toward their 5 percent payout.

On a related matter, foundations need to be more closely regulated by the state and federal governments. As Pablo Eisenberg notes in his book *Challenges for Nonprofits and Philanthropy: The Courage to Change,* "It should be clear by now that self-regulation by foundations has not worked. Public accountability and the eradication of abuses will be achieved only if state and federal governments do an adequate job of oversight." While I agree with Eisenberg that government regulation of foundation practices is about the only mechanism to tide the growing control of social change work and more by foundations, I also believe that foundations can implement some cultural changes to their institutions to diversify their boards and staff to be more representative of the American public and more effectively address critical issues today. As part of a broader vision for social change, we must organize to make foundations accountable to the larger public, mandating that community leaders, working-class men and women, and people of color serve on their boards to redirect grants so these constituents receive a bigger piece of the grant pie.

Last but not least, let's set the record straight by speaking the truth: foundations are created not only from wealth that was made off the backs of hardworking people, but from a social compact they accepted as a result of major tax benefits their donors received. Individuals who have dedicated their lives to working for social and economic justice need a major paradigm shift and recognize that foundation money, often the result of exploited wealth, is public money.

In a meeting of the trusted inner circle of the Open Society Institute (OSI), a private foundation started by the international businessman George Soros, there was a protracted argument that kept the group's discussion going in circles. Finally, an impatient George Soros exerted his authority, slammed down his fists, and said, "This is my money. We will do it my way." This interjection silenced the room, except for a courageous junior member who raised his voice in objection to tell Mr. Soros, "No it isn't." The young heretic went on to say, "Half of it is ours. If you hadn't placed that money in OSI or another of your 25 foundations, sir, about half of it would be in the Treasury."[42] Well, the courageous young staffer is no longer there, but hopefully Soros got the message. Perhaps we will all get the message too and have the courage to reform American philanthropy and democracy.

notes

1 David Cay Johnston, "Very Richest's Share of Income Grew Even Bigger, Data Shows," *New York Times*, June 26, 2003, Business/Financial Desk section, late edition.

2 Using pooled population survey data from 2000, 2002, and 2004, Harry Holzer, professor of public policy at Georgetown University, testified to the United States Civil Rights Commission on April 19, 2006, on disparities in employment and income between white people and people of color, and women and men. Of white men who had some college education, 93.4 percent were employed, compared with just 86 percent of black men with the same level of education. Differences in their earnings were just as stark: White men with a bachelor's degree or higher earned $57,431 (median), compared with $44,675 for black men and $46,753 for Latino men with the same education. Women, irrespective of race, earned significantly less than men. Where white men with college degrees or higher earned $57,431, white women earned $36,400. Unemployment rates were significantly higher for women. In that same category, 96.4 percent of white men were employed, compared with an 86.4 percent employment rate for white women. The disparities were highest according to education (an indicator of class status). White men with less than a high school diploma earned $12,149 (median) and had an unemployment rate of 23.7 percent. Black men with the same level of education earned $17,671 with a comparable unemployment rate (24.4 percent). Black women without high school diplomas had an unemployment rate of 42.4 percent and earned the least—$10,805. Testimony available on the US Equal Employment Opportunity Commission website, http://www.eeoc.gov/abouteeoc/meetings/4-19-06/holzer.html.

3 Lynnley Browning, "U.S. Income Gap Widening, Study Says," *New York Times*, September 25, 2003, Business/Financial Desk section, final edition.

4 For a more detailed analysis of the American charitable tradition—particularly the influence of Christianity on this tendency to seek private solutions to social ills rather than demand government intervention—see Robert H. Bremner, *American Philanthropy* (Chicago: University of Chicago Press, 1988).

5 Marvin Olasky, who was an aide to George W. Bush when he was governor of Texas, coined the term "compassionate conservatism," referring to the work of government in partnership with charities, to "lessen" the pain of the disadvantaged.

6 For example, the world produces enough food to provide 6 billion people each 4.3 pounds of food per day; yet there are over 700 million people who face hunger.

7 In fact, Representative Wright Patman, a Texas Democrat, waged a ten-year battle against the rich, whom he accused of using foundations as a shield for self-dealing. Patman's concern was prompted by advertisements in magazines that blatantly offered to protect rich people from government taxes by helping them establish foundations.

8 "Self-dealing" generally means using a foundation's tax status to enrich oneself without taxation. In a typical scenario, a foundation staff or board member (or their close family members) receives financial compensation outside of a regular salary or nominal trustee fees for services rendered. It's tough to define because you have to think about the family member angle (a transaction that involves a spouse would be clearly self-dealing, but would a great-aunt or great-uncle? A second cousin? And what about friends?), as well as the compensation level (someone receiving $50 to write an article for a newsletter vs. someone receiving a $5 million contract to manage investments).

9 Giving USA Foundation, "Charitable Giving Rises 6 Percent to More Than $260 Billion in 2005," news release, June 19, 2006, http://www.aafrc.org/press_releases/trustreleases/0606_pr.pdf.

10 Akash Deep and Peter Frumkin, "The Foundation Payout Puzzle" (Working Paper No. 9, Hauser Center for Nonprofit Organizations, Kennedy School of Government, Harvard University, June 2001).

11 Mark Dowie, *American Foundations: An Investigative History* (Cambridge, MA: MIT Press, 2002), 266. Dowie writes, "Another verity ignored by Carnegie and most of the philanthropists who followed him is the fact that about 45 percent of any foundation's endowment really belongs to the public, whose state and federal treasuries would hold that portion of any large estate not left to a foundation."

12 Deep and Frumkin, "The Foundation Payout Puzzle," 6.

13 US Senate Committee on Finance, *Recommendations for Reform of the United States Philanthropic Sector* (statement by the National Committee for Responsive Philanthropy [NCRP]), June 22, 2004, 12. Available online at www.senate.gov/~finance/hearings/testimony/2004test/062204rctest.pdf.

14 Ironically, the foundations with the most overhead costs also tend to have the lowest payout rates. According to testimony by the NCRP in 2004 Senate Finance Committee hearings, "The IRS analyzed the payout rates of the 50 largest foundations from 1985–1997, and found that only thirteen actually met or exceeded 5 percent." Ibid.

15 Ibid.

16 Ibid.

17 Deep and Frumkin, "The Foundation Payout Puzzle," 17.

18 Foundation boards are "composed primarily of an elite; people who are accomplished professionals, business leaders, wealthy family members, and well-known educators. They seem to prefer candidates who resemble themselves and belong to their own professional and social circles. They also tend to place a highest priority on 'getting along,'" writes Pablo Eisenberg in "Desperately Seeking Leadership," *Foundation News and Commentary*, November/December 1998. Reprinted in *Challenges for Nonprofits and Philanthropy: Courage to Change; Three Decades of Reflections by Pablo Eisenberg*, ed. Stacey Palmer (Medford, MA: Tufts University Press and University Press of New England, 2004), 66–69.

19 NCRP, "Recommendations for Reform."

20 Jeff Krehely, Meaghan House, and Emily Kernan, *Axis of Ideology: Conservative Foundations and Public Policy* (Washington, DC: NCRP, 2004), 43.

21 Mark Dowie, *American Foundations: An Investigative History* (Cambridge, MA: MIT Press, 2002), 120.

22 Sally Covington, *Moving a Public Policy Agenda: The Strategic Philanthropy of Conservative Foundations* (Washington, DC: NCRP, 1997), 5.

23 Ibid., 3

24 Krehely, House, and Kernan, "Axis of Ideology," 5.

25 Covington, "Moving a Public Policy Agenda," 37.

26 Krehely, House, and Kernan, "Axis of Ideology," 43.

27 Ibid., 6.

28 Ibid., 11.

29 Ibid.

30 Dowie, *American Foundations*, 107.

31 Knowing that the revolution needed massive investment beyond private foundation funding, by the 1960s, the foundations convinced the federal government to finance the agricultural initiative through the Agency for International Development and later the World Bank.

32 See Thomas Robert Malthus, *An Essay on the Principle of Population* (1798; reprint, New York: Oxford University Press, 1999).

33 Dowie, *American Foundations*, 109.

34 Dowie writes that the Ford Foundation's "interest in the revolution seemed even more closely linked to Cold War anxieties than the Rockefeller's." An internal Ford Foundation memo written in 1954 reads, "From the point of view of the West and the preservation of its most cherished values it is of utmost importance whether, in the current efforts to modernize, the underdeveloped countries will lean toward the West, adapting its technology and political ideas to suit their special needs, or instead, accept the Communist promises and eventually the Communist system."

35 Miguel A. Altieri and Clara I. Nicholls, *Agroecology and the Search for a Truly Sustainable Agriculture* (Mexico City, Mexico: United Nations Environmental Program, Environmental Training Network for Latin America and the Caribbean, 2005).

36 Microsoft made net profits of $2.98 billion on $10.9 billion revenues for its financial quarter ending March 31, 2006. Cher Price, "Xbox 360 Drags Down Microsoft Profits," *Inquirer,* April 28, 2006, http://www.theinquirer.net/default.aspx?article=31331.

37 Greg Palast, "Bill Gates, Pres. Bush: Killing Africans for Profit and P.R.—Mr. Bush's Bogus AIDS Offer, " *Idaho Observer,* July 14, 2003, http://www.proliberty.com/observer/20030715.htm.

38 During the Uruguay Round (1986 to 1994), the WTO introduced intellectual property rules into the multilateral trading system for the first time through the Agreement on Trade-Related Aspects of Intellectual Property Rights (TRIPS). According to Anup Shah of Global Issues, an international research and education NGO, "A major criticism then has been that in its current form, intellectual property rights regimes like TRIPS serve to stifle competition and protect one's investments and profits from it in that way. For poor nations it makes developing their own industries independently more costly, if at all possible." Anup Shah, "The WTO and Free Trade," July 28, 2006, http://www.globalissues.org/TradeRelated/FreeTrade/WTO.asp#Trade-RelatedAspectsofIntellectualPropertyRightsTRIPS.

39 Palast, "Bill Gates."

40 Ibid.

41 The National Committee for Responsive Philanthropy (NCRP) is the leading national advocacy organization taking on this task. I encourage interested readers to visit its website and get involved: http://www.ncrp.org.

42 Dowie, *American Foundations*, 247–248.

part ii

Non-Profits and Global Organizing

>>Tiffany Lethabo King & Ewuare Osayande

the filth on philanthropy

*Progressive Philanthropy's Agenda to Misdirect Social
Justice Movements*

THE PROGRESSIVE PHILANTHROPY MOVEMENT THAT EMERGED IN
the mid-1970s with the proposed aim of funding social change has worked in
tandem with the non-profit industrial complex (NPIC) to undermine radical
social change in this country. Of particular interest to this essay is the role that
progressive philanthropy plays in disrupting people-of-color movements seeking
the just redistribution of wealth and power. Proponents of progressive philanthropy place the origins of their movement with the emergence of the Donee
Group.[1] In 1974, the Donee Group, which described itself as a coalition "composed of voluntary action, environmental action, public interest law, housing,
women's rights, community organizing, service to the handicapped, children's
rights, social service, consumer rights and citizen participation activities" convened to provide ad hoc consultation to the Commission on Private Philanthropy
and Public Needs, also known as the Filer Commission.[2]

The Filer Commission, initiated in 1973 by John H. Filer (who was, at the
time, chairman of Aetna Casualty) and John D. Rockefeller III, was formed as a
response to the Tax Reform Act of 1969, which initiated new regulations and taxing of private foundations.[3] Seeking to protect the interests and wealth of private
foundations, Rockefeller and Filer convened the commission and made recommendations to Congress and the public about how the voluntary sector and the
practice of private giving could be strengthened.[4]

The Donee Group, which would later become the foundation watchdog
National Committee on Responsive Philanthropy (NCRP), proposed that the
commission accept additional research and consultation from "non-establish-
ment" perspectives on the deliberations.[5] In 1975, the Donee Group produced its
final report, which raised critical questions and issues for social justice groups
and the philanthropic community. Groups and individuals like the NCRP, David
Hunter (then director of the Stern Family Fund[6]) and former members of the
Donee Group—such as the National Center for Urban Ethnic Affairs (now HUD),

the Center for Community Change, the Council for Public Interest Law, the Grantsmanship Center, the Gray Panthers Youth Project, the NOW Legal Defense and Education Fund, and the National Council of La Raza[7]—would provide the leadership for the progressive philanthropy movement that would seek to address the critical question, "How will philanthropy serve progressive movements for social change?"

Since the mid-1970s, the progressive philanthropy movement has grown. More leaders have emerged, campaigns and strategies have expanded, and social justice groups representing various issues and communities have backed and lent credibility to the movement in leftist communities. Progressive philanthropy's primary work focuses on compelling the philanthropic community, primarily public and private foundations, to be more generous in their grantmaking for social justice causes. This work is supported by additional campaigns and developments within the movement, such as the establishment of alternative funds which participate in workplace giving campaigns, the emergence of social action and community funds, the monitoring of tax breaks (federal credits or deductions) given to private and corporate foundations, and grassroots fundraising. For the past several years, the progressive philanthropy movement has focused on increasing private foundations' annual "payout" rate by one percentage point (from 5 percent to 6 percent) and preventing foundations from including their administrative costs in their payout to non-profits.

On the surface, progressive philanthropy is an attempt by the Left to advance the movement forward by bolstering it with more resources. But rather than putting more money into the hands of non-profits that address the needs of the marginalized, the results have been little more than a few cosmetic adjustments to make capitalist foundations appear progressive and the Left complicit in supporting systems of oppression, exploitation, and domination. In this essay we argue that the white leadership of the progressive philanthropy movement actually protects white wealth and undermines the work of oppressed communities of color.[8]

The white Left's investment in reforming the giving practices of foundations and wealthy individuals through progressive philanthropy directly opposes the work of oppressed communities of color seeking to advance movements for global reparations and the just redistribution of wealth and resources. Within this reformist framework, white people and white institutions continue to control the wealth gained through the exploitation of people of color. Further, as the status quo is maintained within a white supremacist framework, the white Left continues to benefit from their white privilege and relative proximity to the wealth of the white Right (who are the white Left's rich relatives, lovers, good friends, associates, or fellow white-privileged person on the street). When the white Left accepts donations of white capital on behalf of oppressed people of color, they act as brokers between the capital and the oppressed people of color who were exploited to create it.[9] As brokers, they keep white wealth from the grasp of people of color entrenched in movements for wealth redistribution, particularly the movement for reparations. And for their "brokering" efforts, white-led organizations have been able to materially benefit as they garner and maintain control of social justice movements that disproportionately impact and affect the lived reality of people of color.

maintaining racial hierarchies within social justice movements through philanthropy reform

Many white-led social justice non-profits proclaim, in everything from their mission statements to their funding proposals, that they are committed to improving the social and economic conditions of the oppressed communities in which they operate. But alongside these proclamations exist a persisting hierarchy and circulation of capital within the social justice movement. Significantly, the manner in which that capital is circulated among social justice groups, once the wealthy do decide to make a charitable gift to the movement, is often ignored or grossly understated by white leaders within the progressive philanthropy movement.

At a roundtable discussion hosted in 2003 by the Center for Responsible Funding, Rick Cohen, the executive director of the NCRP, remarked that "foundations are institutions with huge concentrations of wealth controlled largely by individuals and families of great affluence."[10] He also noted an "immense social division" that exists between foundations and marginalized social justice groups. While it is true that organizations claiming to be committed to system-wide change (that is, social justice groups) lack the kind of access and funding that mainstream social service non-profits receive, we need to be more specific regarding which social justice groups this "immense social division" exists between. Compared with people of color social justice organizations, the assertion that there is an "immense social division" between white social justice groups and foundations is an exaggeration, if not a complete fabrication. For the white Left capitalist foundations are often only a phone call away. The following example, which illustrates the often close ties with the wealth of foundations enjoyed by the white Left, may be more typical than many realize.

While employed by the Center for Responsible Funding (CRF), coauthor Tiffany King witnessed a discussion between CRF's former and current executive directors. The discussion centered on gaining access to and soliciting a donation from a philanthropist whose funding assets were administered by the Tides Foundation. In this informal strategy session, the former executive director encouraged her successor to approach this funder by establishing relationships with the 2004 Democratic presidential hopeful Howard Dean or folks in his inner circle. (Apparently this philanthropist was a supporter and member of the inner circle of Howard Dean.) Since no directives were given about how to get into Dean's inner circle, one could assume that gaining access would not be difficult for the new executive director.

In contrast, very few people of color engaged in social activism have this kind of access to Howard Dean's white inner circle or other wealthy whites. The conversation between these two white women, in positions of leadership within the progressive philanthropy movement, speaks to the primacy of maintaining relationships with wealthy white people as a method to secure philanthropic contributions. This conversation further illustrates how white capital is circulated among white people and works to maintain systems of white supremacy. Since white-led social justice groups like the CRF often rely on their relationships with wealthy white people to secure their own funding, it is disingenuous for this movement to suggest that there is an "immense social division" that exists between foundations and marginalized social justice groups. Given that white-led social justice groups, claiming to work on behalf of the oppressed and people of color, often rely on their existing and potential relationships with wealthy white people to sustain their organizations at best presents a serious conflict of interest.

Wealthy whites can often count on the white Left to protect their money and interests. Some members of the white Left even offer wealth-related counseling sessions for rich white people. A so-called progressive social justice community fund in Philadelphia holds a support group for wealthy women called Women With Money (WWM). According to their website, WWM "creates a welcoming, stimulating environment where women who have wealth, whether earned or inherited, can gain new perspectives on their lives and their money." The group also provides "a place to explore issues of wealth with safety and confidentiality."[11] A wealthy person talking confidentially with other wealthy people about her money does not put her in a position of accountability to people who are not wealthy. Rather, it simply makes them comfortable about having more money than they know what to do with. Some of the issues explored by WWM include guilt management, accountability, personal relationships, political giving, and best of all, enjoying money. The primary function seems to be to help (by and large, white) women deal with the guilt of having money and how to manage it (not give it up). Although they claim to discuss accountability, the question that begs to be asked is: accountability to whom? Nowhere on the site is there any acknowledgement or articulated participation of people of color or the poor. Within this controlled set-up, accountability exists only between white people with money and the white Left social justice groups that want access to it. This further substantiates our claim that by not openly demanding wealth redistribution, reparations, or justice for exploited workers, white social justice non-profits function as brokers for the wealthy. They simply help them manage their money—and assuage their guilt for having wealth accrued from the stolen and exploited labor of people of color.

The social justice community is also funded by an elitist system of cronyism in which white organizations with the lion's share of resources create and support other white organizations. In Philadelphia, two local foundations—the Philadelphia Foundation and the Bread and Roses Community Fund—have a long history of giving out discretionary funds to favored non-profit organizations such as the Center for Responsible Funding. Discretionary funds are often noncompetitive grants given at the whim of a foundation to friends, be they individuals or organizations. Often these funds do not require the submission of a proposal, just the existence of a "relationship." And it is not unusual for an existing foundation to start a new organization, handpick the leadership (usually a friend or acquaintance), and then provide the organization with resources and its endorsement throughout the duration of that group's life. White social justice non-profits *profit* handsomely from the material privilege of being white in community with their white cronies and cohorts, while the communities they claim to represent languish on the margins of both larger society and the movement for social justice. What are the implications for a social justice movement in which power and resources are transferred based on one's ability to develop a relationship with the right white people?

The implications of this power dynamic are found within valuable critiques of the NPIC that shed light on some of the fundamental problems that impede social justice movements. Annanya Bhattacharjee has offered important insight on how political formations within the NPIC become defenders of the status quo. For example, in Bhattacharjee's address during the 2004 conference The Revolution Will Not be Funded: Beyond the Non-Profit Industrial Complex, she remarked on these attributes of the NPIC: the non-profit structure is predicated on a corporate structure and hierarchy that rewards "bourgeois credentials" and "upward mobility"; the non-profit model makes it easier for young economically privileged people just coming out of college to start a non-profit than to engage in long-term established movements; the model is obsessed with institution building rather than organizing; and it forces social justice activists to become more accountable to funders than to our communities.

When the structural problems that Bhattacharjee points out are understood within the framework of white supremacy, we get a clearer picture of how white people, positioned within the NPIC as the "credentialed" power brokers with access to white wealth are implicated in maintaining the status quo. More specifically, white people become more invested in protecting white wealth than in advancing oppressed people of color's movements to reclaim and redistribute wealth.

how progressive philanthropy uses people of color to maintain the status quo

The progressive philanthropy movement actively recruits people of color into the movement to advance the reform of philanthropy. People-of-color organizations are misled that they too can partake in and benefit from a white model of non-profit social justice fundraising. Organizations such as the CRF and the Grassroots Institute for Fundraising Training (GIFT) provide national models for training social justice activists in fundraising and capacity building. Money for the Movement (MFM) is a project jointly developed by GIFT and the CRF, specifically designed to build the capacity of under-resourced people-of-color social justice groups. The MFM curriculum, offered through the CRF's The Academy for Fundraising Training (TAFFT), trains people of color to become fundraisers and fundraising trainers. GIFT provides the initial training through "training the trainer" sessions.[12]

These training curriculums are designed to be sensitive to and address the reality that people-of-color social justice groups are even more marginalized by foundations than white social justice groups. Given the vulnerable status of people-of-color social justice organizations, the grassroots fundraising model propagated by CRF and GIFT becomes quite alluring. During training sessions, white and people-of-color trainers share the dismal reality that the resources of foundations are difficult to come by for social justice groups and nearly impossible for organizations led by people of color. To drive this point home, such groups often cite statistics from Giving USA, a foundation to advance research, education, and a public understanding of philanthropy,[13] which state that 3 percent or less of all philanthropic dollars come from corporations and that 12 percent or less of all philanthropic dollars come from foundations.[14]

In light of the particularly bleak reality that people-of-color organizations face, GIFT and the CRF often find people-of-color organizations to be a captive audience to which they can sell their grassroots fundraising model. GIFT's model operates on the basic premise that foundation dollars are few and that most philanthropic dollars come from individuals (more than 85 percent).[15] The model instructs social justice activists to stop wasting their valuable time on foundations and invest that time in cultivating relationships with individuals. On the surface, this fundraising rationale appears to embrace a politic that values organizing one's constituency over institution building. Unfortunately, this is not the case.

While encouraging organizers to raise money from their constituencies, the GIFT model also privileges organizations with connections to the wealthy—and does not include among its aims the redistribution of the unearned wealth of foundations. To be successful within this model, organizations must have significant access to wealthy people. Using GIFT's renowned gift-range chart or formula for raising funds, 50 to 70 percent of the gifts must come from 10 percent of an organization's donors (clearly, a few wealthy donors); 15 to 25 percent of the gifts come from 20 percent of an organization's donors; and the remaining 15 to 25 percent comes from 70 percent of an organization's donors.[16] Like the more informal networks of cronyism we've discussed, this model of success is based on building (or "cultivating") relationships with a few rich people and, by direct extension, protecting the interests of those with wealth. In this model, 10 percent of the donor pool (the wealthy) sustains the organization. These few individuals are responsible for upwards of 70 percent of the organization's assets—ultimately, the organization has to answer to these individuals. Cultivating this relationship and protecting the interests of these wealthy few is critical to the success of this model.

Within the "grassroots fundraising" model, valuable time is spent securing cozy relationships with major donors instead of organizing to dismantle the very systems of oppression that allow this owning class to accumulate unearned wealth. Adopting the "grassroots fundraising" model never requires that one fully turn their back on the wealthy and the foundation community in order to organize radical movements that call for the redistribution of wealth. GIFT is a prime example of an organization that receives—and relies on—funds from a number of foundations, including the Ford Foundation, which, historically, has had an infamous role in working with the Central Intelligence Agency to undermine radical movements. (We discuss the relationship that the Ford Foundation maintained with the CIA in the latter portion of this essay.) Above all, GIFT is accountable to the interests of its funders, even when they come in direct conflict with the interests of the oppressed "constituency." Deploying its ostensibly grassroots approach to fundraising, GIFT simultaneously gains credibility with people-of-color communities while co-opting the only viable fundraising option—*true grassroots organizing*—available to oppressed people of color and the poor.

So while some interpret GIFT's fundraising philosophy as an appeal to those seeking justice to turn their backs on the capitalists (foundations), we observe GIFT urging us to simply concede that foundations are not going to give up the money. In other words: Get off their backs. And the foundation community seems pleased with the work GIFT has done in convincing the oppressed to look the other way and not call for an overhaul of the system. (For instance, the Ford Foundation has shown its appreciation by paying GIFT big bucks with multiyear grants for its work.) What has been called "grassroots fundraising training" still does not challenge the fundamental problem of capitalist exploitation, the wealth that has been accrued by white people at the lived expense of people of color in this country and around the world.

Interestingly enough, grassroots fundraising is often made out to be a viable plan for people of color to use to sustain their work. Critical to the success of the white Left's agenda to protect white wealth is the strategic use of people of color as endorsers of these tactics. Yet people-of-color groups rarely find success using this model and are often discouraged by the lack of results. Models based on cultivating relationships with the wealthy do not make sense for people-of-color organizations and movements because we do not have the same access to private wealth, and attempts to encourage us to create alliances with the same capitalists who exploit us are in clear opposition to our struggles for global reparations, which, when waged successfully, will foster the just redistribution of wealth and resources. The progressive philanthropy movement's allied campaign to encourage grassroots fundraising has misdirected the time and resources of people-of-color organizations. People-of-color organizations who adopt these tactics are diverted from the work of organizing around global reparations and the just transfer of resources to people of color around the world.

While some social justice activists acknowledge the injustice that exists in a society where foundations thrive, many remain reluctant to push the movement to its necessary conclusion: to wage organized struggle to eliminate these funding institutions and the need for them. The progressive philanthropy movement has offered some more reformist proposals such as the "spend down" theory, which proposes that foundations gradually spend themselves out of existence. For instance, the Aaron Diamond Foundation spent itself out of existence in 12 years in order to have a greater impact on the HIV/AIDS pandemic.[17] Though few and far between, foundations like the Julius Rosenwald Fund, the Stern Foundation, and the Field Foundation have also spent themselves out of business.[18] While these acts seem to be ones of great personal sacrifice and perhaps left of reformist, they in no way significantly diminish the aggregate wealth that these individuals and families hold and do not challenge the status quo. For example, Julius Rosenwald is an heir to the Sears, Roebuck fortune. When he spent his foundation out of existence, he by no means spent his family out of the owning class.

Notably, the spend-down tactic has been embraced by a number of conservatives as well. Conservative foundations are proposing that they spend themselves out of existence so that "liberals won't get ultimate control of the foundations," as many conservatives claim has happened with the Ford, Rockefeller, Charles Stewart Mott, and Carnegie foundations.[19] Spending down in its conservative form is used to keep the money away from the liberals, and in its leftist version it seeks to gradually rid itself of excess capital as it gives money to causes it deems worthy. Again, these reformist solutions do not advance movements of oppressed people of color for self-determination and the just distribution of wealth. Spending down, even in its leftist manifestation, occurs on the terms of the foundation, not on terms dictated by oppressed people of color. Within this framework, people of color are still not allowed to operate with the agency that would allow them to control wealth and decide how this wealth will be used to benefit their communities. The "spend down" theory does not seek to redistribute wealth stored in foundations or other depositories to the oppressed. Furthermore, it does not seek to dismantle the mechanisms of capitalism that enable white people to attain wealth from the exploitation of oppressed people of color.

This failure to fully commit to eliminating foundations is similar in body and spirit to the posture the white Left often takes on the issue of reparations. For the white Left, the issue of reparations is one that corporations need to deal with, not individual white people. This is similar to their rationale regarding how smaller family foundations should be treated. In reality, the wealth of most family foundations, not just the obvious culprits of oppression like Rockefeller, Ford, Getty, and other corporate foundations, has come from centuries of oppression and exploitation of African Americans, Native Americans, Mexicans, Chinese migrants and other people of color and the poor in this country. Yet the idea that family foundations should be required as a community to pay reparations has never been a part of the analysis of the white Left. The white Left is conspicuously absent in developing an analysis and organizing around the issue of reparations.

some problems of people of color organizing within the npic

The ultimate danger for Black radical movements and other people of color–initiated movements is that they become misdirected and eventually co-opted by a white Left agenda that capitulates in the face of capitalist wealth, thus derailing and subjugating their progressive agendas for real social change. In this vein, certain Black organizations have taken their cue from white leftist groups and have resorted to cultivating relationships with capitalist foundations instead of doing the time-honored work of building relationships with the masses of working and unemployed Black people fighting for reparations. If Black organizations write anything to a foundation or corporation, it should be demands for reparations—not proposals requesting money.

Historically, the Black community has looked upon organizations whose funding sources emerge from outside the Black community with critical suspicion. That suspicion is based on the concern that strings may be attached to the money received and that funders may have ulterior motives and nefarious agendas that would undermine and contain Black self-determination. Often, when Black activists raise critiques of how social justice groups are funded and the possible connection with covert acts by the US government to spy on and curtail liberation and justice movements, they are dismissed by the white Left as conspiracy theorists. But the Ford Foundation's historic relationship to the CIA is not conspiracy theory; it is conspiracy fact:

> In 1976, a Select Committee appointed to investigate US intelligence activities reported on the CIA's penetration of the foundation field by the mid-1960s: during 1963-6, of the 700 grants over $10,000 given by 164 foundations, at least 108 involved partial or complete CIA funding. More importantly, CIA funding was involved in nearly half the grants made by these 164 foundations in the field of international activities during the same period.
>
> "Bona fide" foundations such as Ford, Rockefeller and Carnegie were considered "the best and most plausible kind of funding cover...." The architects of the foundation's cultural policy in the aftermath of the Second World War were perfectly attuned to the political imperatives which supported America's looming presence on the world stage. At times, it seemed as if the Ford Foundation was simply an extension of government in the area of international cultural propaganda.[20]

Given this history, not to mention the FBI's infamous counterintelligence program (COINTELPRO) that monitored radical Black organizations in the late 1960s and early 70s, as well as Army Intelligence's surveillance of civil rights organizations, grassroots trepidation and critical analysis of non-profit funding represents a learned wisdom that has ripened with time, a wisdom that is itself steeped in political struggle. What covert agendas will be discovered in future reports on the relationships being cultivated and developed in this era of the Patriot Act and the Bush administration's so-called war on terror?

The reparations movement and other people of color–led movements for the equitable redistribution of wealth are being co-opted and squashed by the non-profit model and its funding engine, the philanthropy of the white wealthy. Philanthropy is not progressive and never has been. Philanthropy never intends to fund revolutionary struggle that demands the just seizure of wealth, resources, and power that has been gained by exploiting the bodies, lives, and land of people of color worldwide. The time has come for social justice organizations to choose alternative means to fund their initiatives so that their agendas will be executed with integrity and so that they no longer risk colluding in the oppression of those they claim to represent.

notes

1 William A. Stanmeyer, institutional analysis for the National Committee for Responsive Philanthropy (NCRP, Washington, DC, 1978).
2 Ibid.

3 Robert O. Bothwell, "The Decline of Progressive Policy and the New Philanthropy" (paper, Com-Org, 2003), http://comm-org.wisc.edu/papers2003/bothwell/what.htm.

4 Stanmeyer, institutional analysis for NCRP.

5 Ibid.

6 Bothwell, "The Decline of Progressive Policy."

7 Stanmeyer, institutional analysis for NCRP.

8 Ewuare Osayande, *With Allies Like These, You Don't Need Enemies* (Philadelphia: Undaground RR X-Press, 2004), 25. In a speech given on November 12, 2003, at the international headquarters of the American Friends Service Committee in Philadelphia, Osayande explained: "What ends up happening is that these groups [social justice groups] become brokers between the capitalists and the oppressed. These organizations become brokers. Who do you write you proposal to? That's the capital. The oppressed want that. That's what we want. That's how our labor gets exploited. Those are the people we're after. You [white-led non-profits] end up becoming gatekeepers in our struggle to get after the capitalists, those people who own the means of production....We're the folks they hire then fire after they have gotten their due from our labor. That's all we, the oppressed, got."

9 Ibid.

10 Center for Responsible Funding (CRF), "Summary of Conference Roundtable Discussion: Agenda for Progressive Philanthropy," American Friends Service Committee, Philadelphia, February 12, 2003.

11 http://www.breadrosesfund.org/donor/wwm.html.

12 CRF, http://www.responsiblefunding.org/Services/moneyforthemovement.html.

13 Giving USA (2005), http://www.aafrc.org/gusa/index.cfm?pg=aboutgusa.htm.

14 Giving USA (2003), "Giving USA: A Publication of Giving USA Foundation," researched and written by the Center on Philanthropy at Indiana University.

15 Ibid.

16 Kim Klein, "Getting Major Gifts: The Basics," in "Getting Major Gifts," ed. Kim Klein, special bound issue, *Grassroots Fundraising Journal,* 3rd. ed., revised and expanded (2000): 4–5.

17 Frances Stonor Saunders, *Who Paid the Piper: The CIA and the Cultural Cold War* (London: Granta, 1999), 134–35, 139.

18 Robert O. Bothwell, "Should Foundations Exist in Perpetuity?" *The International Journal for Not-for-Profit Law,* September 2003.

19 Ibid.

20 Saunders, *Who Paid the Piper,* 134–35, 139.

>>Amara H. Pérez, Sisters in Action for Power

between radical theory and community praxis

Reflections on Organizing and the Non-Profit Industrial Complex

IN 1999, AFTER GROWING TENSIONS BETWEEN OUR ORGANIZATION, Sisters in Portland Impacting Real Issues Together (SPIRIT), and our parent organization, the Center for Third World Organizing (CTWO), SPIRIT was officially shut down. This suspension of operation would have left the local community we had been organizing for almost four years without the capacity to conduct girl-driven campaigns around critical policy issues such as education, transportation, and safety. This abrupt split left us with the decision to either concede to the closure or spin off and rebuild the organization as an independent non-profit structure.

Many factors contributed to that unexpected and demoralizing split. In hindsight, however, I have come to understand those tensions more as symptomatic of the general state of the movement than as specific conditions of our experience. The initial values, intentions, and politics of an organization can be sound, radical, and inspiring, but it can also be clear from the outset that social change efforts can be susceptible to bad practices. While the history of what has now become Sisters in Action for Power begins with a bitter account of the way we were closed, it is more a thoughtful reflection of the exhaustive steps taken to rebuild the organization, and a critical examination of a movement's struggle to align politics and values to organizational infrastructure, practice, and vision. The nature of non-profit structures, the power and influence of foundation funding, and the relationship of both to social change organizations present complex and challenging questions for the movement.

At the time of our shutdown SPIRIT was just over three years old. I had been working as an organizer almost since its inception and had become the director six months earlier. Our small staff was young and relatively new to community organizing. Collectively, the leadership had virtually no experience in grant writing, strategic planning, or conducting the tasks needed to build the infrastructure of a non-profit. However, our membership, leaders, and the board of directors were committed to our mission of developing the leadership, critical analysis, and community organizing skills of low-income girls and girls of color ages 10 through 18 in Portland, Oregon.

As we worked to do what we thought would ensure a healthy and stable organization, most of the advice we received was about fundraising, administrative development, and infrastructure. First, there was fundraising. We spent a great deal of time dedicated to writing and rewriting letters of interest, proposals, and reports. We secured visits from out-of-town program officers and planned for local site visits. Often applying for grants from foundations resulted in our taking on additional work as required by guidelines that were not always reflective of our own internal priorities. The decision to pursue funding despite the less-than-perfect match was a necessary means of "staying open" to continue our work. Unfortunately, it also required us to overextend ourselves to do both the work we had envisioned *and* the work we had assumed now as grantees.

The foundation dance has always been complex. As organizations with significant budgets and paid staff, foundations are commonly sought after by non-profits as a primary funding source. It is not unusual that we become dependent on grants to fund our work and pay our leadership, and for most of us, the money is difficult to raise, unpredictable, and inconsistent. Nonetheless, private foundations fund many community groups across the country doing amazing work. And some foundations *do* spend a great deal of time thinking about how to best support social justice work—by funding direct action, grassroots leadership development, or providing travel money to take leaders to activist gatherings like the World Social Forums. And there are many program officers who are undoubtedly committed to social justice—many have come from organizing backgrounds—and ensure that some of the radical work we are doing is actually funded. We build relationships with foundations and the leadership within them, turning to them in times of need for support and resources that can often be decisive to the survival of an organization. For example, without foundation support at the time of our split, we might never have had the opportunity to continue and deepen our organizing efforts in Portland. Like many other groups, Sisters in Action for Power struggles to navigate through these complexities and contradictions.

But the reality is foundations are ultimately interested in the packaging and production of success stories, measurable outcomes, and the use of infrastructure and capacity-building systems. As non-profit organizations that rely on foundation money, we must embrace and engage in the organizing market. This resembles a business model in that the consumers are foundations to which organizations offer to sell their political work for a grant. The products sold include the organizing accomplishments, models, and successes that one can put on display to prove competency and legitimacy. In the "movement market," organizations competing for limited funding are, most commonly, similar groups doing similar work across the country. Not only does the movement market encourage organizations to focus solely on building and funding their own work, it can create uncomfortable and competitive relationships between groups most alike—chipping away at any semblance of a movement-building culture.

Over time, funding trends actually come to influence our work, priorities, and direction as we struggle to remain competitive and funded in the movement market. For many activists, this has shifted the focus from strategies for radical change to charts and tables that demonstrate how successfully the work has satisfied foundation-determined benchmarks. Ironically, it is also foundations that most often bring similar social justice groups together from all over the country. And we spend this rare, precious time together walking through the foundations' agendas, meeting their priorities, and contributing to the publications, manuals, and essays they distribute on "the field of organizing." Meanwhile, the occasions we do come together to discuss our own needs, based on our own agendas, and without the gaze of funders, are few and far between.

In addition to the power and influence of foundation funding, the non-profit model itself has contributed to the co-optation of our work and institutionalized a structure that has normalized a corporate culture for the way our work is ultimately carried out. In the initial phase of our efforts to sustain SPIRIT as Sisters in Action for Power, we were overwhelmed with the administrative steps required to become independent. We had to learn to set up accounting programs, a process for paying bills and spending money, legal requirements, insurance, liability, personnel policies, and payroll. We were informed of the need to incorporate as soon as possible and secure our own 501(c)(3). A long list of administrative steps and documents were required, including hundreds of pages of legal credentials, bylaws, articles of incorporation, and other forms and contracts. We registered as a non-profit organization in a dozen state, city, and county offices. For purposes of staffing, we were expected to produce job descriptions, job announcements, a formal hiring process, and official methods of supervision. And, of course, we needed letterhead, business cards, a fax machine, copier, printer, computers, e-mail accounts, and information packets promoting our accomplishments and successes. In the end, the ongoing work to maintain and prospect foundation money, combined with administrative obligations and developing infrastructure, was more taxing and exhausting than confronting any institution to fight for a policy change.

While working to build this complex infrastructure, we were simultaneously running our issue campaign to reduce bus fares for students traveling to and from school. (In fact, we were in the middle of this campaign when SPIRIT was shut down.) We continued to conduct weekly youth nights, leadership meetings, and campaign planning sessions, always engaging longtime members in as much of the organizational development work as possible. But it remained a significant challenge to balance the organizing work, foundation fundraising, and the work of building a non-profit. This "balance" required us to move back and forth between two worlds—and between two areas of work demanding two very different sets of skills. It was always clear which of the two drained us more and seemed more distant from the very purpose for which we had all come into organizing—leaving us to question if the most effective and strategic grassroots organizing can take place in a 501(c)(3) model.

After two difficult years of stabilizing Sisters in Action for Power, we had the essential elements of a non-profit organization in place. Moving out of crisis, we settled into our work. Our long four-year fight finally resulted in a major campaign victory—the creation of a new student bus pass, half of the original fare and available to over 200,000 students in Portland's tri-county area. Our youth leadership model had evolved into a well-structured, successful, and creative program designed to train and support girls in envisioning, planning, and carrying out strategic actions to make social change. Sisters in Action for Power began to receive national recognition, and soon we were encouraged by foundations and supporters to enlarge the scope of our activities—set up chapters, double our membership base, and hire more staff. It was assumed that we could simply take our work and expand it without compromising our project's integrity or our own political goals. It was always a strange conversation to explain why we resisted the pressure to expand. Raising our budget each year was already quite difficult with only three paid staff members. While tempted by the allure of "larger is better," we were daunted by the prospect of needing to raise even more money to function. In addition, inherent to our organizing and leadership development model was the practice of small, deep, and intensive skill building, consciousness-raising, and strategizing. More of everything would have taken away from what we knew worked.

Most social justice allies and supporters encouraged us to do exactly what has become standard practice in building community-based organizations. And in many ways, we moved in the very direction that emphasized building an individual organization over relating to a larger movement or shared analysis: securing 501(c)(3) status without questioning issues of sustainability or strategy; pursuing foundation grants to fund staff and program work with little discussion of other options like volunteer staff; and spotlighting the accomplishments of one's organizing work to seize any opportunity to expand—strategic or not.

Most of our initial work after the split with our parent organization moved us further from social change efforts and toward non-profit building work. We were never asked to articulate and demonstrate a political analysis that would guide our organizing work. No one advised us to explain our niche or role in a larger movement. We were never cautioned against burnout, the external pressure to get bigger, or overextending ourselves by common pulls away from the work. Though we had adopted many businesslike practices, tools, and modes of operation, the threat of mirroring corporate culture within the organization was never anticipated.

Ultimately, critiques of the non-profit model are not just about how the revolution is funded, or the dependency that it creates, or the way foundations have grown increasingly powerful over the course and content of social justice work. Such critiques are also about the business culture that it imposes, how we have come to adopt and embrace its premises and practices, and the way that it preempts the radical work so urgently needed from a social justice movement. It is very difficult, if not impossible, to maintain political integrity in circumstances that demand a professionalized, businesslike practice. And perhaps that is the point.

After the bus pass campaign victory, we carved out a large amount of time to engage in evaluation and reflection—revisiting the split from our parent organization, the "new" organization we were building, our theory and model for change. We returned to the question of how to develop an analysis that not only guided our organizing work but also our vision and practices within the organization. To articulate this political analysis, we read a wide variety of books examining the pan-American legacy of conquest and oppression, and engaged in political discussions about the role of organizing in today's political climate. We discussed the weaknesses in our own model, the missing pieces in our work, and the state of the movement. In addition, we reached out to local social justice groups and set up meetings to explore the ways their organizations used a political framework and articulated their analysis. To our surprise, most organizations could not point to an analytical tool used within their organization to direct their work or strengthen their strategies for change. Certainly, this alarming discovery further motivated us in our search of an organizing tool to understand the historical legacy of oppression, its systemic implications for today, to reveal concrete and strategic direction for our work, priorities, and decision-making.

The political readings, as well as the critical discussions we had both internally and with allies and organizers, resulted in our adopting a systemic analysis of colonialism. As a political framework, we identified four core pillars in this system: taking the land, killing culture, use of force, and the control of mind, body, and spirit. These pillars made up the system we critically talked about and hoped to eradicate. We worked to develop a three-month popular education curriculum to engage members in a critical look at the historical legacy of colonialism. Given our membership was predominately under 16 years old, we began with Columbus as an entry point because that was what was taught in school. We studied the political and social truth about "the discovery of America." We coupled this critical discussion with several weeks of self-defense designed to examine how the control of mind, body, and spirit has been used by this system historically and today. Even after finishing the curriculum, we maintained these critical discussions with members and staff. We used the pillars of colonization to examine national trends, dominant culture, and the current state of the mind and body in our society. We connected the past to the present, seeking knowledge to inform our own tactics and strategies for change.

An essential project, the colonialism curriculum was a genuine attempt to revisit the political nature of our work as it related to a larger movement and a larger legacy of struggle. There was no initial sense of where it would take us, or what would ultimately and concretely be derived from it all. But our ability to operate as a social justice group in a non-profit, foundation-funded organization was made possible by the time we dedicated to collective reflection, evaluation, and political discussion. The challenge, of course, is carving out the space and time with an already overextended workload. Often reflection and evaluation are not prioritized or seen as "the real work." In addition, without elaborate agendas, mapped-out outcomes, or outside consultants to facilitate, this work is also difficult to fund. But in the end, it becomes work one undertakes because of its intrinsic value and merit. It is what one points to when asked about internal priorities and behind-the-scenes work that are often made invisible by the more concrete, measurable tasks. In fact, people were more interested in getting a copy of the colonialism curriculum then in any aspect of the front- or back-end process that insulated and cultivated the very activities which made up the curriculum.

Our current campaign addresses local school closures, high-stakes testing, and sanctions under the federal law known as the No Child Left Behind (NCLB) Act. Beyond the deceitful name itself, NCLB promises education equity, freedom of choice, accountability, bridging the achievement gap, and high-quality teachers. In reality, NCLB discredits, defunds, and dismantles public education and teacher unions. With such a divisive and well-masked law, the development of a political framework was crucial in our own organizing efforts. Many people in the neighborhood we are organizing either don't know about NCLB or view it as a long-awaited answer to institutional inequalities in education. Social justice organizations have ironically supported pieces of NCLB—believing something is better then nothing. Other groups are receiving NCLB funding to work with parents, schools, and districts to implement pieces of the law. But like other critics of NCLB, Sisters in Action for Power recognizes this legislation as a Right-led attack on public schools—the location of some of our most significant fights and victories, the mobilizing grounds for grassroots leaders and communities. By co-opting our language, NCLB proponents deploy real concerns like education inequity, and real desires like accountability and achievement, all with the intention to dismantle the very institutions and safety nets that were fought for decades ago by other social justice efforts.

In addition to developing strategies for institutional change, we also want to incorporate tools for transformation and healing into our organizing efforts. We discuss the challenges of working to change society and also being able to intentionally make strategic changes within ourselves and our local communities. We look at ways to develop an organizational culture and practice inspired more by revolutionary and holistic paradigms than corporate and business models. The work is not just about what we do, but how we do it; the process is just as important as the outcome.

Over the years, we have developed tools and practices that have been shaped by our political framework. We have created a work plan that outlines the larger problems we are seeking to change, our organizational strategies, and our yearly goals. Twice a year, we collectively evaluate and reflect on our work using this political framework. This supports our process to evaluate, plan, and prioritize, as well as test our theory with practice. We meet every week as staff to make decisions together, be informed about our work, and assess workload and capacity. We also include journal writing and space for staff to share personal work as part of building a collective. We dedicate days to staff political education, during which we take turns facilitating critical discussions on issues and our work. Every three months we take half days for team building and bonding. We are very mindful about taking care of ourselves in the work with time off, hours in, and monitoring the pace of our work. We have seen many elders in the movement burn out or become sick from the intense pressure and demands of working faster, harder, and longer—at any cost.

Our model for change now includes leadership development, action campaigns, and modeling the vision—programs, activities, and tools which promote our vision for change in the here and now. This includes integrating mind, body, and spirit work into all aspects of our organizing. We have tried to move from progressive personnel policies to building a culture and practice that reflects our principles and values. We have agreed to maintain a small staff to ensure our ability to do deep skill-development work while maintaining a manageable budget. Many organizations enlarge at the cost of their capacity to engage in consistent reflection and evaluation, a process we consider to be essential in this work.

We have created a grassroots fundraising program to generate support from a wide variety of activities and opportunities. These include an annual event, program advertisement sales, community benefits, a monthly sustainer program, trainings, house parties, selling T-shirts, and more. Everyone raises money, from senior staff to our 11-year-old members. Our goal is to generate 50 percent of our money from grassroots sources to reduce dependency on foundations. The work is slow and painstaking, but essential to sustaining our work over the long run.

These are some steps that can be taken to transform internal cultures and practices in ways that are more congruent with the objectives of radical change. In the last few years, we have received several calls from organizers seeking advice on splitting or spinning off from larger organizations. We share these same lessons as well as new ones we've learned in our ongoing navigation through the non-profit model. But we also remind people that this is only one model for doing social justice work. There are other models that may be very different from our experiences which respond to a specific set of objective conditions at a specific historical moment. (For example, in many of these models organizers do not get paid to do the work.) When beginning to determine the direction and structure of the work to be carried out, be certain you want it to be housed in the non-profit world and be clear of what that will entail. At Sisters in Action for Power it continues to be a work in progress—every year trying to name and address that which takes us away from the work and that which sustains us. Is it reasonable to operate in a 501(c)(3) and still maintain a political edge and revolutionary commitment? This is what we are trying to do by using a political framework that grounds our work, by evaluating our work with this analysis, by staying within a budget that does not deplete us to raise, by integrating grassroots fundraising throughout the organization, and by taking the time to assess and improve on our terms the work we do.

As a young organizer, I was introduced to this work with the idea that it could be a career, housed in a non-profit structure and funded by foundations, and that these structures could sustain the movement. Ten years later, I think we need to re-examine the model, assess its sustainability, and determine its political direction. Foundation funding and non-profit management not only exhausts us and potentially compromises our radical edge; it also has us persuaded that we cannot do our work without their money and without their systems. Many of the problems we face in our organizing work today is derived from the model of business structures and corporate culture that now dominates the movement. In the end, the management skills required to maintain the operation of non-profit organizations become more important than the organizing skills needed to develop grassroots leaders, make institutional change, develop methods to raise community consciousness, or build a movement. I am reminded of the final chapter of George Orwell's *Animal Farm,* in which peering through the farmhouse window the animals see no distinction between the pigs and the farmers—the transformation is complete. For organizers looking at the structures that house the movement, it becomes difficult to distinguish the difference between a social justice non-profit and a small non-profit with a business pursuit.

Adapting to corporate culture and developing business skills have become an additional challenge for those of us who want to develop our members to assume direction and operation of the organizations from which they emerge. We must not develop our members into non-profit managers; we cannot deplete our leadership by burnout due to the administrative demands of this structure and end up replicating the same institutions we are working to change. The organizing skills needed to strategize around a campaign, develop methods for raising consciousness in a community, and developing other leaders have very little in common with the work many of us spend most of our time doing day to day to sustain the agencies that house the community organizing. Our energy and time is limited and should be directed to the assessment, strategizing, and collaboration needed to build a movement for liberation and justice—not to sustain institutions that are dependent on and directed by private foundations.

>>Madonna Thunder Hawk

native organizing before the non-profit industrial complex

I AM A VETERAN OF THE RED POWER MOVEMENT OF THE 1960S
and 70s. I was part of the American Indian Movement (AIM) and am a co-
founder of Women of All Red Nations (WARN). I was involved in several major
actions, including the Occupation of Alcatraz, the Trail of Broken Treaties, and
Wounded Knee. AIM was formed in 1968 by urban Indians, many of whom also
came out of correctional facilities. AIM patterned itself upon the self-defense
model of Huey P. Newton and Bobby Seale's Black Panther Party: AIM patrols
monitored the streets of Minnesota's Twin Cities, documenting and confronting
police brutality against Native people. Chapters sprang up through the country.
The Native people of the Bay Area also took cues from the Black Panthers, especially the 19 Indian people who became the Indians of All Tribes and took over
Alcatraz in an effort to turn it into an Indian cultural center. Several hundred
Indian people joined them, and many non-Indian groups like the Black Panthers
lent their support over a period of two years. The events at Alcatraz inspired subsequent takeovers of federal property and even more militant direct action. When
one of the leaders of the Alcatraz takeover, Richard Oakes, was killed in 1972,
Native groups spearheaded by AIM organized a caravan to Washington, DC, where
they attempted a 20-point treaty renegotiation program with the US government.
As we traveled cross-country to Washington, more and more reservation- and
urban-based Indian people joined our caravan. By the time we got to Washington,
most of the Indians participating were reservation-based. At this event, we ended
up taking over the Bureau of Indian Affairs (BIA) building.[1] In 1973, the Pine Ridge
reservation erupted into conflict when AIM took over Wounded Knee in protest of
tribal chair Dick Wilson in conjunction with the anti-Wilson community members of Pine Ridge. I participated in all of these events.

Because we were dedicated Indian Freedom Fighters, the Federal Bureau of
Investigation (FBI) started targeting the men of AIM. The women of AIM then
realized that we could just about do anything under the eyes of the feds and the
press because we were invisible. So we organized ourselves as WARN in 1978.

We organized around many issues, including environmental contamination in Indian country and sterilization abuse against Native women.

Our goal was to fight for Indian sovereignty and self-determination. We were dealing with the policies of genocide committed by the US government, so our goal was not to assimilate into the US. Consequently, we did not try to become part of any funding establishment, as that would have made our work less radical. We were very dedicated to fighting for freedom for our people.

When we first start organizing, we were rookies. We did not know how to organize but learned as we went along. Today, when young people ask me about my days in AIM and what they could do now, their first question is this: "Where will we get the money?" Often they are surprised by my response. But back then, we did not focus on fundraising. (Nor did we see activism as something we would get paid to do.) We organized first, and then figured out how to make it happen. And we seemed to get a lot more done than what people with funding and non-profits are getting done now. One reason is that organizations today often have to spend so much time raising money for salaries, sending in reports, and schmoozing with funders that they spend more time on fundraising and administration then they do on organizing. In contrast, we put all of our effort into organizing and activism.

Generally, we in AIM and WARN operated on donations. We organized speaking tours and used the honoraria to support our movement. Churches, universities, and non-Indian organizations (e.g., peace organizations, organizations based in other communities of color, women's organizations) supported us. Many lawyers, law students, and others with technical expertise volunteered their time, especially during the Wounded Knee trials. We relied on in-kind donations and were creative with our resources. We also did not travel with the same expectation of comfort as many of today's activists have. Nowadays, if people go to a conference, they often expect to stay at a hotel, while, back in the day, we might camp out or stay in peoples' homes.

For instance, Native communities in reservations and cities would invite us in to support them on various issues. So we might call a church in the town where we were and say, "We have 50 cars going to, say, a town in Nebraska, how can you support us?" The church would usually wire us money or give us supplies. They would also call church groups in the area where we were traveling to and ask them to find us a place to stay (usually in a school gym). Like others, I traveled with my children, and people would make sure we had diapers and other necessities. During that time, even mainline churches supported our work since they were focusing on race relations.

Young people would save up their money or get part-time jobs, and volunteer their time for the movement. Some people would come and work with us for a week; others might stay for a year. (I remember one woman who helped out with the Black Hills Alliance during the day, and played piano for a fancy restaurant in Rapid City during the evening.) We also shared resources communally so that those people who had money shared resources with those who did not, as did the Indian communities we visited. In addition, we developed links with support groups in cities who had more resources they would share with us. Also, back in those days, we did not organize on the basis of single issues. Today, you have groups that, say, only work on peace issues, or only work on violence issues. They won't support your work if it is not specifically part of their mission statement. Back then, organizations were more focused on radical social transformation so collaborations were more frequent. Activists helped each other out regardless of the issue. If we had a pressing issue, other folks would drop what they were working on to support us, and vice versa. For instance, many Black Power organizations supported us in Wounded Knee, and I was active in supporting the farmworker struggles.

One of WARN's big projects was a water study in the Pine Ridge reservation—we were one of the first groups to identity the issue of environmental racism. We began this study when Lorelei Decora (the other co-founder of WARN) mentioned to me that there were so many women having spontaneous abortions in the hospital where she worked that they had to put beds in the hallways. Meanwhile, I was working with the Survival School (an AIM alternative to public and boarding school for Indian children that supports our values of sovereignty and self-determination) and had noticed that people were not really feeling well. It seemed like everyone was always sick with various ailments. After comparing notes, we began to suspect a larger problem, possibly air pollution from the nearby gunnery range or maybe that there something wrong with the water. Certainly we knew a lot about contamination's devastating effects on our communities (such as the high birth defect and miscarriage rates in Indian country that are the result of environmental contamination). WARN had been a founding member of the Black Hills Alliance, which had shut down some of the uranium mining in the Black Hills. The uranium mining conducted in Black Hills could very well have contaminated the Pine Ridge reservation, which is just southeast of the Black Hills.

So we decided to take action. We took water samples on Pine Ridge and then samples from the Cheyenne River reservation as a control group in 1979. We had the samples tested at the School of Mines in Rapid City, South Dakota. High levels of radioactive contamination were found in the Pine Ridge reservation samples compared with the control samples from the Cheyenne River reservation. Our report showed that in one month in 1979, 38 percent of pregnancies reported to the Public Health Service Hospital in Pine Ridge resulted in spontaneous abortions and excessive bleeding. Of the children born, 60 to 70 percent suffered breathing complications as a result of underdeveloped lungs and/or jaundice. Children were born with cleft palates, club feet—diseases uncommon to the Dakota people. Pine Ridge reservation lies southeast of Black Hills, the site of extensive uranium drilling and mining from the late 1940s to the early 70s. At first, both the Center for Disease Control and Indian Health Services condemned us and declared our study was invalid. But later, when they learned that the School of Mines supported our claims, they decided to conduct their own study. What they found were even higher levels of contamination in some areas of the Pine Ridge reservation. The Nuclear Regulatory Commission raised the level of what is considered acceptable contamination, however, instead of attempting to eliminate water contamination. In one area, Indian Health Services started providing bottled water when the water became so contaminated it was visible. After almost 20 years of our organizing, the US Congress finally authorized a new water pipeline in 2003, but the funding for it was halted as resources were diverted to support the Bush administration's "war on terror." So the struggle against environmental racism continues, but at least our efforts have helped raise awareness about environmental racism in Indian country.

How we organized was different from how activists tend to respond now. We didn't wait for permission from anyone. We didn't have people tell us, this is too big of a project for you to do—you should contact the state or some other governing power first. Nowadays, an organization might want to do something more creative, but its board of directors will tell them no. We didn't have a board since we weren't formally organized, so we could just proceed with what we thought was best. We did not worry if our work would upset funders; we just worried about whether the work would help our communities. And we decided to do the study ourselves to ensure the results would be accurate. Today, when the same issue regarding nuclear contamination happens, most people go to an Indian Health Services or county commission meeting, and ask them to do something instead of doing something themselves. These bodies then don't do anything, and the people just go back home and complain. I have seen this happen where ranchers complained to a commission about water contamination near an air force base. They went to a city council meeting with water samples, and then did nothing else.

WARN had tax-exempt status once, but we let it lapse. It was too complicated. No one wanted to sit in the office and write reports with time and energy that could be used to advance our movement. We also had security concerns with COINTELPRO (the government counterintelligence program designed to destabilize radical organizations), so we were careful about being too organized. We did not want to have membership lists and chapters. We learned that the FBI would fabricate information, so we were a loose-knit group. If women in Cleveland wanted to organize, they could be autonomous and be WARN. Once you get too structured, your whole scope changes from activism to maintaining an organization and getting paid.

When we first heard about non-profits in the late 1970s and early 80s, it seemed like a good thing. We did not necessarily see what might happen if we started pursuing our work through non-profits; instead non-profits seemed to be just another way to raise money. But over the years, it has changed the scope of activism so that non-profits are just part of the system. The focus turned to raising money to keep the organization going, while the actual work of activism became secondary and watered down. And when the money disappeared, the work did too. Before, we focused on how to organize to make change, but now most people will only work within funding parameters. People work for a salary rather than because they are passionate about an issue. In Native communities, the economy is so bad that people just need jobs. So they might work for a non-profit primarily because they need the income, but they do not have the motivation to really push the issue. Of course, not everyone in a non-profit is like that—many people in non-profits really try to do good work. But the point is, when you start paying people to do activism, you can start to attract people to the work who are not primarily motivated by or dedicated to the struggle. In addition, getting paid to do the work can also change those of us who are dedicated. Before we know it, we start to expect to be paid and do less unpaid work than we would have before. This way of organizing benefits the system, of course, because people start seeing organizing as a career rather than as involvement in a social movement that requires sacrifice.

As a result, organizing is not as effective. For example, we first started organizing around diabetes by analyzing the effects of government commodities on our health: Indian communities were given unhealthy foods by the government in exchange for our having been relocated from our lands, where we engaged in subsistence living, and now damming and other forms of environmental destruction impact our ability to be self-sustaining. Today you can get a federal grant to work on diabetes prevention, but rather than get the community to organize around the politics of diabetes, people just sit in an office all day and design pamphlets. Activism is relegated to events. Many people will get involved for an event, but avoid rocking the boat on an ongoing basis because if they do, they might lose their funding. For instance, if the government is funding the pamphlet, then an organization is not going to address the impact of US colonialism on Native diets because they don't want to lose funding. People in non-profits are not necessarily consciously thinking that they are "selling out." But just by trying to keep funding and pay everyone's salaries, they start to unconsciously limit their imagination of what they *could* do. In addition, the non-profit structure supports a paternalistic relationship in which non-profits from outside our communities fund their own hand-picked organizers, rather than funding us to do the work ourselves.

Today the Bush administration is wreaking havoc on environmental protection, but where is the big outcry? People are too busy building organizations. So who is left to do the work? People are also very narrow in their scope of work. Previously, organizers would lay down their issue when necessary and support another issue. Now, most organizers are very specialized, and cannot do anything unless they have a budget first. More, foundations will often expect organizations to be very specialized and won't fund work that is outside their funding priorities. This reality can limit an organization's ability to be creative and flexible as things change in our society. Of course, when we did our work as WARN we also got crushed by the FBI and COINTELPRO, so it can be understandable that people are reluctant to think in terms of more radical organizing approaches. Also, nonprofits have so changed the culture of organizing that we would have to really change that culture now to do organizing differently. It is also true that in the computer age, it feels like we do need more expensive equipment to do work that we didn't need before. Maybe when we start paying $8 a gallon for gas, people will start being activists again because we won't have a choice.

Activism is tough; it is not for people interested in building a career.

note

1 At the end of the BIA takeover, AIM negotiated with the US government to leave without arrests. However, this takeover served to harden differences between AIM leaders and many more conservative tribal government leaders. These differences furthered conflicts between tribal and AIM leaders on the Pine Ridge reservation, contributing to the Wounded Knee Massacre.

▸▸**Stephanie Guilloud & William Cordery,**
Project South: Institute for the Elimination of Poverty
and Genocide

fundraising is not a dirty word

Community-Based Economic Strategies for the Long Haul

WHEN YOU CONVENE ORGANIZERS, NON-PROFIT STAFF MEMBERS, and activists together, fundraising is rarely the center of passionate debate. Though an important component of most organizing efforts in the United States, fundraising is usually perceived by activists as our nasty compromise within an evil capitalist structure. As long as we relegate fundraising to a dirty chore better handled by grant writers and development directors than organizers, we miss an opportunity to create stepping stones toward community-based economies.

In fundraising, there is foundation income and grassroots income. For the purpose of this essay, grassroots income is defined as all income generated from individuals, fee-for-service, and non-foundation sources. One of the staunchest critiques of the non-profit industrial complex (NPIC) is that non-profits have become over dependent on foundation funds as their primary source of income. We cringe about questionable investment policies or association with the elite, so foundations ostensibly provide a nice buffer between social movement work and finance capitalism. But relationships with foundations, like all things in capitalism, come at a cost. Relying on foundations removes an accountability mechanism from our work. In this current political moment in the US, the non-profit structure is the primary model used to organize, launch campaigns, and respond to attacks. Though grassroots fundraising does not completely free us from the limitations of the NPIC, it is a method that can increase and strengthen out accountability to the communities most affected by injustice.

grassroots fundraising as an organizing strategy

Project South is a scrappy organization located in Atlanta, Georgia, focused on movement building for racial and economic justice. More than just a necessity, fundraising is a crucial element to our organizational purpose and direction.

Grassroots fundraising is a strategy to maintain a firm connection to our base and to initiate community-based economic structures. We define *organizing* as building relationships and institutions to sustain community power, and it follows that fundraising *is* organizing. Project South doesn't hire fundraisers to fundraise; we hire organizers to fundraise. While our model may not work for everyone, we believe that part of building community power is creating a community economy in line with our principles and analysis.

Project South works to tie local and immediate struggles to the systemic root causes of oppression. Using popular education models, we partner with grassroots organizations and communities to step back and focus on the patterns of social movements, government politics, and economic trends. We create spaces to develop leadership, strengthen analysis, and plan strategies for more effective organizing. We believe in movement building, and we believe in community power. We connect grassroots fundraising to our central program goals for two reasons: foundation dependency limits effectiveness and to create a community-based economic model while building a base of allies and community members to whom we are ultimately accountable.

fickle foundations

Project South's experience has shown foundations as a whole to be fairly unreliable. With the media and financial institutions regularly declaring economic scarcity, non-profits are willing to meet foundations' programming and even political mandates. Our work becomes compartmentalized products, desired or undesired by the foundation market, rated by trends or political relationships rather than depth of work. How often do we hear that "youth work is hot right now"? Funders determine funding trends, and non-profits develop programs to bend to these requests rather than assess real needs and realistic goals. If we change our "product" to meet foundation mandates, our organizations might receive additional funding and fiscal security. But more often than not, we have also compromised our vision and betrayed the communities that built us to address specific needs, concerns, and perspectives.

Competition does not enhance movement-building work. Weeding out the "weak" to create three or four perfect organizations does not meet the many and complicated needs of diverse communities. Competing for resources with our partner non-profits aggravates the tendency toward turf wars and territorialism. Small organizations located in the US South face these dynamics. The South has fewer regionally based foundations than anywhere else in the US. The foundations we do have are small and fund small organizations. The only option for small organizations like Project South is to appeal to national foundations and compete at a national level. We are told time and again that resources for the South are limited and shrinking, and on a particularly bad day, a grant even disappears in the middle of a three-year award. Struggling community-based organizations are at an extreme disadvantage.

As an organization that works with many other grassroots groups to define and implement strategies that connect to long-term movement building, we see common barriers. Bound to yearlong grant cycles, foundation-funded organizations are discouraged from taking the long view and forget to expect the slow push to real change. Organizers working to connect local issues to broad transformation strive to build relationships and examine root causes of inequities. Though short-term projects and goals may move us along in the right direction, developing leaders and carving out integrated, multi-issue strategies does not happen in a year.

So, we still need money. How are we going to get it?

community-based economics

Fundamentally, economies are about the give and take of resources. In a community-based economy, resources flow from and return to that same community. Connecting organizing and fundraising allows those affected by the work of an organization to determine its course. Project South receives 40 percent of its income from grassroots fundraising. Our goal is to increase that percentage every year through publication sales, fee-for-service, community collaborations, and membership.

Publishing our curriculum is a simple example of providing needed resources and generating grassroots income. Community members (low-income people of color, students, and community organizers) request accessible education tools about globalization. Project South researches the historical dynamics and develops interactive, popularly based exercises to explore the effects of corporate globalization on our communities. We sell that tool kit for $15. The community receives a needed resource, and the organization receives income to sustain itself and our program work.

Another basic method used by Project South to support the community while sustaining our organization is serious collaboration with other organizations. We plan, coordinate, and share costs of community events with other groups in the area. All the organizations expand their base and visibility, the events are at cost or free, and there is a give and take for community members who may donate or pay a few bucks for raffle tickets. On the surface, these events may look similar to traditional fundraising parties, but there is an important difference. The folks attending, performing, and soaking up the politics are the same folks (youth, low-income organizers, community members) who participate in the organizing projects. We don't throw parties to raise money but to develop a culture of economic give and take that places value on community, collaboration, and resource sharing.

building a base

Project South also works to integrate fundraising goals and strategy with our overall efforts around base building. Just as we are intentional in ensuring that our leadership positions reflect those most affected, and that our programs address the institutionalized marginalization of so many communities, so must we integrate our fundraising efforts along these same lines. We believe it is better to be dissolved by the community than floated by foundations. Members who contribute to an organization will stop contributing when the work is no longer valuable. Tangible ways used by Project South to do this include hiring from within affected communities (staff, consultants, caterers, performers, researchers, tech support) and creating a membership base that participates in the give and take of all kinds of resources. Some provide financial resources, others provide cultural support, and still others provide links to organizations or people in the community.

Regardless of individual contribution levels, we need to ask the same hard questions about our membership as we do of our leadership and staff. Do they reflect the communities most affected? Are we building intergenerational, multiracial, multigendered membership? Simple structures can help ensure a base that is truly reflective of the broader community's composition. For example, Project South offers annual membership on a sliding scale: $25 if you earn a full-time, living wage; $10 if you are employed part time or at minimum wage; and $1 if you are incarcerated or unemployed. The system of value goes both ways. We express value and acknowledgement of all levels of work, and members express their support of the organization's work. Paying attention to who values us and who we value keeps our organization focused on those building a stronger movement for long-term change.

Grassroots fundraising through income-generating projects and base-building work also provides a solid structure to determine the effectiveness of our organizations. Program work with income-generating elements (like registration fees for workshops) has helped Project South gauge community interest and investment in our various projects. And when people do not respond or seek out opportunities to participate with us, it forces us to ask questions, especially this one: Do our programs/publications/resources reflect the priorities in the community? Grassroots fundraising provides a checks-and-balances structure.

The danger in this practice, as our organization still operates within a capitalist framework, is that we might be tempted to follow the money rather than follow the work. Generating income while maintaining relationships built on a commitment to long-term social justice requires consistent examination and evaluation so that organizations do not compromise principles for the sake of increasing revenue.

Project South has not, by any means, perfected this approach. We are not fully funded by grassroots sources. Our membership is still unorganized and uncharted. But we strive for a process that prioritizes grassroots sustainability over limited (and dwindling) foundation relationships that chart our success on a short-term rather than long-haul basis. We consistently ask ourselves: Could we survive if we didn't have foundation money tomorrow? Our answer is yes, but at a reduced level. We make a commitment to increase our financial independence not only for our own sustainability in a dangerous political climate, but also to be accountable to the communities who support us and whom we work to support.

To think of fundraising as a dirty word does not make our vision of a better world more viable or pure. Developing a real community-based economic system that redistributes wealth and allows all people to gain access to what they need is essential to complete our vision of a liberated world. Grassroots fundraising strategies are a step in that direction.

»»Ana Clarissa Rojas Durazo

"we were never meant to survive"

Fighting Violence Against Women and the Fourth World War

ON JANUARY 1, 1994, THE ZAPATISTAS LAUNCHED THEIR INSUR-
gency in Mexico. The date signified opposition to NAFTA (the North American
Free Trade Agreement), one of the greatest neoliberal projects, set to commence
that day. Globalization policies like NAFTA deem expendable the life and lands
of indigenous peoples. This is why, in 1997, Subcomandante Marcos declared in
an article in *Le Monde* that "the fourth world war has already begun."[1] Following
the cold war, which Marcos refers to as the third world war, the fourth world war
doles out violence and intimidation in dollars, in market bombs.[2] The fourth
world war is where the logic, organization, and violence of the market is deployed
in always increasing disbursements to all corners of the world and to all aspects
of life. Violence, in all its myriad manifestations—economic, environmental,
militarized borders and wars of terror, attacks on language and culture, and
more—is deemed a natural phenomenon by imperial and corporate powers. Like
the sun, the market also rises, and money is naturalized as that neutral ingredi-
ent which makes the world go round. The same is true of our social movements,
which, like many of us, took the bait hook, line, and sinker. The non-profit industrial complex (the NPIC) emerges from these processes of privatization and
globalization, and the non-profitization of our social movements is wielded as a
weapon in the fourth world war.

How did it happen? How did our movements come to look the way they look?
Is the way we work, the way we prioritize and engage in social change reflective
of the change we're seeking? What kinds of communities and societies are our
current social movements creating? Is the daily minutiae of our work consistent
with our vision for a more just and peaceful reality? Who do we name as allies in
our work? What is our accountability to each other, and do our "partners" share
our commitment to ending violence against women? And what's money got to do
with it? In our efforts to fight violence against women, have we become complicit
partners in the fourth world war?

Let me tell you about the sinker. After over 10 years in the antiviolence movement, I reflect in awe at the courage and leadership of so many sisters across the generations who have given and continue to give of their hearts to create more just and peaceful communities, to stand in solidarity with a sister going through it in the middle of the night. My work humbly rests on the strategies for survival unearthed by many who call out violence against women, insisting on dignity and humanity for all. In that spirit of calling out, I recall a few moments when I witnessed the movement sinking, when I noticed that our practices had become inconsistent with our vision; when we were usurped by capitalism and the state and became complicit with the violence of racism *and* violence against women (not mutually exclusive forms of violence, but rather interrelated and interdependent forms of violence[3]). These "sinking the movement" moments speak specifically to how funding steered our labors toward reproducing instead of eliminating violence against women.

1995. While working in the "Latina program" at the Support Network for Battered Women, I learn that an immigrant Latina has been brutally beaten by *"la Migra"* (immigration law enforcement). I approach the executive director with an op-ed I wrote on behalf of the program that speaks out against all forms of violence against Latinas, including both domestic violence and anti-immigrant state violence. (The executive director's approval is needed prior to publishing anything.) She tells me the board would never allow such an opinion to represent the organization because it is not allowed to take a political stance and "this" (the INS beating, not domestic violence) is clearly a political issue.

1997. After a racist and professionalist takeover of La Casa de las Madres, the new white managerial and directorial staff explicitly hire with a bias toward specialized and licensed degrees, while queer and immigrant Latinas are targeted for harassment. Many of us gather at a forum in New College, in San Francisco, where we tell our stories and critically assess the professionalization of the domestic violence movement and the increasing divide between social work and social justice.

1998. An attempt to rule out bilingual education is underway with the Unz Initiative (aka Proposition 227) in California, a measure that would seriously impede Latin@s' access to education and employment. I work with Sor Juana Inés: Services for Abused Women, a Latina organization assisting predominantly Latina survivors and their families. While exploring ways that Sor Juana can take a stance, I am reminded at a meeting of the state's Maternal and Child Health funders that agencies will risk losing their funding if they take a political stance. I go back and read the bylaws and find that upon accepting funding, agencies forfeit their right to take a stance on political matters especially those pertaining to elections.

2005. After facing over a year of threats to its very existence, not to mention threats directed at staff, San Francisco Women Against Rape loses most of its city funding as well as some foundation money. Many point to the harassment and loss of funding as a Zionist response to the organization's stated position against Israeli-imposed colonial violence and sexual violence against Palestinian women.[4]

Let's take a closer look at how these moments reflect the sinking of the movement, diverting our work toward a project that colludes with violence against women.[5]

antiviolence organizations reproduce racist violence against women

In the first case scenario, we note the existence of a "Latina program." Now a staple in many antiviolence programs, ethnic- or race-specific specialty programs exist within a larger "general" operation. Embedded within this organizational strategy is an assumption of universal whiteness. Within many antiviolence organizations, the distribution of resources (salary, benefits, and travel, for example) is consistent with the racial disparities that shape this process in the larger society; more often than not, the programs serving communities of color within larger organizations receive the smallest share of their organization's economic resources. Since most antiviolence organizations have become hierarchically ordered, decision-making power is another significant resource that is doled out unequally. Although this arrangement seems inconsistent with organizational objectives to foster and promote relationships in which power is shared equally and not abusively, it nonetheless perseveres, and, again, inequality manifests itself across racial lines.

The existence of "special" and "non-white" programs emerges from the logic of the liberalist project of multiculturalism. While there are clear racial hierarchies structured into organizations, these programs are developed under a multiculturalist model that renders race marginal by heralding the primacy of culture. Multiculturalist ideology is a remnant of early-20th-century modes of studying ethnicity, which were modeled on the experiences of white European immigrants who, through processes of assimilation and acculturation to dominant culture, became new white Americans. Although this model is mute on the issue of race—a silence which is part and parcel to the project of whiteness—it often conflates the experiences of communities of color with the experiences of white European immigrants. Thus culture becomes the dominant framework in establishing support to communities of color, yielding the institutionalization of "culturally competent" services across domestic violence organizations. Cultural competence models also falsely assume that culture is fixed and static, often dismissing great heterogeneity and inequalities internal to a particular nation, race, or ethnicity. While culturally specific services and programs might appear to address the injuries of racism, this organizational strategy actually displaces race from the broader analysis—effectively ignoring the power structure of white supremacy and the structured subjugation of people of color, which effects countless forms of violence against women. By adding a program ostensibly designed to serve the needs of a given community of color, the larger organization avoids direct accountability to that community. In other words, the organization's own white supremacy remains intact and fundamentally unchallenged, as are the countless forms of violence against women perpetuated by racism.

Further, as this example illustrates, the larger organization's white supremacy clearly shapes *all* its work, programming, and decision-making, including its "specific" projects. Certainly, institutional white supremacy dictated the work of the "Latina program," with the Support Network for Battered Women taking a position that silently supported state racist violence against Latinas by muzzling an attempt to publicly denounce it. Thus, "culturally competent" and/or multicultural organizational structures collude with white supremacy and violence against women of color, namely because this logic enables organizations to dismiss the centrality of racism in all institutions and organizations in the United States. These structures also help protect the state, whose Department of Justice was at once responsible for the brutal beating of a Latina immigrant *and* the funding of several staff positions and programs at the Support Network for Battered Women, including my own.[6] Conversely, this funding relationship encourages the organization to privilege its own "fiscal well-being" above all else, including the imperative to challenge state violence against women. Here, as the Sor Juana Inés example affirms, we see the paradoxical depoliticization of movements to end violence against women, an insidious process which obscures and protects the tyrannies of the state while diverting these movements' energies away from projects of resistance.

the non-profitization of the antiviolence movement

In her speech at the 2004 conference The Revolution Will Not Be Funded, veteran antiviolence activist Suzanne Pharr pointed to the significant injuries progressive social movements incurred through McCarthyism, COINTELPRO, and as an effect of establishing an alliance with the state by joining the non-profit sector. At first, she said, women doing antiviolence work sought tax-exempt status for shelters. But the price of achieving non-profit status became obvious early on as organizers were taunted with lesbian-baiting and misogynist jokes—and as funders demanded of the institution certain policies and practices, including professionalization. Soon funders were expressing their preference for degree-bearing professionals instead of community organizers; organizations were expected to have hierarchical structures; and therapeutic social services were funded over popular education work. Ideologically, violence against women became more and more a behavioral, criminal, and medical phenomenon, rather than a social justice issue. When violence against women is understood this way, interventions and attempts at prevention are overly reliant on therapy and the courts—all individualized methods of intervention that fail to address and combat the social organization of violence against women. These methods are also inextricable from institutional arrangements that carry steep histories of racism like the medical industrial complex and the prison industrial complex; as a result, the re-victimization of women of color becomes more likely.[7]

Ronald Reagan, a key player in the emergence of the fourth world war, made massive attempts to extend privatization to social movements and academia.[8] Through the non-profitization (a kind of corporatization) of social movements, a non-profit organization's economic structure, survival, and identity (that is, tax classification) became a dominant aspect of the organization. Ideologically, and in practice through the strict regulation of finances, the "rest" of the organization's work is understood as a consequence or byproduct of the funding. As organizations became non-profitized they began to lose political autonomy (from the state and funders), and their sense of accountability shifted from their constituents to their funders. The movement was literally split in two when funding came in to work discretely on *either* domestic violence *or* sexual assault, but not both, as if they were so neatly divisible and mutually exclusive. (In reality, sexual assault is one of the most common forms of domestic violence, and most survivors of sexual assault knew their assailants prior to the attack.[9])

Moreover, executive directors and managers are often given tyrannical say and power while hierarchies are entrenched, usually in line with social axes of inequality such as class, race, nationality, sexuality, and ability. The growing heterosexist and racist harassment pointed to this entrenchment at La Casa de las Madres, and the INS incident at the Support Network confirm the tangible power inequality. Ironically, it appears that our corporate-modeled hierarchical organizational structures are actually reproducing the same cycle of violence we seek to eliminate.

Let me tell you about the line. Through funding and non-profitization, the movement was called in to sleep with the enemy, the US state, the central organizer of violence against women in the world. In an effort to maim the movement, the state made its interests seem compatible with the interests of women. As Patricia Hill Collins observes, "Domination operates not only by structuring power from the top down but by simultaneously annexing the power as energy of those on the bottom for its own ends."[10] Through policy, ideology, and the NPIC, the state began to break into pieces the radical social justice agenda of the movement against violence against women. First, by prohibiting non-profits from engaging in "politics," it separated interpersonal violence against women from state-based, economic, and institutional violence against women. This individualization of violence excluded the experiences of women of color surviving the multiple forms of state violence.[11] Then the state splintered anti–sexual assault work from the movement to end domestic violence, while certain state-based forms of sexual assault were kept out of the discourse of violence against women (for example, militarized and prison sexual assaults, militarized border rapes, and sterilization and other population control practices.)[12]

The production of knowledge consistent with this agenda is a key strategy to get us to "buy" the line and to further the project of the non-profitization, professionalization, and social servicization of the antiviolence movement while escalating the criminalization and medicalization of violence. Academic research, under attack by "academic capitalism" and the extension of privatization to academia, has become increasingly dependent on federal and foundation funding. This funding develops a problematic allegiance to the state and foundation capital and steers the production of knowledge toward those ends. It is in this aforementioned context that the history of domestic violence research is produced. Thus, the historical legacy, the trends and directions in the literature on domestic violence, for example, reflects the trends and directions of the "sinking movement" in so far as they follow the subterfuge of the state's ideology on violence against women.

the state's line on the criminalization of domestic violence

In a move to align itself alongside the antiviolence movement, the state increasingly came to structure violence as a crime. This ideology naturalized violence as a crime, and thus emerged normative contemporary vernacular on "violent crimes" and "hate crimes" that conflates violence with crime. Violence is not naturally a crime, yet the interests of the state and the economy are served when violence becomes a crime.[13] The criminalization of domestic violence created a dual advantage for the state: the perpetrator became the sole party responsible for violence against women while the state positioned itself against the perpetrator and thereby as an ally of battered women. Criminalization also buttressed the state's claim that prisons were the solution to domestic violence, a framework that has been proven to the contrary while yielding disastrous results for women of color and their communities.[14] Interestingly, this development closely parallels the growth of the prison industrial complex (PIC) and the heightened criminalization of domestic violence through mandatory arrest policies, development of new crime legislation, and steepening sentences for existing crimes.

Federal funding to address violence against women was a key strategy to align the antiviolence movement with the criminalization project. In 1976, the Center for Women Policy Studies received a grant from the Law Enforcement Assistance Administration, the first federal monies made available to address domestic violence. The Center published *Response,* a newsletter intended to reach a national audience with the hope of fostering support for the funding's objective: the criminalization of domestic violence, specifically, by improving criminal prosecution rates.[15] Through this newsletter and funding, the interests of the criminal justice system and the battered women's movement were made to look compatible, and domestic violence came to be seen increasingly, both within the movement and in larger society, as a crime. Federal funding pitched the need for a "system-based" response to domestic violence, a move that partnered the antiviolence movement with the prison industrial complex, the medical industrial complex and state social service agencies. The criminalization project ensued, then heightened when two policies that created the largest pools of state funding for antiviolence work became law: the Violence Against Women Act in 1994 (VAWA) and the Violence Against Women Act II in 2005. VAWA I and II merged in policy the interests of the state—to criminalize society, populate the cheap labor force of the PIC, manage the nation's shifting racial demographics (specificallly, a declining white population) by quarantining more people of color in prison, and deflect attention from its role in the production and reproduction of domestic violence—with the interests of the antiviolence movement.[16] To affirm and structure this merger, VAWA created the US Office on Violence Against Women and housed it in the Department of Justice, the federal arm of the PIC. Thus, federal funding has entrenched the ideology of the criminalization of violence against women, doling out "the line" inside billions of dollars of funding.

One of the dangerous effects of the criminalization process is that it has inhibited grassroots organizing and creative community thinking about real solutions to domestic violence. Instead, the now-naturalized response to domestic violence is to "call the cops," a tactic that doesn't work too well for communities already under attack by the racism of law enforcement, immigration laws and enforcement, and the prison industrial complex. Additionally, mandatory arrest laws, which are pervasive throughout the country, require an arrest be made if there is a domestic violence call. But rather than protecting women against domestic violence, these policies often revictimize the survivor by either leading to her arrest (if she so much as scratched her abuser in self-defense) or to the arrest of the abuser without survivor consent. In 2004, INCITE! Women of Color Against Violence and Critical Resistance released a joint statement regarding the criminalization of domestic violence that revealed the state's true colors:

As an overall strategy for ending violence, criminalization has not worked. In fact, the overall impact of mandatory arrest laws for domestic violence has led to decreases in the number of battered women who kill their partners in self-defense, but they have not led to a decrease in the number of batterers who kill their partners. Thus, the law protects batterers more than it protects survivors.[17]

the state's line on the medicalization of violence against women

The Western medical model of disease deflects political causation and individualizes the origin of the problem/illness. Likewise the medical industrial complex (MIC), yet another partnering of the state and capital, co-opts social justice issues by taking them under its jurisdiction.[18] Through policies such as health practitioner mandatory-reporting policies, the MIC interfaces with the PIC to support state and economic interests in the criminalization of violence against women. For instance, these policies require that health care providers report suspected abuse to law enforcement. But survivor advocates argue that mandatory-reporting policies disregard survivors' choice to contact law enforcement, and in the process they are revictimized with the increased danger of being arrested or deported.[19] The MIC and PIC are principally interested in promoting profit, often at the expense and victimization of the most marginalized members of society, such as women of color. Just as the criminalization of violence against women emerged alongside the growth of the PIC, the medicalization of violence against women is closely linked to the growing privatization and corporatization of health care.

The criminalization and medicalization of violence against women intersect in that they promote an agenda to depoliticize the movement. The racist, corporate, and hierarchical organizational structures of the MIC and the PIC are extended to social movements, and more and more, the antiviolence movement mirrors these violent organizational structures. Private and public funding that encourage, or require, a "system-based" response coerce antiviolence organizations to work alongside these industrial complexes by extending the criminalization and medicalization of violence against women.

calling out the "antiviolence" state

As argued earlier, the state used funding as a strategy to ally itself with the antiviolence movement while diverting our attention from state violence. But our efforts to fight violence against women must account for the ways the state deploys violence; we cannot plan and create just and peaceful realities without calling out the state that deceptively positions itself as the "antiviolence" state.

As Angela Davis poignantly argued in her opening address at the first Color of Violence conference, violence is constituted in the very fabric of society.[20] In no way an unexpected aberration in the order of things, violence is the knife that cuts *and* the thread that sews this racist imperial nation together; violence *is* the order of things. It creates and separates nation-states, slices us into genders and sexes, Global North and South, distances the suburbs from the inner cities, brown and black from white.[21] Indeed unequal and oppressive social arrangements are engendered through acts of violence.[22] It takes violence to breed injustice, it takes violence to keep injustice.

The specific contours of violence today glare with a neocolonial empire building agenda that has conjured "the war of terror," the 21st-century invention of an ideological weapon wielded to maneuver public consent for abhorred attacks on humanity. It has been estimated that more than 100,000 Iraqi civilians were killed in just the first 18 months of military occupation—this, in addition to the many more hundreds of thousands killed through economic sanctions and the Gulf War invasion in 1991.[23] All expressions of violence are interconnected, and physical and military violence require ideological violence for legitimation and to enlist our participation. A war could not be without acquiescence to the logic of war.

The US-Mexico border reminds us that mass rapes, the mutilation of bodies, and murder have been integral ingredients in the concoction of neocolonial, neoliberal relations—the fourth world war. The Juárez femicides and the entire continuum of violence against Mexicanas and other migrants follow the violent incision of an increasingly militarized US-Mexico border into these lands and peoples.[24] Violence is an attempt to mark domination. Paolo Freire argued that violence is a tactic in the pursuit of power, a tool of domination that is centrally deployed by the state.[25] This is consistent with the work of Yvette Flores-Ortiz and Antonia Castañeda, who trace the foundational acts of domination in the United States—acts of conquest and colonial violence against native women and black women.[26]

Where violence is the constant and the context, multiple forms of violence are co-constituted, carried out in an organized manner that drives the mission of empire and its hues of a heteronormative, white supremacist patriarchal capitalist order. Domestic violence is a manifestation of unequal, or the pursuit of unequal, intimate relationships, and it emerges from and within a social context marked by inequality and the pursuit of inequality.[27] The state cites the exclusive primacy of gender oppression in its ideology on domestic violence. This emphasis is dangerous, as it obscures how other central social processes such as race and class are implicated in the production of domestic violence, not just as effects but as constructive forces. For example, the feminization and racialization of poverty don't just create additional barriers for poor survivors of domestic violence who are women of color; these social processes are actually constitutive elements in domestic violence.

Violence itself, as Angela Davis also noted, is a "powerful ideological conductor, whose meaning constantly mutates."[28] Discourses of violence are situated and produced amid specific political and historical interests and contexts. So it is compelling to note that the state has ushered in what have become dominant narratives on violence against women that do not consider the intersection of state and interpersonal violence.[29] Antiviolence groups who do consider this intersection, such as San Francisco Women Against Rape, are considered a threat and have had to endure organized attacks. When the state defines violence against women, it excludes from the definition among the most egregious attacks in the history of the human experience, dismissing many experiences of colonial and racist violence. In fact, the state narrative on violence against women excludes just about every form of violence, including military violence.[30] When we ask the question, "What counts as violence against women?" we come to find that the state's narrative not only fails to consider the experiences of women of color, but it also fails to represent the scope of violence against us. In doing so, it ignores the roots of domestic violence, therefore missing any opportunity to arrive at real solutions.

Through the criminalization process, the state also produces a racist, sexist, and heteronormative discourse on violence that works to purport men of color as hyper-violent, legitimating the racist practice of containing, detaining, invading, criminalizing, and splitting people-of-color communities.[31] The ideological work of a hegemonic discourse on violence against women that avoids many other prevalent forms of violence, particularly those experienced by women of color and our communities, sets up a pretense to address violence while simultaneously protecting white supremacist, patriarchal, and capitalist social arrangements. This analysis begins to reveal not only the state's complicity in maintaining violence against women, but the state's interest in deploying violence against women. This is the state's double discourse on violence against women: expressing interest in care, definition, and intervention of certain forms of violence (individual) on one hand, while dismissing, negating, and deploying other forms of violence.[32] In practice, the state legitimates violence as "legal," excluding its own practices from the very nomenclature of violence.[33] Violence is defined as separate, even oppositional to the state, in order to evade accountability. During the civil rights era, the state's concern with the threatening rise of social movements reinvigorated its interest in violence. In direct response to that summer's "urban riots," in 1967 the federal government commissioned the National Advisory Commission on Civil Disorders (popularly known as the Kerner Commission), which established a link between civil disorder and violence. A year later, the first federally appointed body to ascertain the "problem of violence" in the US, the National Commission on the Causes and Prevention of Violence was born.[34] The commission was given the following tasks:

> To investigate and make recommendations with respect to: (a) the causes and prevention of lawless acts of violence in our society, including assassination, murder, and assault, and (b) the causes and prevention of disrespect for law and order, of disrespect for public officials, and of violent disruptions of public order by individuals and groups.[35]

This ideological maneuvering positions violence outside the jurisdiction of the state, as "lawlessness." From this it seems clear that the commission's assigned task was to quell popular uprising which could potentially pose a threat to the state by any available measures, particularly the law-and-order state itself.[36] To that end, this historic panel's work assigned violence to the state's "control" and tagged myriad resistant activities as criminal. It sets violence as an expression of opposition to the state/law, as well as a crime and behavioral issue. The latter two frameworks are rooted in the individual, and with this swift move, the state slips itself out of the realm of violence. Undergirded by this ideological foundation, the social servicization of violence against women is made a dominant feature of the antiviolence movement through funding that effectively discourages social change, a recurring tactic of the NPIC.

While the state posits itself as an ally in ending violence against women, the antiviolence movement grows ever more dependent on its funding and ideology. Antonio Gramsci argued that the consent of the ruled is achieved through the state's education of the masses. In other words, the feeding of the line is key to establishing hegemony, the way the dominant group, through culture, folklore, and an array of social institutions, creates what comes to be known as "common sense."[37] And through the ideological disbursements in funding, we come to expect prisons, therapists, and medicine to eliminate violence against women. The NPIC has delivered the line.

And the hook? Money, money, and more money. The US Office on Violence Against Women diffuses the state's ideology on violence against women through the more than $1 billion of funding it administers each year. The context is key here because the non-profitization of social movements occurs in a globalizing context, in which privatization is extended more and more to all aspects of life, including resistance. In this way, non-profitization becomes a weapon of the fourth world war. Everyone, whether an educator, a health care worker, or a domestic violence advocate is working in pseudo-corporate environments where the culture and organization of the market is increasingly encroaching on our lives. Instead of organizers, we have managers and bureaucrats, receptionists and clients. Instead of social change, we have service deliverables, and the vision that once drove our deep commitment to fighting violence against women has been replaced by outcomes.

Globalization also sets out to heighten need and dependence on money by impoverishing and crippling economies and then fostering dependence on the institutions and national currencies capable of distributing it. The same is true for social movements that arise out of severe injustice that cripples and impoverishes the marginalized members of society. So in many ways, social movements for justice and liberation are made to *need* money. To the hungry fish in the sea, the bait on the hook looks real good. But soon enough, the fish learns that the hook ain't worth it, that the bait ain't just a meal, after all. Do we take to the hook because we need it? And when do we come to know the hook ain't worth it, and the money ain't worth it because it's actually killing the change we set out to create while signing us up to become complicit partners in the fourth world war? What will it take to resist the hook, to disinvest from the NPIC?

going global: the mcdonaldization of a movement

Subcomandante Marcos asserts, "What is to be done when violence derives from the laws of the market?" The greatest casualties of the fourth world war are undoubtedly endured by the most disenfranchised: lands, nations, and indigenous peoples in the Global South. Movements of resistance and justice also stand among the casualties. Like McDonald's franchises on the global market, movement-sinking ideology from the state, non-profits, and nongovernmental organizations (NGOs) is handed out alongside billions of dollars in funding. Globalization extends the logic and organization of the market to all aspects of life; imperialism extends the state ideology. The two work hand in hand while the criminalization, social servicization, medicalization, and non-profitization of social movements proliferates. Under the guise of transnational feminist projects, many US-based organizations and funders partner with organizations in the Global South in their fight against domestic violence. In a move reminiscent of the prior discussion on multiculturalism, institutionalized racism, and cultural-competency models, US-based "maimed movement" approaches are signed, sealed, and delivered throughout the world, with minor adjustments to protocol and practice based on the cultural and social particulars of the Global South partner. Caren Kaplan and Inderpal Grewal reveal that the fallacy of supposed transnational feminist projects lies in their inability to commit to engaging an international and critical analysis and practice that recognizes asymmetries of power and multiple expressions of agency.[38] In effect, the imposition of US models of intervention in violence against women dismisses the context of globalization and imperialism, falsely casting the United States as interested in the safety and well-being of women in the Global South. Further, this imposition frames US antiviolence models as superior to all others, jeopardizing the practices, traditions, and epistemologies of indigenous women and communities in the Global South.

The antiglobalization movements throughout the world are leading the way in fighting privatization and the fourth world war. Given that they share the same enemies, what will it take for the antiglobalization movements to ally with the antiviolence movement? First, both movements would have to jointly resist non-profitization, the process which extends privatization to social movements and allies them with profit-seeking interests like the PIC and MIC. And second, both movements would have to jointly articulate and engender visions of social justice and liberation that account for the ways the fourth world war deploys violence against women and sets out to co-opt the antiviolence movement.

getting there

I was recently riding a taxi in Ann Arbor, Michigan, and the driver, a middle-aged man from Mumbai, India, commented that we should always be skeptical of research findings and design, and that we should look very closely at who is funding the research. "Through funding they tell you how to think," he said....

In 2003, in Delhi, India, INCITE! met with a grassroots activist group doing work around AIDS. The group refused any money except that raised through grassroots means. We were reminded that money corrupts and always carries strings.

Suzanne Pharr asked the audience at the Revolution Will Not Be Funded conference, in a time of rapacious capitalism, "what might we do to fund a radical movement?" Many sisters are leading the way, disinvesting from the NPIC, disinvesting from the state, and redirecting energies and precious resources and time to grassroots organizing, political education, and community mobilization. As I write this article, Sista II Sista is de-501(c)(3)izing,[39] INCITE! still refuses to incorporate as a non-profit, and we remember the rejection by the NCAVP (National Coalition of Antiviolence Programs) of $600,000 from the Department of Justice, the federal agency that refused the group's references to lesbian battering, racism, and commitment to organizing.

In spite of the dismal landscape, we persevere with fierce and strong determination as more radical and grassroots movements against violence against women are born. These movements insist on recognizing all forms of violence against women, including state and racist violence. More interested in ending violence against women than in winning the largest grant, pandering to funders, or worrying over government regulations, we are reminded to take a close look and notice what path we're headed down. This is a call to remember why funding takes the directions it takes, why some things get funded and others don't, and what we become complicit in by pursuing and accepting certain funds.

Funding, whether government or foundation money, emerges from the deepest ravages of capitalist inequality. Simply put, the government will not dole out dollars to organize against privatization, against the fourth world war, or against itself—in other words, it will not fund the movement to end violence against women. Paolo Freire once said that violence is an instrument of terror intended to immobilize the opponent; it stands then that the non-profit industrial complex is guilty of deploying the violence of non-profitization, an attempt to sink our movements. And, just as we have always done, we will not stand for violence. We will call out injustice wherever we see it and continue our long, hopeful fight to end violence against women *and* the fourth world war.

notes

The title of this essay is inspired by Audre Lorde, who wrote: "For to survive in the mouth of the dragon we call America, we have had to learn this first and most vital lesson—that we were never meant to survive." Audre Lorde, Sister Outsider (Freedom, CA: The Crossing Press, 1984).

1 Subcomandante Marcos, "Why We Are Fighting: The Fourth World War Has Begun," *Le Monde Diplomatique*, September 1997, http://mondediplo.com/1997/09/marcos.

2 Subcomandante Marcos, "The Fourth World War Has Begun," in *The Zapatista Reader*, ed. Tom Hayden (New York: Thunder's Mouth Press/Nation Books, 1997), 270–275.

3 For further discussion of the intersection of the violence of racism and violence against women, see the work of Antonia Castañeda and Yvette Flores-Ortiz, and INCITE! Women of Color Against Violence, ed., *Color of Violence: The INCITE! Anthology*, (Cambridge, MA: South End Press, 2006).

4 For further discussion on Zionism, please see *Color of Violence*, specifically Nadine Naber, Eman Desouky, and Lina Baroudi's "The Forgotten –ism: An Arab American Women's Perspective on Zionism, Racism, and Sexism" and Nadine Naber's "A Call for Consistency: Palestinian Resistance and Radical US Women of Color."

5 My observations stem from my own direct personal experience working in the movement and the emergent patterns noted from countless conversations and statewide and national meetings. These formations are not present in every organization; rather, such organizational structures have become dominant and mainstream within the antiviolence movement as a whole.

6 Violence Against Women funding is administered through the Department of Justice, which, up until the creation of the Department of Homeland Security, also housed and administered immigration enforcement.

7 Beth E. Richie, *Compelled to Crime: The Gender Entrapment of Battered Black Women* (New York: Routledge, 1996).

8 See the following: Jennifer Washburn, *University, Inc.* (New York: Basic Books, 2005) and Andrea del Moral, "The Revolution Will Not Be Funded," *LiP: Informed Revolt*, April 4, 2005.

9 Rape, Abuse, and Incest National Network, "Statistics," http://www.rainn.org/statistics/index.html.

10 Patricia Hill Collins, *Black Feminist Thought* (Boston: Unwin Hyman, 1990).

11 Gail Garfield, *Knowing What We Know: African American Women's Experiences of Violence and Violation* (Piscataway, NJ: Rutgers University Press, 2005).

12 See the following: Cynthia Enloe, *Maneuvers: The International Politics of Militarizing Women's Lives* (Berkeley: University of California Press, 2000); Sylvanna Falcón, "Securing the Nation

Through the Violation of Women's Bodies: Militarized Border Rape at the US-Mexico Border," in INCITE!, *Color of Violence;* Andrea Smith, "'Better Dead than Pregnant': The Colonization of Native Women's Reproductive Health," in *Policing the National Body: Race, Gender, and Criminalization,* ed. Jael Silliman and Anannya Bhattacharjee (Cambridge, MA: South End Press, 2002).

13 Urvashi Vaid asked in her speech at INCITE's first Color of Violence conference in Santa Cruz, "If hate violence is motivated by prejudice, why is there an over-reliance on the law through the pro-criminalization of hate crimes and an under-reliance on education?" Urvashi Vaid, opening plenary (Color of Violence conference, University of California, Santa Cruz, April 2000).

14 See Justice Now, www.jnow.org, and "INCITE!/Critical Resistance Joint Statement," www.incite-national.org.

15 Susan Schechter, *Women and Male Violence: The Visions and Struggles of the Battered Women's Movement* (Boston: South End Press, 1982), 189–191.

16 Antonia Castañeda, "History and the Politics of Violence Against Women," in *Living Chicana Theory,* ed. Carla Trujillo (Berkeley: Third Woman Press, 1998); Yvette Flores-Ortiz, *"La mujer y la violencia:* A Culturally Based Model for the Understanding and Treatment of Domestic Violence in Chicana/Latina Communities," in *Chicana Critical Issues,* ed. Mujeres Activas en Letras y Cambios Sociales (MALCS) (Berkeley: Third Woman Press, 1993); Andrea Smith, "Looking to the Future: Domestic Violence, Women of Color, and Social Change," in *Domestic Violence at the Margins: Readings on Race, Class, Gender, and Culture,* ed. Beth E. Richie, Natalie J. Sokoloff, and Christina Pratt (Piscataway, NJ: Rutgers University Press, 2005).

17 Critical Resistance and INCITE! Women of Color Against Violence, "Gender Violence and the Prison-Industrial Complex," in INCITE!, *Color of Violence,* 223.

18 For further discussion, see my essay "The Medicalization of Domestic Violence," in INCITE!, *Color of Violence.*

19 Ariella Hyman, *Mandatory Reporting of Domestic Violence by Health Care Providers: A Policy Paper* (San Francisco: Family Violence Prevention Fund, 1997).

20 Angela Y. Davis, keynote speech (Color of Violence conference, University of California, Santa Cruz, April 2000).

21 For discussion on the production of normatively sexed bodies and gendered subjects through medical violence, specifically through sex assignment surgeries, see Cheryl Chase, "Hermaphrodites With Attitude: Mapping the Emergence of Intersex Political Activism," *Gay and Lesbian Quarterly* 4, no. 2 (1998): 189–211

22 Paolo Freire, *Pedagogy of the Oppressed,* trans. Myra Bergman Ramos (1970; repr., New York: Continuum, 1982), 26–40.

23 Dorothy Roberts, *Killing the Black Body: Race, Reproduction, and the Meaning of Liberty* (New York: Pantheon, 1997).

24 See INCITE!, *Color of Violence,* especially Rosa Linda Fregoso's "The Complexities of 'Feminicide' on the Border" and Sylvanna Falcón's "'National Security' and the Violation of Women: Militarized Border Rape at the US-Mexico Border."

25 Freire, *Pedagogy of the Oppressed,* 26–40

26 Flores-Ortiz, *"La mujer y la violencia"* and Castañeda, "History and the Politics of Violence Against Women."

27 Over and over again, I have been told by women in Chiapas, Colombia, and Palestine that as military violence escalates, they see forms of intimate gender-based violence escalate. See Enloe, *Maneuvers* and Clarissa Rojas, Margo Okazawa-Rey, and Marisol Arriola, "War Hits Home for US Women," *War Times,* no. 6 (October 2002).

28 Davis, keynote speech.

29 For further information, see the work of Nadera Shelhoub Kevorkian, Nada Elias, Margo Okazawa-Rey, and Cynthia Enloe. For recent findings that female US female military personnel have been dying from complications resulting from holding their urine, for fear of being raped by men in their own armies if they went to the restroom in the middle of the night, see Marjorie Cohn,

"Military Hides Cause of Women Soldiers' Deaths," truthout, January 30, 2006, www.truthout.org/docs_2006/013006J.shtml.

30 Office on Violence Against Women, http://www.usdoj.gov/ovw/.

31 Gayatri Chakravorty Spivak stated that colonialism (in the minds of some colonizers), as in the invasion in Afghanistan, involves "white men saving brown women from brown men." See also Nadine Naber et al., "The Forgotten –ism."

32 Another double discourse exists with regard to the state's narrative on other forms of violence. For example, a February 26, 2006 headline read, "Bush Urges Iraqis to Stem Wave of Violence" (AP). Simultaneously Bush addresses Iraqi violence while dismissing the violence of the US military invasion. This also exists with the prison industrial complex, where prisoner violence is noted yet the many institutional acts of violence that prisoners endure are ignored. These double discourses are also racialized—they are specifically intent on pinning the tag of violence on people of color, while the violence of white supremacy and colonialism is evaded.

33 Alexander Passerin d'Entreves, The Notion of the State (Oxford: Clarendon Press, 1967).

34 Albert J. Reiss, Jr., Understanding and Preventing Violence, ed., National Research Council (Washington, DC: National Academy Press, 1993), ix–27.

35 Ibid., x.

36 The commission was also set up in response to the National Science Foundation's Program on Law and Social Sciences, which was interested primarily in studying violent behavior, and the National Institute of Justice, which sought assistance with preventing violent crime.

37 Rosemary Hennessy, Materialist Feminism and the Politics of Discourse (New York: Routledge, 1993); Antonio Gramsci, Selections From the Prison Notebooks of Antonio Gramsci, ed. Q. H. Smith and G. N. Smith (1971; repr., New York: International Publishers, 1999.

38 Inderpal Grewal and Caren Kaplan, Scattered Hegemonies: Postmodernity and Transnational Feminist Practices (Minneapolis: University of Minnesota Press, 1994), 3, 19.

39 To learn more about Sista II Sista's decision to disinvest from the non-profit system, see Nicole Burrowes, Morgan Cousins, Paula X. Rojas, and Ije Ude, "On Our Own Terms: Ten Years of Radical Community Building With Sista II Sista," which appears in this volume.

>>Paul Kivel

social service or social change?

CAN WE PROVIDE SOCIAL SERVICE *AND* WORK FOR SOCIAL CHANGE, or do our efforts to provide human services maintain or even strengthen social inequality?

I first began thinking about this issue when the Oakland Men's Project was established in 1979. At that time, we were responding to women in the domestic violence, sexual assault prevention, and child sexual assault prevention movements. When asked what we could do as men, they said that they had their hands full dealing with the survivors of male violence and trying to get institutions to respond to these issues. But we were told that since it was men who were the perpetrators of most of the violence, men were needed to address other men.

Many men in the country who heard that initial call started batterer intervention programs, working with men individually and in small groups to help them stop their violent behaviors. At the Oakland Men's Project we were involved in these efforts, yet we felt that in order to end male violence we needed more than groups for individual men who were violent. We committed to build an organization which, through community prevention and education, could contribute to ending violence, not just "reforming" individual perpetrators.

Nearly 30 years later, I look around and see many shelters and services for survivors of domestic violence, but no large-scale movement to end male violence. I see many batterer intervention programs, but few men involved in challenging sexism. The loss of vision that narrowed the focus of men's work reflects a change that occurred in other parts of the movement to end violence, as activists who set out to change the institutions perpetrating violence settled into service jobs helping people cope. Why does this narrowing of focus continue to happen in so much of our community work?

Social service work addresses the needs of individuals reeling from the personal and devastating impact of institutional systems of exploitation and violence. *Social change work* challenges the root causes of the exploitation and violence. In my travels throughout the United States, I talk with many service providers, more and more of whom are saying to me, "We could continue doing what we are doing for another hundred years and the levels of violence would not change." I meet more and more people who are running programs for batterers who say, "We are only dealing with a minute number of the men who are violent and are having little impact on the systems which perpetuate male violence."

We need to provide services for those most in need, for those trying to survive, for those barely making it. We also need to work for social change so that we create a society in which our institutions and organizations are equitable and just, and all people are safe, adequately fed and sheltered, well educated, afforded safe and decent jobs, and empowered to participate in the decisions that affect their lives.

While there is some overlap between social service provision and social change work, the two do not necessarily go readily together. In our violent world, the needs and numbers of survivors are never ending, and the tasks of funding, staffing, and developing resources for our organizations to meet those needs are difficult, poorly supported, and even actively undermined by those with power and wealth in our society. Although some groups are both working for social change and providing social services, there are many more groups providing social services that are not working for social change. In fact, many social service agencies may be intentionally or inadvertently working to maintain the status quo. After all, the non-profit industrial complex (NPIC) wouldn't exist without a lot of people in desperate straits. The NPIC provides jobs; it provides opportunities for professional development. It enables those who do the work to feel good about what we do and about our ability to help individuals survive in the system. It gives a patina of caring and concern to the ruling class which funds the work. While there is always the risk of not securing adequate funding, there is a greater risk that if we did something to really rock the boat and address the roots of the problems we would lose whatever funding we've already managed to secure. In this essay I will explore the rise of this paradox and what activists might do to combat the deleterious effects imposed by the NPIC on our work for lasting social change.

the economic pyramid

To get to the root of the social service/social change dilemma we must examine our current political/economic structure, which can be thought of as a pyramid (see next page). In the United States, 1 percent of the population controls about 47 percent of the net financial wealth,[1] and the next 19 percent of the population controls another 44 percent. That leaves 80 percent of the population with just 9 percent of the remaining financial wealth. The result is that large numbers of people in the United States spend most of our time trying to get enough money to feed, house, clothe, and otherwise support ourselves and our families, and many end up without adequate housing, food, health care, work, or educational opportunities.

The US Economic Pyramid

1 percent
of the population
holds 47 percent of the nation's wealth
RICH/OWNERS
Independently wealthy
Over $3 million/household net worth
Average income over $374,000/year

19 percent
of the population
holds 44 percent of the nation's wealth
PROFESSIONAL/MANAGERIAL
Over $344,000/household net worth
Average income over $94,000/year

80 percent
of the population
holds 9 percent of the nation's wealth
MIDDLE AND WORKING CLASS/UNEMPLOYED/WELFARE/HOMELESS
$56,000/household net worth
Average income $41,000/year

The economic pyramid[2] is only a rough instrument for measuring income distribution, as there are many gradations it overlooks. Nevertheless, it offers a snapshot of devastating social and economic inequality. Most notably, among the 80 percent at the base of the pyramid, there is a vast difference in the standard of living between those nearer the top and those at or near the bottom. And a substantial number of people (nearly 20 percent of the population) actually live *below* the bottom of the pyramid with negative financial wealth (that is, more debt than assets).

▷ **Questions to ask yourself**

Where did you grow up on the pyramid, or where was your family of origin on the pyramid? Where are you now?

Historically, the United States has always had a steep economic pyramid with a large concentration of wealth in the two richest classes. But in the last 25 years, since the beginning of the Reagan administration in 1981, the distance between the ruling and managerial classes and the rest of the population has increased dramatically. Class mobility has decreased, and the economic well-being of the poorest 80 percent has substantially deteriorated. Those on the bottom of the pyramid have fared the worst. During this period, most of those in the top 20 percent have thrived because they have substantial assets providing them with social and economic security as well as access to power, resources, education, leisure, and health care. Of this group, those at the very top have consolidated their power and privilege.

I refer to the top 1 percent as the ruling class because members of this class hold positions of power as corporate executives, politicians, policy makers, and funders for political campaigns, policy research, public policy debates, and media campaigns. The ruling class maintains the power and money to influence, and often to determine, the decisions that affect our lives, including where jobs will be located and what kinds of jobs they will be; where environmental toxins are dumped; how much money is allocated to build schools or prisons and where they will be built; and which health care, reproductive rights, civil rights, and educational issues will be discussed and who defines the terms of these discussions. In other words, when we look at positions of power in the US, we will almost always see members or representatives of the ruling class. We cannot call our country a democracy when 1 percent of the population controls nearly half, and the top 20 percent controls 91 percent, of the wealth and the access to power that wealth produces. This vast concentration of wealth produces the conditions of impoverishment, ill health, violence, and marginalization that necessitate the services so many of us provide.

While the ruling class might not all sit down together in a room and decide policy, members of this class *do* go to school together, vacation together, live together, and share ideas through various newspapers and magazines, conferences, think tanks, spokespeople, and research and advocacy groups. They *do* meet in Congress, corporate offices, foundation boardrooms, elite law firms, and in national and international gatherings to make significant social, political, and economic decisions for their collective benefit. Perhaps most important, members of this class sit together on interlocking boards of directors of major corporations and wield great power on corporate decisions. Because multinational corporations have larger economies, greater security forces, and more political clout than most countries, those who sit on boards of corporate directors collectively wield tremendous influence on political decisions through lobbying, government appointments, corporate-funded research, interpersonal connections, and advisory appointments, as well as the power they wield through direct economic and political intervention in local communities and in the affairs of other countries.[3]

The next 19 percent of the economic pyramid, the professional/managerial class, consists of people who work for the ruling class. Members of this class may not gain the same level of power and financial rewards as people at the very top, but their work provides the research, managerial skills, expertise, technological development, and other resources which the ruling class needs to maintain and justify its monopolization of political and economic power. This class also carries out the direct management of the largest public, private, and non-profit enterprises in the country.

But it is the majority of the population, the bottom 80 percent, which produces the social wealth benefiting those at the top. Laboring in factories, fields, classrooms, homes, sweatshops, prisons, hospitals, restaurants, and small businesses, the individuals composing this enormous class keep our society functioning and productive. Meanwhile, entire communities remain entrapped in endless cycles of competition, scarcity, violence, and insecurity that those at the top are largely protected from.

Certainly the gradations within the bottom 80 percent (middle class, working class, and the dependent and working poor) produce additional security and benefits for some of its members, specifically those in the middle class, those who are white, or male, or citizens, or not incarcerated, or straight, or able-bodied, and keep many of us blaming and attacking those like—or even worse off than—us, rather than looking to the economic system and the concentration of wealth at the top of the pyramid as the source of our problems. The role of the NPIC is to keep our attention away from those in power and to manage and control our efforts to survive in the bottom of the pyramid. These functions are necessary to maintain the concentration of wealth and power because people have always resisted economic and political inequality and exploitation.

People on the bottom rungs of the pyramid are constantly organizing to gain more power and access to resources. Most of the progressive social change we have witnessed in US history resulted from the work of disenfranchised groups of people who have fought for access to education, jobs, health care, civil rights, reproductive rights, safety, housing, and a safe, clean environment. In our recent history, we can point to the civil rights movement, women's liberation movements, lesbian and gay liberation movements, the disability rights movement, labor movements, and thousands of local struggles for progressive social change.[4]

▷ **Questions to ask yourself**

Are you part of any group which has organized to gain for itself more access to voting rights, jobs, housing, education, or an end to violence or exploitation—such as workers, women, people of color, people with disabilities, seniors, youth, lesbians, gays, bisexuals and trans people, or people whose religion is not Christian?

How have those struggles benefited your life?

How have those struggles been resisted by the ruling class?

What is the current state of those movements you have been closest to?

the buffer zone

People in the ruling class have always wanted to prevent people at the bottom of the pyramid from organizing to maintain the power, the control, and, most important, the wealth that they have accumulated. At the same time, they have generally wanted to avoid directly managing people on the bottom of the pyramid. To maintain this separation and to prevent themselves from becoming the objects of people's anger, they have used legal, educational, and professional systems to create a network of occupations, careers, and professions to deal directly with the rest of the population. This buffer zone comprises all occupations that carry out the agenda of the ruling class without requiring ruling-class presence or visibility. Some of the people employed in the buffer zone fall into the 19 percent section of the pyramid; however, most have jobs that put them somewhere near the top of the bottom 80 percent. These jobs give them a little more economic security and just enough power to make decisions about other people's lives—those who have even less than they do. The buffer zone has three primary functions.

The first function is *taking care of* people at the bottom of the pyramid. If it were a literal free-for-all for that 9 percent of the nation's wealth allocated to the poor/working and lower-middle classes, there would be (particularly in the eyes of those who benefit most from the economic pyramid) "chaos": many more people would be dying in the streets (as happened during the Depression, for example) instead of invisibly in homes, hospitals, prisons, rest homes, and homeless shelters. Individual, hidden deaths and personal tragedies caused by AIDS, cancer, occupational dangers, environmental pollution, unsafe consumer products, diabetes, heart disease, asthma, family violence, lack of health care, homelessness, poverty, discrimination, and neglect keep people from adding up the total cost of the concentration of wealth. There are many occupations—social welfare workers, nurses, teachers, counselors, case workers, advocates for various groups—to either manage or sort out (generally based on class, race, gender, immigration status, and other social categories) which people get how much of the 9 percent and to provide minimal services for those in need. These occupations are performed mostly by women and are primarily identified as women's work.

Taking care of those in need is valuable and honorable work, and most people do it with generosity and good intentions. But it also serves to mask the inequitable distribution of jobs, food, housing, and other valuable resources. When temporary shelter becomes a substitute for permanent housing, emergency food a substitute for a decent job, tutoring a substitute for adequate public schools, and free clinics a substitute for universal health care, we have shifted our attention from the redistribution of wealth to the temporary provision of social services to keep people alive.

The second function of jobs in the buffer zone is *keeping hope alive* by distributing opportunities for a few people to become better off financially. There are still many people who believe the myth that anyone can make it in this society—that there is a level playing field. To keep that myth believable there have to be examples of people who have "made it"—have gone to college from a poor family, moved from homelessness to stable housing, found a job despite having few "marketable" skills. Some of those who have buffer-zone jobs determine which people will be the lucky ones to receive jobs and job training, a college education, housing allotments, or health care. Those who gain access to these benefits are held up as examples that the system works and serve as proof that if one just works hard, follows the rules, and doesn't challenge the social order or status quo, she or he, too, will get ahead and gain a few benefits from the system. Sometimes getting ahead in this context means getting a job in the buffer zone and becoming one of the people who hands out the benefits.

When the staff of a housing agency enables three families out of a hundred in a community to get into affordable housing, or a youth program enables a handful of students out of hundreds in a neighborhood to get into college or into job-training programs, buffer-zone organizations can honor the achievements of those who have made it, validate that the system does work for those who play their cards right, and pat themselves on the back for the good work they have done in helping a few succeed. At the same time, by pointing to those few who succeed, they provide a social rationale for blaming those who didn't make it because they did not work or study hard enough. The focus on the individual achievements of a few can distract us from looking at why there is not enough affordable housing, educational opportunities, and jobs for everyone.

The final function of jobs in the buffer zone is to maintain the system by *controlling* those who want to make changes. Because people at the bottom keep fighting for change, people at the top need social mechanisms that keep people in their place in the family, in schools, in the neighborhood, and even in other countries. Police, security guards, prison wardens, highway patrol officers, sheriff's departments, national guard members, soldiers, deans and administrators, immigration officials, and fathers, in their role to provide discipline in the family—these are all traditionally masculine roles in the buffer zone designed to keep people in their place in the hierarchy.[5]

co-opting social change

During the latter half of the 20th century, multiple groups were demanding—and, in some cases, gaining—crucial changes in US society, such as better access to jobs, education, and health care. The ruling classes recognized the need for new strategies to suppress dissent among the oppressed and to curtail demands for structural change.

One strategy used by the ruling class to maintain the social order has been to fund social welfare programs through government and non-profit agencies. This creates the appearance that the government is responsive, creating an illusion of "progress" while recruiting buffer-zone agents from the groups of people demanding change of the system. But more often than not, the programs are severely underfunded and overregulated; more, they merely provide services, without addressing the structural issues as required to actually eliminate the injustice or inequality motivating people to organize in the first place. In addition, hiring community leaders into paid program and administration jobs separates them from their communities by making them beholden to the governmental and non-profit bureaucracies that employ them, rather than to the people they are trying to serve.

An example of how this process of co-optation works can be seen in the 1960s civil rights movement, a grassroots struggle led by African Americans for full civil rights, for access to power and resources, and for the end of racial discrimination and racist violence. Significantly, the civil rights movement did put pressure on the government, those in middle management and academic jobs, corporations, and non-profits to hire some African Americans, which has created a small Black middle class. But while those struggles succeeded in dismantling legalized segregation, many forms of structural racism still exist and the broader goals of political and economic justice have largely remained unfulfilled.

Indeed, the issue of racism is now frequently "addressed" in our social institutions by a multiracial group of professionals who work as diversity or multicultural trainers, consultants, advisors, and educators. Although the ruling class is still almost exclusively white and most African Americans, Native Americans, and other people of color remain at the bottom of the economic pyramid, conservatives and the media advance the illusion that substantial change has occurred because there are a few very high-profile, wealthy African Americans and a larger Black middle class—"proof" that any person of color has the opportunity to become rich and powerful if she or he works hard enough.

The civil rights movement is not the only arena in which demands for social change have been co-opted by the ruling class. Another example is the battered women's movement. Again, gains were made in identifying the issue, in improving the response of public institutions to incidents of male violence, and in increasing services to battered women. But systematic, large-scale efforts to mobilize battered women and end male violence have not been attempted. Instead, we have a network of (still largely inadequate) social services to attend to the immediate needs of battered women, and a new network of buffer-zone jobs in shelters and advocacy organizations to administer to those needs.

Neither the roots of racism nor the roots of male violence can be addressed by the present network of narrowly focused social services or the new cadres of professionals administering to the needs of those on the bottom of the pyramid. In fact, I would argue that in combating racism and male violence through the engines of the NPIC, we have lost some ground because we now have more controlling elements—more police, security guards, and immigration officials than ever before monitoring, interfering with, and criminalizing the family lives of people of color, as well as poor and working-class white people. We need to examine the impact of our work very carefully to make sure that it does not perpetuate a narrow social service perspective and that we ourselves have not been co-opted by the jobs and privileges we have been given in the non-profit industrial complex.

▷ **Questions to ask yourself**

What are the historical roots of the work that you do?

What were your motivations or intentions when you began doing this work?

Who are you in solidarity with in the pyramid? That is, who would you like to support through the work that you do—the people at the top of the pyramid, the people in the buffer zone, or the people at the bottom?

Who actually benefits from the work that you do?

Are there ways in which, through your work, family role, or role in the community, you have come to enforce the status quo or train young people for their role in it?

the role of the non-profit

The ruling class created the non-profit legal status primarily to establish foundations so they could park their wealth where it was protected from income and estate taxes. The foundations allow them to retain control over their family wealth. The trade-off they made with the government was a legal mandate to distribute a very small percentage of each foundation's income every year for the public good. A vast network of non-profits was set up to receive and distribute this money. The non-profit tax category grants substantial economic benefits to the ruling class: even today, most charitable, tax-exempt giving from the ruling class (either as direct donations or through foundations) directly benefits those at the top of the economic pyramid by going to institutions and programs such as ruling class think tanks and foundations, ruling class cultural institutions (e.g., museums, operas, the theater, art galleries), elite schools, and private hospitals.

In 2000, non-profits controlled over $1.59 trillion in financial assets and had expenditures of over $822 billion.[6] Non-profits also control significant amounts of federal and state monies through contracts for the provision of public services such as health care, education, housing, employment training, and jobs. The ruling class, through the non-profit sector, controls billions of dollars of private and government money ostensibly earmarked for the public good, but subject to virtually no public control.

The non-profit industrial complex was not always so huge. During the civil rights period, when there were large-scale marches, sit-ins, protests, and demonstrations, policy makers at the largest foundations decided that they should fund some of the more moderate leadership in the Black community both to elicit their cooperation and to provide some measure of services that might lessen dissent. Money began to be funneled into "acceptable" (that is, non-radical) community groups as a way to forestall and co-opt further protest and to steer public policy towards the provision of individual services.[7] Until that period, most activists and community members working for social change were not employed by non-profits. Although some were paid for their work, most worked voluntarily in neighborhood associations, unions, church groups, and cultural and other civic organizations.

During the 1970s, the NPIC increased dramatically as a response to the continued protests of antiwar, women's liberation, queer liberation, and other social movements. Soon it became common for people to be paid to do "good work" by providing services for people in the community. Non-profit management became a career path and many subspecialties of non-profit programming were developed, such as youth work, violence prevention work, senior services, domestic violence services, housing services, and job training programs.

Organizations on the right also used the non-profit sector to advance their agenda. As author Beth Shulman notes, "Right-wing funders invested in the building blocks or skeletal structure of their movement, such as publications, research centers, think tanks, and academic fellowships and chairs designated for rightist scholars, campus organizations, and youth groups." Labor activist Jean Hardisty goes on to comment,

> Instead of underwriting movement-building, liberal and progressive founda-
> tions funded social service programs and advocacy programs that promised to
> ensure better living conditions and promote equality and tolerance. Much of
> this funding could be classified as humanitarian aid....Unable to ignore need
> and suffering, liberal and progressive funders lacked the ideological single-
> mindedness of the right's funders. The right's funders got greater political
> mileage for each dollar invested, because the organizations and individuals
> funded focused on a strategic plan for seizing power.[8]

Beginning in the 1980s with the Reagan-era cutbacks in social services, many non-profits experienced even more pressure to provide basic human needs services to growing numbers of people. As they became completely reliant on private donors, private foundations, or dwindling government dollars to cope with ever-increasing demands, many non-profits began spending inordinate amounts of time writing proposals, designing programs to meet foundation guidelines, tracking and evaluating programs to satisfy foundations, or soliciting private donations through direct-mail appeals, house parties, benefits, and other fundraising techniques. Their work had to be developed and then presented in such a way as to meet the guidelines and approval of the ruling class and its representatives.

Today, funders generally support non-profit programming that fills gaps in the government's provision of services, extends outreach to underserved groups, and stresses collaboration among social services providers to use money and other resources more efficiently, that is, to stretch less money further to cover greater need. Although many took jobs in this sector to avoid working in the corporate sector and to work in solidarity with those at the bottom of the pyramid, the professionalization and corporatization of the non-profit sector, coupled with the expanding needs of the population and decreasing government funding, meant that many became disillusioned and burned-out from the demands of the work.

co-opting community leadership

The ruling class co-opts leaders from our communities by providing them with jobs in non-profits and government agencies, hence realigning their interests (i.e., maintaining their jobs) with maintaining the system. Whether they are social welfare workers, police officers, domestic violence shelter workers, diversity consultants, therapists, or security guards, their jobs and status depend on their ability to keep the system functioning—and to suppress potential opposition from community members—no matter how illogical, exploitative, and unjust the system is. The existence of these jobs serves to convince people that tremendous inequalities of wealth are natural and inevitable. Institutionalizing soup kitchens leads people to expect that inevitably there will be people without enough to eat; establishing permanent homeless shelters leads people to think that it is normal for there not to be enough affordable housing. In his discussion of co-optation, sociologist Raymond Breton makes clear that integrating the leadership of our communities into the bureaucracies of the buffer zone separates the interests of those leaders from the needs of the community:

> Co-optation is a process through which the policy orientations of leaders are influenced and their organizational activities channeled. It blends the leader's interests with those of an external organization. In the process, ethnic leaders and their organizations become active in the state-run interorganizational system; they become participants in the decision-making process as advisors or committee members. By becoming somewhat of an insider the co-opted leader is likely to identify with the organization and its objectives. The leader's point of view is shaped through the personal ties formed with authorities and functionaries of the external organization.[9]

Ruling-class policies, including development of the non-profit sector and support for social services, have led to the co-optation of substantial numbers of well-intentioned people. In this group I include all of us whose intention is to "help" people at the bottom of the pyramid, but whose work, in practice, helps perpetuate their inability to change the circumstances which force them to need this assistance in the first place. Ultimately, our efforts end up benefiting the ruling class by actively supporting the current exploitative structure. Rather than helping others, we need to develop ways to work together to create community power.

▷   Questions to ask yourself

Do you work in a government-funded or non-profit organization?

Where does the funding come from for your work?

In what ways does funding influence how the work gets defined?

How much time do you spend responding to the needs of funders as opposed to the needs of the people you serve?

In what ways has the staff of your program become separated from the people they serve because of the following: the demands of funders; the status and pay of staff; the professionalization of the work; the role of your organization in the community; the interdependence of your work with governmental agencies, businesses, foundations, or other non-profit organizations?

In what ways have your ties with governmental and community agencies separated you from the people you serve?

In what ways have those ties limited your ability to be "contentious"—to challenge the powers that be and their undemocratic and abusive practices?

getting ahead or getting together?

Getting ahead is the mantra of capitalism. Getting ahead is what we try to do in our lives. Getting ahead is what we urge our children to do. Getting ahead is how many of us, including activists for social change, define success. Many people in the US believe that it is the responsibility of our society not to guarantee material security for all, but merely to ensure that everyone has an "equal opportunity" to get ahead. Those who are deserving, the myth continues, will get ahead; the rest will fail because of their own laziness, ignorance, or lack of discipline. Ironically, some of the recent political struggles organized by women, queer communities, people with disabilities, people of color, and recent immigrants have become defined as struggles for equal opportunity, for everyone to be able to compete to get ahead.

But in a pyramid-shaped economic system, only a few can get ahead. Many are doomed to stay exactly where they are at the bottom of the pyramid, or even to fall behind. With so much wealth concentrated at the top of the pyramid there are not enough jobs, not enough housing, not enough health care, and not enough resources devoted to education for most people to get ahead. In this economic system, equal opportunity for some groups inevitably means more exploitation of others. If we are only fighting for equal opportunity—to eliminate discrimination and level the playing field—we will still end up with a huge concentration of wealth and power in the ruling class and not enough resources for the rest of us to meet our needs. We need to engage in battles against specific kinds of exploitation, exclusion, marginalization, discrimination, and violence while *simultaneously* engaging in a longer-term struggle for a redistribution of wealth and power.

How does the system change? How do people gain access to money, jobs, education, housing, and other resources? Historically, change happens when people get together. In fact, we have a long history of people getting together for social change, such as the civil rights and women's movements. Both of these efforts involved people identifying common goals, figuring out how to work together and support one another, and coming up with strategies for forcing organizational and institutional change. When people get together, they build community by establishing projects, organizations, friendships, connections, coalitions, alliances, and an understanding of differences. Identifying common goals, supporting each other, working for organizational and institutional change, building community—these are the elements of creating a better world and fighting against the agenda of the ruling class. These activities put us into a contentious relationship with ruling-class power.[10]

Those of us who are working for progressive social change must do that work subversively. We must make strategic decisions about what the fundamental contradictions are in the system and how we can work together with others to expose and organize around those contradictions. We can use our resources, knowledge, and status as social service providers to educate and agitate, and to support organizing for social change. We can refuse to be used as buffer-zone agents against our communities. Instead, we can come together in unions, coalitions, organizing projects, alliances, networks, support and advocacy groups, and a multitude of other forms of action against the status quo.

Many of us are doing work which is defined as providing social services. People in our communities need the services, and those of us who are providers need the work. Others do non-service-providing work. All of our work is situated within the economic pyramid, and in whatever part of the economy we find ourselves, we have a choice. Either we can go along with a ruling-class agenda dictated through grant proposals, donors, foundations, government agencies, "best practices," quantified evaluations, standards, and traditional policies, or we can take on the riskier work of engaging in consciousness-raising, organizing, organizational and institutional critique, and mobilization for change. We are doing subversive work that is not within buffer-zone job descriptions when we support people's efforts to get together with others for greater collective power.

The problem is not with providing social services. Many radical groups, such as the Black Panthers and the Zapatistas, have provided social services as a tool for organizing. The problem comes when *all* our time and energy is diverted toward social services to the detriment of long-term social change. Clearly, there is a tremendous difference between helping people get ahead individually and mobilizing buffer-zone resources to help people get together, a difference activists working within the NPIC should be mindful of in thinking about whether we are empowering people to work for social change at the same time we are providing them with social services.

▷ **Questions to ask yourself**

Is the primary goal of the work you do to help people get ahead or to help them get together?

How do you connect people to others in the same situation?

How do you nurture and develop leadership skills in the people you serve?

How do you ensure that they represent themselves in the agency and other levels of decision-making that affect their lives?

Do you provide them not only with information related to their own needs, but also with information on how the larger social/political/economic system works to their disadvantage?

Do you create situations in which they can experience their personal power, their connection to others, and their ability to work together for change?

Do you help people understand and feel connected to the ongoing history of people's struggles to challenge violence, exploitation, and injustice?

domestic violence

Let's look at domestic violence work as an example. If we accept the dominant paradigm, which frames domestic violence as an interpersonal issue and the result of a breakdown in the normative heterosexual nuclear family, and views battered women as victims, that framework will lead us to try to protect the "victims" from further violence, provide them with services, and try to help them get ahead (and, even better, eventually into a healthy heterosexual nuclear family). We will treat them individually, as clients, and hold the people (primarily men) who beat them individually accountable for their violence through stronger criminal justice sanctions and batterer groups. We will try to help survivors escape battering relationships and to move forward in their lives. We will be advocates for more services, better services, culturally competent services, multilingual services, and we will advocate for strong and effective sanctions against men who are batterers. We will measure our success by how many battered women we served, and our success stories will be about how individual women were able to escape the violence of abusive families and get on with their lives. Our advocacy success stories will be about how various communities of women were provided better services and how batterers were either locked up or transformed.

Rather than accept this social service (and racist, sexist, and heterosexist) framework, however, we could understand family violence (in both heterosexual and queer families) as a direct result of economic inequality, colonization, and other forms of state violence, and of patriarchal and heterosexual norms—and that, in particular, women who are battered are caught in cycles that are the result of systematic exploitation, disempowerment, and isolation. This analysis would further acknowledge the structural forces that keep women in battering relationships: community tolerance for male violence, lack of well-paying jobs, lack of decent childcare and affordable housing, and, most of all, their isolation from one another and from the information and resources they need to come together to effect change. As organizers and resource providers, we would provide organizational and structural support for battered women to organize on their own behalf. We would not be working *for* battered women; we would be working *with* them. "They" would be "us"—battered women would be in leadership in the movement to end violence against women, holding the jobs that currently many non-battered women do. We would measure success by the strength of our programs for leadership development and the community response to domestic violence. We would work for changes in the economic, educational, penal/law enforcement (including immigration law), military, and social service institutions which condone, encourage, or perpetuate violence against women and keep women trapped in abusive relationships. Our success stories would be about how battered women became leaders, educators, and organizers, and how communities of people came together to develop strategies and wield power.

Whether we are domestic violence workers or other types of workers in the non-profit industrial complex, even with the best of intentions, it is easy to be co-opted by a ruling-class agenda. The buffer-zone strategy of the ruling class works smoothly, so smoothly that many of us don't notice that we are encouraged to feel good about helping a small number of individuals get ahead, while large numbers of people remain exploited, abused, and disenfranchised. It works so smoothly that we often don't notice that we have shifted from helping people get together to helping ourselves and our families get ahead. Some of us have stopped imagining that we can end domestic violence and have, instead, built ourselves niches in the edifice of social services for battered women or for batterers. The only way to avoid settling into patterns that perpetuate ruling-class dominance is through accountability to grassroots community struggles led by people at the bottom of the pyramid.

> **Questions to ask yourself if you work in a domestic violence agency (if not, adapt the questions to reflect the work you do)**

Can you imagine an end to domestic violence?

What do you think it will take?

Does the work that you do contribute to ending domestic violence? How?

How are battered women viewed in your agency?

Are you providing social services and/or are you working for social change?

Are you helping battered women see that they are not alone, their problems not unique, their struggles interrelated?

Are you helping them come together for increased consciousness, resource sharing, and empowerment?

accountability

Even if it is not possible to change the system from within, an individual's actions within the system do matter. We can accept or reject, promote or hinder the state's agenda.—Taiaiake Alfred[11]

So the question is, how do we maintain a critical transformative edge to our politics when we are building that politics in an organizational environment that is shaped by institutions outside of our community that don't necessarily want to see us survive on the terms that we are defining for ourselves?
—Tamara Jones[12]

As Taiaiake Alfred and Tamara Jones note, relationships between those working in the buffer zone and those in the community are complex and often difficult because of the ruling class's use of the buffer zone to co-opt both social change movements and leaders drawn from those struggles. Only a "critical transformative edge" from those in the community will prevent co-optation.

How do we know if we are being co-opted into contributing to a ruling-class agenda and just providing social service, or if we are truly helping people get together? We cannot know by ourselves. We cannot know just from some people telling us that we are doing a good job or even telling us that we are making a difference. We cannot know by whether we feel good about what we do. Popularity, status, good feelings, positive feedback—our institutions and communities provide these to many people engaged in immoral, unethical, dangerous, exploitative, abusive, and illegal activities.

As a member of the buffer zone, whether by job function or economic position, the key question we must confront is this: To whom are we accountable? Since our work occurs in an extremely stratified and unequal economic hierarchy, and in an increasingly segregated and racially polarized society, we can begin to answer this question by analyzing the effects of our work on communities at the bottom of the pyramid. Are we perpetuating inequality or promoting social justice? Are we raising awareness of the roots of our social, political, and economic problems? With whom? How many are we reaching? Are they more powerful and able to develop more creative strategies as a result? Are we providing information, resources, and skills for people to get together? Are they able to be more politically effective as a result? What impact do we see from the work we are doing? If we keep doing what we are doing what impact will there be in five years? Ten years? Twenty-five years? These are some of the questions we can be asking about our work.

Wherever we are within the economic pyramid, whatever work we are doing, it is possible to work for social justice. It is possible to more effectively serve the interests of the poor and working class, people of color, women, queer people, and people with disabilities. But doing so is challenging. It is easy to forget that we are only able to work *inside* non-profits, schools, and other social service organizations because so many people organized from the *outside* as part of the civil rights movement, the women's movement, the queer liberation movement, and

disability rights movement. As we become dependent on this work for our livelihood, professionalized, and caught up in the demands of doing the work, there
is a strong tendency for us to become ever more disconnected from the everyday
political struggles in our communities for economic, racial, and gender-based
justice, for an end to various forms of violence and for collective power—those
social justice issues which our work originally grew out of.

None of us can stay connected to social justice organizing and true to social
justice values while working in isolation, inside of a non-profit organization. Our
work is part of a much wider network of individuals and organizations working
for justice from outside of the non-profit industrial complex. To make effective
decisions about our own work we need to be accountable to those groups and
take direction from their actions and issues. This accountability then becomes a
source of connection that breaks down isolation and increases our effectiveness
as social justice activists.

In closing, here are several suggestions for thinking about accountability to
grassroots communities and struggles for social justice. I offer six questions we
should ask ourselves in the current political context.

Who supervises your work? I don't mean who employs you or hires or
funds you, although these are important considerations in a conservative political climate when jobs are scarce. Who are the grassroots activists who advise you
and review your work? If you are a male antiviolence activist, it is particularly
important that you be accountable to women who are doing different kinds of
antisexist organizing. If you are white, it is critical for you to be accountable to
people of color with a progressive antiracist agenda so that your work doesn't
inadvertently fuel the backlash to the gains of the civil rights movement or otherwise collude with attacks on people of color. If you are a person with economic
privilege, you need to be listening to the voices of poor and working-class people
struggling for economic justice. Of course, these are not isolated identities. We
can and should be accountable to groups and organizations which have a multi-
issue social justice perspective.

Regardless of your ethnicity, race, gender, or economic position, as an activist (particularly, as one who has gained access to the buffer zone) you need to be
accountable to people who are on the front lines of movements for social justice.
You have to be engaged in a critical dialogue, while recognizing that because of
your race, gender, class, sexual orientation, educational level, or other form of privilege you most likely have been socialized by our culture to expect to have all the
answers and not to listen to those who have less social and political power than you
do (that is, internalized supremacy). Therefore, I think it is important that privileged activists participate directly in some form of grassroots struggle, making sure
to consult thoroughly and extensively with other activists similarly engaged.

Are you involved in community-based social justice struggles? If you are not actively involved in a specific movement—be it the struggle for the redistribution of wealth, for immigrant rights, against environmental dumping, against police brutality, for access to health care, against male violence, or for peace—how are you learning? What are you modeling? What practice informs your work? For example, can you be accountable to communities struggling to end male violence if you are not politically involved yourself in some aspect of that struggle? Can you be an effective antiracism trainer if you are not involved in antiracism action?

Is political struggle part of the work you do? Do you connect the participants in your programs/services/trainings to opportunities for ongoing political involvement? Do you work with participants on issues they define or on issues you or funders or others located in arenas of greater access and power define? Do you give participants tools and resources for getting involved in the issues they identify as most immediate for them, whether those are public policy issues, such as immigration, affirmative action, welfare, or health care, or workplace, neighborhood, and community issues, such as jobs, education, violence, and toxic waste? After experiencing contact with you, can they connect what they have just learned to the violence they experience in their lives? Are you responsive to their needs for survival, safety, economic well-being, and political action?

Are you in a contentious relationship with those in power? The ruling class—those at the top of the pyramid—have an aggressive and persistent agenda to disempower and exploit those at the bottom. If you are accountable to those at the bottom of the pyramid, you will necessarily be challenging that agenda. Are you willing to speak truth to power, even at the risk of losing your current job or future employment by certain agencies? Or do you hold back your real opinion so as not to make waves when you are at the "power-sharing" table? How have you come to justify your reluctance to challenge power?

Are you sharing access to power and resources with those on the front-lines of the struggle? Do you systematically connect people in grassroots efforts to information, resources, supplies, money, research, and each other?

Do you help people come together? It would be simple and ideal if there were a cohesive or coherent community to be accountable to. Few such communities exist in our society and even fewer of us are connected to them. I believe that being accountable means supporting the growth and stability of cohesive communities. For example, do the battered women who leave your program understand themselves to be in connection to other battered women and their allies? Do the students in your classroom see themselves as part of a community of learners, activists, and change agents? Social change grows out of people understanding themselves to be interdependent, sharing common needs, goals, and interests. Are you helping people see that they are not alone, that their problems are not unique, and that their struggles are interrelated? Are you helping them come together for increased consciousness, resource sharing, and mobilization?

In the non-profit industrial complex, accountability is directed toward the ruling class and its managers—toward foundations, donors, government officials, larger non-profits, research institutes, universities, and the media. These are all forms of top-down accountability. I am suggesting a bottom-up accountability guided by those on the frontlines of grassroots struggles for justice. In which direction does your accountability lie?

We live in conservative political times and in a contracting economy in which racial, gender-based, religious, and homophobic violence is widespread and accepted. You may be discouraged about the possibility of doing effective political work in this context. You may be fearful of losing your job and livelihood or lowering your standard of living if you take risks. These are real concerns. But this is also a time of increasing and extensive organizing for social justice. It is an opportunity for many of us to realign ourselves clearly with those organizing efforts and reclaim the original vision of an end to the violence and exploitation which brought us into this work. This is a vision of social justice and true equity, built from community leadership and collective power.

acknowledgments

My thanks to Bill Aal, Allan Creighton, Luz Guerra, Micki Luckey, Nell Myhand, Suzanne Pharr, Hugh Vasquez, and Shirley Yee for their encouragement and suggestions.

notes

1 Net financial wealth refers to all assets excluding housing and subtracting debt. It would include checking and savings accounts, stocks and bonds, commercial land and buildings, and so on.

2 Edward N. Wolff, *Recent Trends in Wealth Ownership, 1983-1998*, (Annandale-on-Hudson, NY: Jerome Levy Economics Institute, April 2000). Figures are for 1998.

3 A full analysis of how the ruling class and power elite control power and wealth, can be found in my book *You Call This a Democracy? Who Benefits, Who Pays, and Who Decides?* rev. ed. (New York: Apex Press, 2006).

4 For a history of these struggles and movements, see Howard Zinn, *A People's History of the United States: 1492–Present* (1980; repr., New York: Harper Perennial, 2003).

5 These distinctions in function are not always so separate in practice. For instance, many caretaking roles, such as that of social workers, also have a strong client-control element to them, and the police are now trying to soften their image by resort to community policing strategies to build trust in the community.

6 National Council of Nonprofit Associations, *The United States Nonprofit Sector* (annual report, Washington, DC: National Council of Nonprofit Associatons, 2001).

7 Kivel, *You Call This a Democracy?* (New York: Apex Press, 2006), 120–124. For a detailed look at the role of foundations, see Joan Roelofs, *Foundations and Public Policy* (Albany: State University of New York Press, 2003).

8 Jean Hardisty, *Mobilizing Resentment: Conservative Resurgence From the John Birch Society to the Promise Keepers* (Boston: Beacon Press, 1999), 16.

9 Raymond Breton, *The Governance of Ethnic Communities: Political Structures and Processes in Canada* (Westport, CT: Greenwood Press, 1990), quoted in Taiaiake Alfred, *Peace, Power, Righteousness: An Indigenous Manifesto* (Don Mills, ON: Oxford University Press Canada, 2000), 74.

10 I am indebted to Taiaiake Alfred for this terminology from his book *Peace, Power, Righteousness.*

11 Alfred, *Peace, Power, Righteousness,* 76.

12 Tamara Jones, "Building Effective Black Feminist Organizations," *Souls: A Critical Journal of Black Politics, Culture, and Society* 2, no. 4 (Fall 2000): 55.

▸▸Alisa Bierria,
Communities Against Rape and Abuse (CARA)

pursuing a radical antiviolence agenda inside/outside a non-profit structure

IN THE SUMMER OF 1999, SEATTLE RAPE RELIEF (SRR), ONE OF THE first three rape crisis centers in the US, was closed by its board of directors. Founded in 1972 by women who had organized a Speak Out on Rape at the University of Washington campus, SRR began as a volunteer organization with explicitly feminist politics. Through its 27-year history, SRR witnessed the transformation of the US antiviolence movement, whereby organizations became less associated with a progressive feminist politic and more invested in gaining legitimacy with professional fields such as the criminal justice system, the medical industry, and the social services industry. SRR itself was impacted by the professionalization of a once grassroots antiviolence movement, and SRR's volunteers identified this shift in the organization's political identity as the main reason for its demise. Eventually SRR closed in a dramatic turn of events that included resignations of nearly the entire paid staff, the dissolution of the 70-member volunteer corps by the acting executive director, and significant speculation by the local press. SRR's board of directors identified a $50,000 shortfall in its nearly $500,000 budget as the reason why they felt forced to close.[1] However, SRR's volunteers argued that an organization that had become such a mainstay within the Seattle community for nearly 30 years would not pursue the shutdown of the entire organization for a financial loss that was far from devastating. Instead, we identified a political assessment of the closure of SRR within a larger movement-based context. In a letter to all former volunteers and staff, we wrote:

> So why is [this closure] happening now? What is happening in Seattle Rape Relief is part of a larger national movement occurring in sexual assault and domestic violence agencies. The movement is attempting to streamline these organizations into being more professionalized and less grassroots oriented. This means less critique of institutions that perpetuate sexual violence, no connection between anti-oppression theory and violence against women theory, less outreach to marginalized survivors (sex workers, prisoners, etc.), no community based fundraising initiatives, thinking about survivors as "clients"

rather than people, and perhaps, most importantly, little to no organizational accountability to the community, specifically survivors.[2]

Later that same summer, former SRR volunteers established a new organization, Communities Against Rape and Abuse (CARA). Unlike SRR, CARA did not include crisis-based services for sexual assault survivors such as counseling, hotlines, and legal advocacy, mostly because these services were offered by other existing organizations in Seattle. Instead, CARA prioritized community organizing as the primary tool to increase support for survivors. The organization's founders also wanted to work specifically with survivors from marginalized communities. Such communities have a disproportionately high rate of sexual violence, and survivors from these communities are less likely to have access to support from crisis-based institutions. Assessing the "gaps in service" by reviewing the work of other local antiviolence organizations, CARA built projects specifically for people with disabilities, Black people, and young people.

CARA did not yet have a clear and public analysis of institutional oppression and its relationship to the prevalence and experience of sexual violence, though we acknowledged that these things existed. We asserted a somewhat vague distinction between being a "social service" organization and a "social change" organization, meaning that we did not simply want to "manage" sexual assault, but to seek strategies to transform the way communities confronted sexual violence. However, this distinction, though meaningful, did not carry with it a clear political analysis of violence and oppression, making us interesting to city funders but not necessarily threatening.

asserting legitimacy

After the closure of SRR, the city government reallocated SRR's abandoned funding to other non-profits addressing sexual assault. Ultimately, the city decided to distribute the funding that was specifically for crisis services to other organizations that did similar work, and the rest of SRR's funding was allocated to CARA. The staff at the Domestic and Sexual Violence Prevention Office, most of whom were white liberal feminists (and one of whom was as an original founder of SRR), supported funding CARA for two reasons. First, they endorsed community organizing as an important strategy to address sexual violence, and they recognized that, with the other existing organizations providing medical and legal services, a group that used a community-organizing approach could offer a useful complement. Second, the women endorsed a multicultural approach to service delivery; they supported organizations that worked with identity-based communities recognized as "underserved."

However, the decision by the city to fund CARA immediately disrupted the relationship between CARA and the other two major anti–sexual assault agencies in Seattle (one is based in a hospital and primarily does medical advocacy and therapy and the other maintains a crisis line and offers legal advocacy services), who felt entitled to the money left over by Seattle Rape Relief. The executive directors of these two established agencies—both older, middle-class white women—were astonished that the city would want to support an organization started by a group of 20-somethings who were virtual unknowns in the sexual assault "field." The volunteer who represented CARA in most of these early meetings was a 25-year-old queer Black woman. (This same woman eventually became staff leadership at the burgeoning organization.) Her experience of racism and ageism was explicit in the early meetings with the executive directors and the city funders. In one meeting, for example, an executive director called her incompetent and said that CARA had not earned the "right" to this funding. Despite the conflict, the city provided CARA with $250,000 in 2000, allowing us to establish ourselves quickly and hire four full-time staff members.

re-centering our work

From 2000 to 2002, CARA staff created a critical shift in our identity and work from being a "social change" organization that provided a multicultural approach to antirape services to being an organization with a radical feminist of color and disability politic which manifested as grassroots antiviolence projects and campaigns. There are three factors that provoked this shift. First, CARA staff spent significant time reading and discussing *Pedagogy of the Oppressed* by Paulo Freire, which taught us to critique the way organizers objectify their constituents rather than learn from them. This critique informed our organizing model of centering the experiences of the communities we organized and letting those experiences reframe the work we chose to do, and how we chose to do it. The staff began to figure out not just how to make antiviolence services more "accessible" to marginalized people, but how to have the marginalization of people inform how we define violence and what kind of work we would do. Andrea Smith, co-founder of the national grassroots organization INCITE! Women of Color Against Violence, describes this method of organizing as "re-centering" rather than "inclusion." She writes:

> All too often, inclusivity has come to mean that we start with an organizing model developed with white, middle-class people in mind, and then simply add a multicultural component to it. We should *include* as many voices as possible, without asking what exactly are we being included in? However, as Kimberlé Crenshaw has noted, it is not enough to be sensitive to difference,

we must ask what difference the difference makes. That is, instead of saying, how can we *include* women of color, women with disabilities, etc., we must ask, what would our analysis and organizing practice look like if we centered them in it? By following a politics of re-centering rather than inclusion, we often find that we see the issue differently, not just for the group in question, but everyone.[3]

The process of re-centering created political agendas at CARA is illustrated in the development of our campaign against the sterilization abuse organization Children Requiring a Caring Kommunity. CRACK pays $200 to women currently or formerly addicted to drugs to get sterilized or to take long-term dangerous birth controls. When we centered the experience of women of color and poor women who had been raped, we noted that many women used illegal drugs as a strategy to cope with trauma. We also noted that, as a result of the mass criminalization of drug users that occurred throughout the 1980s and 90s, women of color and poor women were experiencing an unprecedented rate of incarceration. Further, their reproductive capacity was being demonized and targeted by groups such as welfare offices, public hospitals, and organizations like CRACK. Members of CARA's Black People's Project found CRACK's flyers on buses that went to low-income neighborhoods and in front of homeless shelters and recovery programs. They were outraged at CRACK's racist approach to addressing the problem of drug addiction and reproduction. Members of CARA's Disability Pride Project also critiqued the anti-disability component of CRACK's agenda. As a result of centering marginalized survivors, CARA recognized how rape and abuse places women of color, poor women, and women with disabilities at the intersection of multiple kinds of violence. Following the wisdom of their constituents, CARA developed a campaign opposing CRACK, which contributed to CARA's multi-movement approach of undermining sexual violence by also organizing for issues such as reproductive justice and disability rights.

The second factor that contributed to CARA's political shift was our emerging relationship with INCITE! Women of Color Against Violence. INCITE! organized its first Color of Violence conference in Santa Cruz, California, in the year 2000. It brought together over two thousand women of color to articulate a more radical conception of what is entailed under the category of "violence against women." CARA sent two staff members to this conference, both of whom were deeply moved by the comprehensive analysis of violence, which included a critique of the prison industry, colonization, imperialism, and capitalism. These members returned to CARA with a radical revisioning of the kind of work they wanted to see happen within the organization. Over the next several years, CARA worked with INCITE! on projects such as contributing to the INCITE!/Critical Resistance joint statement, "Gender Violence and the Prison-

Industrial Complex."⁴ Working on this statement pushed us to develop a political assessment of the prison industry as antiviolence activists. As a result, we organized a film festival in collaboration with Critical Resistance (a prison-abolition organization), the first of its kind in Seattle and the first Critical Resistance film festival organized by an outside group. CARA also began to organize community-based accountability responses to sexual and domestic violence as alternatives to the criminal justice system.

The third factor was the inauguration of George W. Bush as the president of the United States in 2001. Bush's radical conservatism deeply impacted the women at CARA and the kind of work we felt compelled to do. After 9/11, the Bush administration built an unapologetically nationalist, war-based agenda, explicitly citing imperialistic political ambitions. In a moment when many mainstream antiviolence organizations were silent about the war on Afghanistan because of the liberal feminist stance that war would dissolve the Taliban and, therefore, liberate Afghan women, CARA took a public stance against the war and mobilized its constituents for anti-war organizing. In their statement on the 9/11 attacks, CARA makes a connection between our primary political issue—sexual violence—and militarism and racism. We wrote, "We recognize that rape is often used as a tool of war and know that women are often the most brutally impacted by war. We also challenge our leadership's tokenization of the plight of Afghan women to justify carpet-bombing their country and their people."⁵ The devastating political context of Bush's "war on terrorism" facilitated CARA's process of incorporating a clear feminist-of-color analysis on militarism and colonization into our local antiviolence agenda.

These developments at CARA contributed to an increasingly clear and radical politic deeply grounded in our primary accountability to local survivors of sexual and domestic violence. However, as CARA became more articulate about our radical feminist-of-color, pro-queer, and pro-disability politic, the local government became increasingly conservative.

tactics for survival: solidarities and disguised identities

Though we were funded in 2000 by the city of Seattle, each new year saw the executive directors of the other mainstream antirape organizations appeal to conservative city council members to revoke CARA's funding. This process continued over the course of three years—every year, CARA applied for funding, and every year, the organization had to answer to the city council for some political action or stance it had taken.

Mainstream, white-led antiviolence organizations questioned whether it was appropriate for CARA to receive public funding because of our analysis of rape as a political problem. One city council member, Richard Conlin, wanted to reduce CARA's funding by 75 percent, because he didn't like that we used the term "rape culture" in our materials. In his words, "This is a culture that has had the courage to confront these problems directly, unlike many other cultures."[6] (A post-9/11 world in which liberals support wars in Afghanistan and Iraq because of racist assessments of the "backwardness" of Arab cultures contributes to this kind of thinking. Conlin, generally a liberal member on the city council, was not unique in his knee-jerk defense of US culture, a culture in which a third of its women experience physical and sexual abuse from a husband or boyfriend at some point in their lives.[7]

In 2002, faced with a shrinking revenue base, Seattle's new mayor, Greg Nickels, decided to reduce funding for many antiviolence programs, particularly those that emphasized community organizing. He justified the funding cuts by asserting that he wanted to prioritize "core" or "vital" human services. Although Mayor Nickels never clearly defined which services he identified as core or vital, his 2002 budget significantly cut antiviolence programs that were using community organizing as a strategy and that were working with marginalized populations. Apparently, according to the Nickels administration, shelters and crisis lines were vital antiviolence services, but community organizing in communities of color and queer communities was not.

Mayor Nickels's proposal included a significant 25 percent reduction for CARA's funding, which, by this time, had already been reduced to $200,000. When the mayor's proposal went to the city council, council member Conlin suggested that the city actually reduce CARA's funding by *75 percent* and reallocate this funding to restore the cuts the mayor had made to the other, smaller antiviolence programs. Because CARA had not significantly diversified our revenue, this dramatic funding reduction could have shut down all our programs. Most likely Conlin anticipated that the other programs would support this proposal because they presumably only cared about their own program's financial resources and not about the survival of CARA. We call this tactic "divide and conquer."

However, most of the other organizations that would have benefited from this fiscal decision were longtime advocates of CARA. Like CARA, they were small and scrappy, worked with communities that are marginalized from mainstream approaches to domestic and sexual violence, were politicized to various degrees, and identified community organizing as a primary tool to address sexual and domestic violence. They recognized that CARA was like a canary in the mine—because we were the most explicit about our politics and the need for community organizing, we would be targeted first as a result of any hostile policies. CARA promptly contacted the other antiviolence programs that would have "profited" from this proposal to explain Conlin's strategy to them. Though some of these organizations chose to not express concern about Conlin's tactics because of worries about their own funding problems, most of the programs were upset about the divide-and-conquer approach and wrote letters expressing their solidarity with CARA. They refused to allow their programs to be pawns in a political struggle that would have resulted in the closure of an organization that had quickly come to be a crucial resource in the community. This organizational solidarity was key in demonstrating to council members that this kind of manipulative funding shift would actually win them more enemies than friends. Further, because CARA was a community-organizing program, we had, by this time, successfully built a significant base of supporters, who deluged the mayor and city council with hundreds of letters, phone calls, and e-mails, pressuring the council members to come up with a different plan that did not include reducing our funding so drastically. Ultimately, CARA was saved. We call this tactic "having each other's backs."

After this experience, CARA tried to avoid being targeted by learning to negotiate the process of lobbying with local government, and subverted its language to fit a program that was more palatable to local politicians. We created a kind of dual identity—a disguised one for the city funders and an authentic one for our constituents. For example, in all materials designed for city officials we replaced the phrase "community organizing," which seemed overtly political, with the phrase "community engagement." Though politically and throughout our organizational culture we shifted from a "multicultural inclusion" approach to a more radical "re-centering" approach, we used the former framework with the city to describe what we were doing. When we organized people with disabilities to mobilize against disability institutions or sponsored a teach-in for people of color about slave rebellions, we represented these activities to the city as working with "underserved communities" to engage in "community building" and "community conversations" about sexual violence. This description was not untrue. Though CARA is a multi-movement organization, we center antirape work and thinking in all that we do. But the fact that another purpose of these activities was to undermine institutional oppressions that directly contribute to sexual violence was simply not included in our city report. In short, we developed ways to frame our work that seemed "reasonable" enough for the local government to support.

While the city attempted to control and direct our work, CARA continued to create ways to use city resources to do the work that our constituents led us to do. As CARA organizer Theryn Kigvamasud'Vashti puts it, "We realized that even though this is where we are right now, being stuck in a non-profit structure does not necessarily dictate who we are going to collaborate with in order to fully support those communities that we identify or who have identified us as resources to build community and safety and support."[8] We also began to fund our explicitly political work with resources we received from progressive foundations and grassroots support. Through trial and error, we figured out a strategy to maintain our public funding and continue to maintain our identity as a radical feminist organization.

While we remained consistent in our political work and ideas and our final accountability to our constituents, creating and maintaining a dual identity comes at a cost. This kind of "doublespeak" and "dual identity" is a common practice among people of color and poor people who spend time in spaces dominated by white people and middle-class and wealthy people. We do not necessarily endorse this method as a sustainable practice, but we recognize that oppressed people develop creative strategies for survival as we move across the boundaries of our own communities and communities we do not identify as ours. The goal is not about ensuring that our presentation to the city and to our constituents is the same, but to ensure that this process of strategic disguise does not undermine our actual projects and our accountability to the survivors and communities with whom we work. It isn't easy, and we're not sure it's worth it. The dissonance of maintaining a real identity and a disguised one creates significant amounts of stress and consumes considerable amounts of precious time and resources that should be spent organizing.

By 2004, the city of Seattle's Human Services Department (HSD) experienced a transition in staff. The women in HSD who initially supported CARA left their jobs in local government in part because of the increasingly corporate style in which the Nickels administration sought to distribute funding to non-profits. The new HSD staff issued requests for funding to antirape organizations which included rhetoric defining the relation between organizational staff and survivors as one that is fundamentally capitalist and demanded practices that deeply objectified survivors of sexual violence. For example, the request for proposals (RFP) referred to survivors as "customers" and providers as offering "products" rather than services.[9] City officials wanted CARA to promise absurd things in its contract, such as ensuring that survivors would not experience another sexual assault after working with CARA staff. CARA's strategy of maintaining a dual identity became increasingly more untenable. As of this writing, CARA members anticipate that they will not pursue another RFP from the city of Seattle, effectively eliminating city funding altogether. Again, we do not choose to do so as a way of maintaining a "purely" consistent organizational identity, but because we have come to recognize that we can no longer bend to the degree that the local government demands us to without our work and our values becoming compromised to such an extent that we lose focus on our bottom line accountability to our constituents.

rethinking "communities"

> I spent a lot of time in the battered women's movement from 1976 onward.... In the beginnings of that movement, there was so much community-based work. All of us thinking about our constituency being battered women, that we are battered women, battered women are us...[10]

Early in the antiviolence movement, women made intimate connections between their own experience of violence and violence that survivors who sought support in their organizations and groups experienced. Organizers often understood themselves as belonging to a mutual community of women who had suffered from patriarchal violence. Seattle Rape Relief, for example, began from a speak-out, a mutual sharing of stories about the experience of abuse. As the movement developed and became increasingly professionalized, workers were expected to be not "battered women" but experts with a master's degree in social work. Andrea Smith explains:

> As the antiviolence movement has gained greater public prominence, domestic violence and rape crisis centers have become increasingly professionalized to receive accreditation and funding from state and federal agencies. Rather than develop peer-based services in which large groups of women can participate, they employ individuals with the proper academic degrees or credentials. This practice excludes most women from full participation, particularly women of color and poor women.[11]

Additionally, professionalization of antiviolence work encouraged a climate in which survivors became increasingly objectified (as clients or as customers) and pathologized. A distance between advocates and survivors was enforced throughout most organizations and considered much more professional and healthy. In fact, whereas in the beginning of the antiviolence movement, survivors were prioritized as workers in organizations, it is currently the case that if an advocate identifies herself as a survivor of rape and abuse, she could provoke a warning flag for employers, for if she was one of *them*—the damaged ones—how could she possibly effectively advocate on their behalf?

Ultimately, this attitude rooted in professionalization, oppression, and internalized oppression undermined opportunities for rich community building in the antiviolence movement. By the 1990s, Seattle Rape Relief volunteers, most of whom fielded calls on the crisis line, barely knew each other, meeting only at a mandatory monthly training. Though most volunteers were survivors of sexual violence, we were trained to protect ourselves from callers on the crisis line. "Don't get too involved," we were told, "Don't be afraid to end the call." CARA member Xandra Ibarra says that in a different antirape organization she worked at before coming to CARA, she was "pathologized as having secondary trauma" because she was "investing too much time in trying to organize communities or help them organize themselves."[12]

CARA intentionally rejected the idea that there is a fundamental difference between ourselves and the survivors we work with.[13] We understand ourselves as community members who are survivors of sexual and domestic violence and whose experience as survivors helps to inform our work and accountability to our constituents. Staff/community boundaries are disrupted in a number of ways. We prioritize leadership development among the people we organize, which results in many of those individuals eventually being hired as interns or staff, or becoming board members. We organize regular community gatherings, parties, and meals to facilitate community building among CARA workers, our families, our constituents, and even the people who live in the neighborhood where our office is located. CARA's office location is not confidential and is instead open to organizational members; they can come in, use computers and other resources, or hang out in the meeting space to work on projects, peruse our library, watch videos, have conversations and debates, or just take a nap. We attend weddings, funerals, baby showers, and graduations of our members. We have arguments and conflicts among staff, among members, and between staff and members, and we figure out ways to move through it. To illustrate, Theryn Kigvamasud'Vashti discusses how and why her own family is integrated in the CARA space.

> Our own families are what we're talking about when we're organizing these communities and if I was working for a non-profit that was really following those kinds of corporate non-profit policies and structures, I would not actually be able to have my son at work with me. I would have to figure out a way to spend more money on daycare and things like that. This way, I get to actually access the community of women that are already doing organizing within CARA because everybody takes care of this little guy right here.[14]

We wouldn't say that there should be *no* boundaries between staff and our constituents or that paid staff and CARA members have equal access to institutional power within the organization.[15] We believe in a balance in power and responsibility—people with certain organizational responsibilities need the institutional power to attend to those responsibilities effectively. However, we've developed a structure in which CARA members also individually have institutional influence and collectively have institutional power such that the decisions of CARA's staff and board remain accountable to our constituents.

While some boundaries are healthy, the particular kind of distancing so prevalent within antiviolence organizations is counterproductive to any goal of creating connection and communities of struggle. Eliminating this difference increases the potential for mass-movement building because the approach becomes flexible enough to allow survivors to create the kind of relationship they want between themselves and the organization, including political work or healing work that they want to pursue. For example, one CARA member is a young Chicana who was first interested in CARA as a survivor of abuse, but then became intimately involved in the CARA community by participating in events or simply hanging out at the CARA space and building projects such as women's poetry and spoken word groups. She was eventually hired as a part-time organizer. She explains why it was so easy to not only become integrated into the CARA community, but then to go out and build community informed by CARA's political values with other young women of color.

> It's really alienating and scary when you come into organizations—even organizations that focus on your community—and it's like wait, it doesn't feel like it's in my community, it feels outside my community. But [CARA] is really flexible and open to my lifestyle. I'm really blessed to be working at CARA because everything is really flexible and fluid. And everything moves with you. It's kind of like dancing. Like, organizations that are radical should embrace the movement and fluidness and listen to the rhythm of the movement of the people in their space and begin to check in with each other and embrace each other and move with each other and CARA feels like that.[16]

CARA's practice of community building is deeply connected to our political goals. At INCITE!'s second Color of Violence conference in 2002, Angela Davis captures how we understand the concept of "community" when she asserts,

> I do think it is extremely important not to assume that there are "communities of color" out there fully formed, conscious of themselves, just waiting for vanguard organizers to mobilize them into action. You know some people might say that there are communities in themselves waiting for someone to transform them into communities for themselves, but I think that's a mistake. I think it's a mistake because we have to think about organizing as *producing* the communities, as generating community, as building communities of struggle.[17]

We do not believe that there are "healed" survivors that are allowed to work in antiviolence organizations and "unhealed" survivors that must be clients within those organizations. We understand the process of surviving as just that—a process. Therefore, we understand ourselves as building communities of struggle with survivors that connect with CARA through our programs, events, and campaigns. When survivors access CARA for support, we see them less as clients and more as potential comrades in a struggle for social justice. CARA works to actualize a vision in which we understand ourselves as equally vulnerable to being abused, as equally valuable to the survivors we work with, and, potentially, as equal participants in a movement for justice and a world free from violence and oppression.

Finally, as Kigvamasud'Vashti's experience illustrates, CARA's integrated conception of community necessarily prioritizes strategies for accessibility to include as many people with as many different circumstances as possible. Engaging a radical disability politic has taught us to put accessibility in the front of what it means to build communities of struggle and think critically about who finds this process inviting and who doesn't. Ensuring that we have ASL interpretation, wheelchair-accessible office spaces and event venues, accessible transportation options for participants and staff members, and so on, is critical—and sometimes expensive. We've found that, when organizations both inside and outside the non-profit structure have fewer financial resources, what gets cut first is resources for accessibility—for people with disabilities, for children, for parents, for people whose first language is not English, for poor people, and for all of us who need support to participate in movement building. Though CARA's funding from the city sometimes undermines our community-building work, divesting from these funds would undermine accessibility, which also threatens our community-building work. We do not argue that it is necessary to receive funds from the state or to be a non-profit to ensure accessibility (of course, other non-profit organizations that receive government funding sometimes fail to prioritize accessibility—an ethical and political commitment is needed as well). However, we do assert that, as we work ourselves out of the non-profit system to fully realize our revolutionary potential, we must create alternatives to sustain the rich standard of accessibility that these resources have sometimes allowed us to achieve.

conclusion

CARA's story and strategies are not offered here as a model for how radical anti-violence organizations can survive within a non-profit structure, but more as an illustration of how, although the non-profit structure specifically works to undermine and threaten our organizations, we can work to practice an ethic of resistance and creativity nevertheless. This practice is not clean or simple and there are some difficult contradictions. However, because we are discussing a practice instead of a "model," we offer our story in a context of ongoing discourse, learning, discoveries, and transformations. Creating a movement outside and inside the boundaries of the non-profit structure (as well as somewhere in between) is a dynamic exercise, one that we expect to refine and improve as our work continues.

acknowledgments

The ideas in this paper were developed in critical dialogue with the following CARA members: Joelle Brouner, Onion Carrillo, Eboni Colbert, Xandra Ibarra, Theryn Kigvamasud'Vashti, and Emily Thuma.

notes

1 Judi Hunt, "Financial Problems Force the Seattle Rape Relief Agency to Close," *Seattle Post-Intelligencer,* June 23, 1999.

2 Alisa Bierria, "Letter to Seattle Rape Relief Volunteer Advocates" (June 30, 1999).

3 Andrea Smith, "Re-Centering Feminism," *Left Turn,* no. 20 (May/June 2006).

4 Critical Resistance and INCITE! Women of Color Against Violence, "Gender Violence and the Prison-Industrial Complex," in *Color of Violence: The INCITE! Anthology,* ed. INCITE! Women of Color Against Violence (Cambridge, MA: South End Press, 2006), 223–226.

5 Communities Against Rape and Abuse (CARA), "September 11, 2001 and Next Steps," CARA, http://www.cara-seattle.org/response_sept11.html.

6 Erica C. Barnett, "Buzz: City Hall," *Seattle Weekly,* November 20, 2002.

7 Commonwealth Fund, "Health Concerns Across a Woman's Lifespan: 1998 Survey of Women's Health" (May 1999).

8 Theryn Kigvamasud'Vashti, "Panel Discussion" (see note 8).

9 City of Seattle Human Services Department, "Request for Proposals" (2004).

10 Suzanne Pharr, "History of the Non-Profit Industrial Complex" (lecture, The Revolution Will Not Be Funded: Beyond the Non-Profit Industrial Complex, INCITE! Women of Color Against Violence conference, Santa Barbara, spring 2004).

11 Andrea Smith, "The Colors of Violence," *ColorLines* 3, no. 4 (Winter 2000–2001).

12 Xandra Ibarra, "Panel Discussion"

13 Researcher Emily Thuma has helped CARA rethink and articulate our analysis of the concept "communities."

14 Kigvamasud'Vashti, "Panel Discussion" (see note 8).

15 For example, CARA has a policy that prohibits romantic relationships between staff and survivors coming for specific kinds of support (direct service advocacy or support group).

16 Onion Carrillo, "Panel Discussion" (see note 8).

17 Angela Y. Davis (keynote speech, Color of Violence II conference, Chicago, IL, March 2002).

>>Andrea Smith

the ngoization of the palestine liberation movement
Interviews with Hatem Bazian, Noura Erekat, Atef Said, & Zeina Zaatari

AROUND THE GLOBE, NON-PROFITS AND NONGOVERNMENTAL organizations (NGOs) have worked closely with the US government to influence and direct the shape of liberation movements. As can be seen by the Ford Foundation's defunding of INCITE! Women of Color Against Violence (reported in greater detail in the introduction to this volume) and other organizations over the issue of Palestine, it is clear that NGOs are very much involved in efforts by the US government to steer the course of the Palestine liberation movement. The impact of NGOization on this movement is analyzed through interviews with the following longtime activists in the struggle:

Hatem Bazian has been involved in the Palestinian struggle for over 20 years through such groups as the Free Palestine Association, the Islamic Association for Palestine, the Union of Palestinian Association, the American Arab Anti-Discrimination Committee, American Muslims for Jerusalem, American Muslims for Palestine Solidarity Committee, Students for Justice in Palestine, and Al-Awda. He currently lives in northern California.

Noura Erekat is a New Voices fellow working on grassroots activism and a legal project using American laws to give Palestinians recourse against Israeli military officials. She is a steering committee member of Arab Movement of Women Arising for Justice (AMWAJ) and a founding member of the Divestment Support Committee, which seeks to support students, communities, and institutions in their efforts to divest from Israel. A recent graduate of the University of California, Berkeley, School of Law, Erekat is also a cultural worker—writing, performing, and producing pieces meant to transcend the otherwise formidable structures we battle daily.

Atef Said has been involved in human rights organizations, including NGOs, since 1995. He has worked with the Center for Human Rights Legal Aid and the Arab Center for Independence of the Judiciary and the Legal Profession. He worked as a research assistant and research director. His field of research includes labor rights and political prisoners rights' and torture. Said worked at the Hisham Mubarak Law Center, and he volunteered at the Socialist Research Center (a key contributor to the Egyptian antiwar and antiglobalization movements).

Zeina Zaatari is the program officer for the Middle East and North Africa at the Global Fund for Women. She is also involved in the National Council of Arab Americans, Sunbula: Arab Feminists for Change, and the Free Palestine Alliance.

a brief history of the palestine liberation movement[1]

Palestinians are among the indigenous inhabitants of historic Palestine Mandate, a land stretching from the Mediterranean coast east across the Jordan River, and from the Gulf of Aqaba north beyond the Sea of Galilee. Today, this geographical area is divided between the state of Israel (established in May 1948), and the West Bank (including eastern Jerusalem) and Gaza Strip, which Israel occupied in 1967. Palestinian cities, villages, and most of the 19 official refugee camps in the latter areas were transferred to a self-governing Palestinian Authority in the 1990s under the Madrid/Oslo "peace process." The bulk of this land area, however, remains under full Israeli military control.

Over the course of the 20th century, the Palestinian people have experienced several periods of major displacement: beginning during the first Arab-Zionist/Israeli war in 1947–48, followed by a second major displacement in the 1967 Arab-Israeli war, and again, as recently as 1991, when some 350,000 Palestinians were displaced from Kuwait during the Gulf War. Additional displacement has resulted from Israeli government policies and practices in Israel and in the 1967 occupied Palestinian territories, including land confiscation, house demolition, revocation of residency status, and deportation, as well as from government policies and armed conflict in various countries of asylum in the region.

Palestinian refugees from the 1948 displacement and their descendants make up the bulk of the Palestinian refugee population today, numbering over 5 million persons, and constituting nearly two thirds of the Palestinian people. If one includes Palestinians displaced for the first time in the 1967 war and internally displaced Palestinians inside Israel, approximately three quarters of the Palestinian people have been uprooted from their traditional lands over the past five decades, making them the largest and one of the longest-standing unresolved refugee groups in the world today. The majority of these refugees reside within 100 miles of their places of origin inside Israel, in the occupied West Bank and the Gaza Strip (from which Israel withdrew its troops in 2005), but are unable to exercise their right of return to their homes and lands of origin. The state of Israel opposes the return of Palestinian refugees, based on its desire to maintain Israel as a "Jewish state" characterized by a solid demographic Jewish majority and Jewish control of the land.

The right of the Palestinian people to self-determination was first recognized by the League of Nations in 1919. Palestine, which had been part of the Ottoman Empire until its collapse at the end of WWI, was among a number of non-self-governing Arab territories in the Middle East that were placed under temporary "tutelage," or administration of foreign powers under the League of Nations mandate system, until the peoples of these territories were deemed "ready" for independence. In 1922, the League of Nations entrusted the Mandate for Palestine (considered to be "Class A" or closest to independence) to Great Britain.

Contrary to the intent and purpose of the mandate system (that is, to administer Palestine and its peoples through to independence), Great Britain also recognized the demand of the Zionist movement to establish an exclusive Jewish state in Palestine. Under the terms of the 1922 Mandate for Palestine as drafted by the British government (which incorporated the 1917 Balfour Declaration whereby the British government first recognized Zionist demands for an exclusive Jewish state), the British administration in Palestine was required to "secure the establishment of the Jewish national home" in Palestine through Jewish immigration and settlement. As for the majority of the inhabitants of the country (that is, Palestinian Arabs), who were referred to as the "non-Jewish communities," the 1922 mandate only recognized their civil and religious rights; their political rights, including the right to self-determination, were ignored.

In early 1947, the British government informed the United Nations of its intention to withdraw from Palestine, ending more than two decades of mandatory rule. Despite the fact that the League of Nations had recognized the provisional independence of Palestine, the UN General Assembly decided to establish a special committee of inquiry to formulate recommendations for the future status of Palestine. Repeated requests by key Arab states, including former mandated territories, to obtain an advisory opinion from the International Court of Justice (ICJ) concerning the legal obligation of the UN to recognize the independence of Palestine under the terms of the League of Nations mandate system were rejected by the General Assembly.

In November 1947, the General Assembly adopted a plan (under Resolution 181), based on recommendations of the majority of the members of the special committee of inquiry, for the division of Palestine into two states—one Arab and one Jewish. The recommendation was adopted despite the wishes of the majority of the inhabitants. Irrespective of unresolved legal issues and provisions in the plan for the protection of minority rights in each state, opponents of Resolution 181 argued that its terms were inequitable: the proposed Jewish state was allotted 56 percent of the territory of historic Palestine even though Jewish inhabitants of Palestine constituted less than one third of the population and owned not more than 7 percent of the land. The collapse of the UN-sponsored initiative, after key supporters backed away from implementing it by force, and the subsequent war in 1948 led to the depopulation of some 530 villages and the displacement/ expulsion of some 750,000 Palestinians.[2]

Some 20 years later, the United Nations Security Council adopted Resolution 242, calling upon Israel to withdraw from the territories it occupied in the 1967 Israeli-Arab war (also known as the Six-Day War), including eastern Jerusalem, the West Bank, and the Gaza Strip. Several hundred thousand Palestinians, including refugees from 1948, were displaced during the 1967 war and have been denied the right to return to their homes and lands in these territories (which make up only 22 percent of the land of the historic Palestine Mandate) due to Israel's continued military occupation.[3]

The mass exodus and displacement of Palestinians is also related to gross and persistent human rights violations. During the 1948 war, the Palestinian Arab population was displaced and expelled in large numbers, first by Zionist militias and later by Israeli forces after the unilateral establishment of the state of Israel in May 1948, through a combination of tactics that violated basic principles of international law. These tactics included indiscriminate military attacks on civilians (including those fleeing areas of conflict), massacres, looting, destruction of property (including entire villages), and forced expulsion. Israeli military forces later instituted "shoot to kill" policies at the frontlines to "prevent infiltration" (that is, the spontaneous return of refugees to their homes). After the signing of armistice agreements in 1949 between Israel and its Arab neighbors, Israel subsequently adopted a series of laws concerning citizenship and nationality which effectively prevented Palestinian refugees from returning to their homeland, as well as a series of "abandoned property" laws to dispossess refugees of their property and transfer it to full Jewish control.

Many of these same violations of international law were committed against Palestinians during the 1967 Arab-Israeli war, leading again to mass displacement and imposed exile. Palestinian residents of villages near the ceasefire lines, including, for example, the villages of Imwas, Yalu, and Bayt Nuba in the Latrun area and the Moroccan quarter of the old city of Jerusalem, were expelled from their homes, which were completely demolished by Israeli military forces. Palestinian civilians who were fleeing areas of conflict were strafed by Israeli aircraft, while others were transferred out of the West Bank on Israeli buses. In some cases, young Palestinian men were forced to sign documents that they were leaving voluntarily. As in 1948, Israeli forces shot at Palestinian civilians, including women and children, attempting to cross the border and return to their homes and lands.

The violation of the human rights of Palestinians inside Israel, the 1967 occupied territories, as well as in Arab states such as Jordan, Lebanon, and Kuwait has led to further cycles of displacement. While there are no exact figures to illustrate the impact of these policies, it is estimated that over three decades of Israeli policies of land confiscation, house demolition, revocation of residency rights, and deportation have led to the forced displacement of several thousand Palestinians. The 1970 conflict between the government of Jordan and the Palestine Liberation Organization (PLO), the civil war and Israeli invasion of Lebanon in the 1980s, the 1991 Gulf War, and the violation of basic human rights of Palestinian refugees residing in these areas—including the massacre of several thousand Palestinian refugees in the camps of Sabra and Shatila in Beirut by Lebanese Christian Phalangists allied with Israel—has led to further displacement, with many Palestinians having experienced multiple displacements in their lifetime.

▷ ▷ ▷

On December 11, 1948, the United Nations General Assembly set forth the basic framework for addressing Palestinian refugees in Resolution 194. Based on principles of international law, Resolution 194 affirms the right of each Palestinian refugee to choose to return to his or her home (this includes restitution of properties) and receive compensation for damages. Palestinian refugees choosing not to return are to be compensated for their losses and damages and are entitled to resettlement. The United Nations established a special regime to facilitate the implementation of durable solutions: the UN Conciliation Commission for Palestine (UNCCP) and the UN Relief and Works Agency (UNRWA). The UNCCP was established in 1948 under Resolution 194 to facilitate the return and compensation or resettlement and compensation of Palestinian refugees based on their individual choices. One year later, the UN established the UNRWA (under Resolution 302) to facilitate relief and a works program for Palestinian refugees until they were able to exercise their right to return to their homes.

These two bodies, the UNCCP and UNRWA, were respectively to provide protection and assistance to Palestinian refugees. All other refugees receive protection and assistance from the Office of the UN High Commissioner for Refugees (UNHCR), which was established in 1950; however, if for any reason protection or assistance for Palestinian refugees ceases to exist vis-à-vis the UNHCR, the 1951 Refugee Convention stipulates under Article 1D that the protection or assistance gap should be filled by the UNHCR within the framework of relevant UN resolutions, namely Resolution 194. In other words, UNHCR would be obligated to facilitate the return of Palestinian refugees who choose to do so, and would not be free to facilitate resettlement elsewhere, except for refugees who have made a free and informed choice not to exercise the right to return to their homes.

Several years after it was established, the UNCCP ceased to provide protection to Palestinian refugees, due in large part to Israel's opposition to the return of refugees and the lack of international will to uphold basic principles of international law applicable to Palestinian refugees. The UNCCP, however, did complete an identification and assessment of refugee properties, which is archived at UN headquarters in New York. While UNRWA assistance provides a significant degree of protection of the daily economic and social rights of Palestinian refugees, the collapse of the UNCCP has left Palestinian refugees without legal and diplomatic protection, physical protection, and protection related to durable solutions (that is, implementation of their right of return and restitution based on refugee choice).

Under the Oslo/Madrid process, which began in the early 1990s, the Palestinian refugee issue—among a set of other issues such as Jerusalem, settlements, borders, and water—was left for so-called final status negotiations, as set forth in the 1993 Declaration of Principles signed by Israel and the PLO. The agreement does not make explicit reference to Resolution 194—the guiding framework for durable solutions for Palestinian refugees—nor does it make explicit reference to international law as the foundation for a comprehensive agreement. In fact, during final status talks in July and December 2000, Israel's position and US bridging proposals on the refugee issue attempted to secure a political agreement whereby Israel would "recognize" the right of return, in principle; Palestinians, in turn, would agree to forego the right of return in practice in order to maintain the Jewish demographic majority in Israel and Jewish control of refugee properties.

Palestinian refugees and the Palestinian political leadership have rejected this formula as a basis for a resolution of the refugee issue. Palestinians argue, rather, that for a solution to be durable, it must be based on international law and practice as applied in other refugee cases, such as in Kosovo, Bosnia, Guatemala, and Mozambique. This includes the individual right of refugees to return to their homes (a right which has been affirmed also by major international human rights organizations such as Human Rights Watch and Amnesty International), restitution of properties, and compensation.

Between September 16 and 18, 1982, several thousand Palestinian refugees—men, women, and children—were brutally slaughtered by Lebanese Christian Phalangist forces allied with Israel, while Israeli forces looked on and prevented refugees from fleeing the camps. The massacre happened within weeks of the US-brokered withdrawal of PLO fighters from Lebanon in the late summer of 1982. Left without protection, Israeli-allied Lebanese forces were able to enter the camps of West Beirut without opposition. On September 16, the day the massacre began, General Amos Yaron, commander of Israeli forces in Lebanon—and later director general of the Israeli Defense Ministry—provided Lebanese Forces Intelligence with aerial photographs to facilitate entry into the camps.[4]

When Israel finally ordered the withdrawal of the Lebanese forces two days later, the camps had been destroyed and several thousand refugees had either been slaughtered or had disappeared. Today, one of the mass graves is used for dumping garbage and another has been paved over for a golf course. An Israeli commission subsequently found then–defense minister Ariel Sharon indirectly responsible for the massacre.

This poem by Noura Erekat speaks to the lived realities of colonization and occupation in Palestine that ground the current liberation struggle.

Three home demolitions and one pending order
For the al-Atrash family in Hebron, Occupied Palestine

The first time the bulldozers came
I was at school
Challenged with negative numbers
Who thought zero had an inferior?

I ate a hard-boiled egg for breakfast
And drank mint tea sugared
By Mama's sweet fingers

In break, Lena and I clapped our hands
And sang "Sister, sister, where is Mama?
Mama's in the city. What's she doing?
Kneading dough. Where is Baba?"

The second time they came
I stood in the doorway
Israeli bulldozers needed to crush me
If they wanted to trample my home
 Again
But the soldiers didn't care that I was
Fifteen and female
Long hair just made it easier to pull me
Away

They spit on Mama but she wouldn't move,
Not her baby's home she screamed
She looked so strong, I swear
I thought her fingers would shoot lightning
It took three soldiers to take her down
Expose her breasts to the watchful sky
Spill her hair from her God-fearing hijab
And push her into the wailing dirt

Baba choked on his own screams
I think breathing got too hard for him
Because he stopped crying and
The Israeli soldier clenched his curly head
To keep him watching the stones
Of his 15-hour work days selling hot sesame seed bread
Crumble

After a while Baba couldn't taste
his bloody mouth
Couldn't see
His littered teeth through
His purple swollen eyes
I bet he even forgot about the rifle's eyes
Glaring into his neck.

My brother Hasan jumped
Without thinking
Ran for his books
It was his final year
3 more weeks he would take his matriculation exams and
Graduate to university
He was going to be an engineer
Going to build bridges
To connect Palestine's torn back
But one Israeli soldier kicked his
Hands with a
Sharp black boot
So hard
His books flew into suffocating mud
Sealed their pages silent
Those aren't cheap
Cost Baba 40 hours work just to buy
2 books
The mud ate 6 and Hasan watched his bridge collapse
Now he drives a taxi
17 hours in our 24-hour days

The third time they came
I lay in my husband's bed
Staring at the ceiling
Mama, Baba and Hasan did not, could not know
Because the bulldozers always came back
Before we could finish rebuilding our home

I lay in my husband's bed awake
I couldn't sleep
Stopped sleeping with marriage
Because I knew

Mama, Baba and Hasan couldn't fall asleep
In half-built homes without roofs
But Mama and Baba wanted
One of their babies to know
The inside of an undemolished home

The next time they come
I'll be strapped with a ticking vest
Missiles loaded on my shoulders and
Land mines beneath my feet
A sling shot on my ears and
Rocks on my belt

Daring the Israeli soldier to
Take
one
more
Step.

How have non-profits impacted Palestinian and other Arab liberation struggles?

Hatem Bazian: NGOs control the purse strings. Through this funding or through the staff they hire, they assert their political agenda. For example, the largest coalition of organizations that work on Palestine do not insist on US divestment from Israel or devote organizing resources into achieving this agenda. But look at the solidarity movements that developed around apartheid South Africa and Central America: they made divestment central to their struggle. These movements recognized that economic sanctions and pressure are central to change a government's policies; but when it comes to Palestine, NGOs do not want to offend certain segments of the liberal Zionist community. So they shift their focus to changing Israel's mind without making Israel suffer. This kind of strategy was dismissed as ineffectual in the South African and Central American solidarity movements.

The Palestinian struggle (which does not differentiate between land stolen from Palestinians in 1948 and land stolen in 1967) has demanded the right to return for all Palestinian refugees and calls for Palestine to be a complete whole. But today, almost all NGOs and foundations call for a "two-state solution" that insists Israel, as it's currently constructed, must exist as is, and that Palestinians must learn to accept colonization and occupation. The two-state solution defends Israel's "right" to define itself on racially exclusivist criteria, and hence exist as a racially apartheid state. Further, by proposing that Palestine exist as a divided, demilitarized state whose resources are fully controlled by Israel, this approach effectively eliminates the possibility of Palestinians having a real state that encompasses their historical and international rights. In other words, this "solution" would essentially dispense with the 6 million Palestinian refugees.

In other solidarity movements, there is often the understanding that they exist to support liberation struggles, not to dictate the terms of those struggles. However, when it comes to Palestine, NGOs feel they have the right to tell Palestinians what to do. In their framework, the problem is not Israeli colonization and occupation; the problem is that Palestinians need to be trained to develop "civil society" and learn to cooperate with Israel. Consequently, funding is often focused on developing joint "Israeli-Palestinian" ventures and projects rather than address the issue of occupation. Furthermore, the NGOization of the solidarity movement in the US has been so thorough that anyone who criticizes this position is silenced and marginalized. (For instance, in the Bay Area there used to be an annual demonstration for Peace, Jobs, and Justice throughout the 1980s, and no speakers on Palestine were allowed to speak unless they supported the two-state solution.)

Without exception, every foundation that funds work on Palestine (from the most conservative to the most "progressive") does so from the understanding that Israel, as it currently exists, should stay intact, and the solution is to change Palestinians so that they will adapt to their colonial situation. Now, for instance, the [Open Society Institute] wants to bring Palestinian intellectuals to the US to "train them." Train them to do what? Train them to see the situation the way the US does and facilitate the continued colonization of Palestine?

Zeina Zaatari: Organizations that are able to operate and function and have enough resources to hire staff—these organizations are careful and strategic about what they say. There are lines they do not cross, or else they are penalized. United for Peace and Justice (UFPJ) has more foundation support than Act Now to Stop War and End Racism (ANSWER), although both coalition efforts organize against war. A big difference is that ANSWER includes Arab organizations with a clear political view, groups UPFJ doesn't invite into its leadership. Basically, it is not okay for organizations to address Zionism or historic Palestine. You can talk about occupation, but you cannot talk about discrimination within the Israeli state or the right to return. For instance, San Francisco Women Against Rape lost funding when it started to address the issue of Zionism in its organization. On the issue of Lebanon, it is okay to send money for support services, but it is not okay to talk about liberation. If you talk about violence, you must denounce the liberation movement in Lebanon; you cannot focus on the violence perpetrated by Israel. Follow the money, and it's clear that foundations are driving these and other political agendas.

For another example of how deeply foundation funding impacts this movement, compare the American Arab Anti-Discrimination Committee (ADC) with the National Council of Arab Americans. The ADC works with the FBI, supports US interventions in Afghanistan, does not take clear stands on Palestine, and works with US government officials (such as Colin Powell and Madeleine Albright) who are responsible for killing our people. Its focus is to make Arabs acceptable to the mainstream US, not grassroots organizing. The National Council of Arab Americans, meanwhile, calls for an end to the colonization of Palestine, addresses Zionism, and does not support the two-state solution. Consequently, it has a much more difficult time getting funding. Additionally, as a result of the Patriot Act, even individuals are afraid to support Arab liberation organizations because they are targeted by the US government.

Atef Said: In Egypt, NGOization often competes with grassroots organizing work. For instance, in labor organizing, NGOs encourage workers not to clash with business owners, thus pacifying labor struggles. Sadly, most NGO leaders were previously involved in the country's Left movements, but were seduced into the NGO world because they can be funded (including personal benefits like travel and luxury hotel accommodations) and incur less trouble with the establishment. A significant problem with this model, of course, is that NGOs depend on foundations for their resources, not the people; thus, they spend little if any time organizing and are instead accountable only to their funders. For example, since NGOs are dependent on foundation support, directors of NGOs focus on quantity rather than quality of work (that is publish more reports in less time).

In 1997 and 1998, I started to observe from my work in these human rights NGOs that they are a bit isolated, and while they claim to defend people's human rights, they are not invested in the question of social change and social justice. For instance, if we look at the case of workers who are fired or on strike—a labor organizer would work with them to continue their activism and organization. But the NGO legal aid staffer would ask to be authorized legally to sue the employer on the worker's behalf. In other words, the NGO asks the worker to stop her/his activism: "Go home and just authorize me to sue him." After 1998, I continued to work in these NGOs with no big hope that they will really do genuine human rights work. I started to work voluntarily with labor as well as the Palestine solidarity movement, and it became clear that my work for human rights NGOs was just a paid job.

On the positive side, because of growing social movements that are not NGOized, particularly those in support of Palestine, some NGOs are focusing more on grassroots work, even if it impacts their funding.[5]

Historically, how has the NGOization of the Palestinian struggle developed?

Hatem Bazian: Beginning in the 18th century, Christian missionary workers emerged in the Middle East and set about influencing policy through education.

Banking institutions also developed that became involved with Christian elites. European countries, in turn, often claimed themselves as the protectors of Christians in the area to justify political intervention in the region. Using educational exchange programs, England, France, and, later, the US aspired to create an elite within the region that would support their interests.

After Israel was created in 1948, the Palestinian liberation movement was often shaped by Arab states. They tried to control the movement and its interaction with Israel so that it would not negatively impact their diplomatic relations with Western countries. The PLO, which was constructed from outside Palestine, mirrored the authoritarian structure and corruption of the neocolonial Arab states. However, since the uprising of the 1980s, the shaping of this movement has shifted from outside Palestine to inside of it. It is now less susceptible to being co-opted into the Arab state structure and can assert a different vision for struggle. This vision, of course, is fluid and the movement has diverse sectors.

After the 1970s, NGOs emerged as key shapers of the movement. But they too attempted to influence the movement in ways that accorded with US and Western interests. So, while NGOization is a more recent phenomenon, it is part of a legacy of outside interests attempting to shape a liberation struggle in a way that supports imperial forces rather than the Palestinian people.

Zeina Zaatari: Oslo helped set the framework for what is and is not acceptable. Pre-Oslo, or during the first intifada, political movements were still strong, organizing within Palestine, and, to a lesser extent, in refugee camps outside Palestine. But Oslo isolated the Palestinian issue as unrelated to larger Arab-Israeli conflicts, and transformed the movement by shifting its focus from liberation to statehood and from decolonization to peace. Funders supported the Oslo agenda by rewarding projects concerned with mutual coexistence, and forced the collaboration between Israeli and Palestinian groups. Within Palestine, organizations previously concerned with a broader vision for justice—such as freedom for historic Palestine, the right of return, and the land—turned their attention to smaller issues such as social services and other structures necessary for statehood, representational politics, and constitutional development. Donors put much money behind this kind of work, and the work of liberation became much more compartmentalized: for instance, the issue of refugees became separated from the larger liberation struggle, its emphasis redirected in the post-Oslo political and funding climate from the right of return to humanitarian relief.

In South Africa, foundations were instrumental in directing the antiapartheid struggle away from an anticapitalist framework. Has any similar process happened in Palestine?

Hatem Bazian: Yes. Eighty percent of the infrastructure in Palestine is funded by international granting agencies. These agencies stifle critiques of capitalism and try to normalize the free market economy in the occupied territories. They train elites within Palestine to integrate into the global economy. Now, maquiladoras are being constructed in the Gaza Strip, with the elites in Palestine negotiating with Israel to develop these economic units. The result is the development of an economic elite that will become invested in the well-being of Israel. All such efforts are funded by granting agencies which require that these economic development programs be connected to Israel structurally.

Similar strategies to tie economic elites to Israel are being used in Egypt and Jordan, primarily through the development of free trade zones. In Jordan, Israel is developing joint venture companies with Jordan elites that rely on cheap labor from Jordan and Palestine. Establishing these zones in Jordan essentially ensures that Jordanians will not try to cross into Israel, while encouraging Palestinians to migrate to Jordan so they will be less inclined to press for their right to return. Egypt has also signed an economic agreement with Israel to expand markets with Israeli investment. Again, NGOs are supporting the integration of Palestine into the capitalist global economy so that it will be dependent on Israel.

Zeina Zaatari: Funding agencies can only exist in a capitalist structure. Tax cuts is what make these foundations able to make money. Foundations and corporations are talking about corporate responsibility. They want to provide resources to address workers' rights, and will take some steps toward issues for justice. But a full-fledged discussion of capitalism and its impact on the world is not happening. Instead, NGOs are geared toward integrating people into capitalism. In Palestine, most of the population is barely working, while NGOs use their resources to create a class of people who live comfortably on donor dollars. This class of people becomes less angry and are less compelled to transform the system.

What are some alternative approaches to supporting Palestinian liberation?

Zeina Zaatari: In Palestine, the alternative to NGOs is political parties. However, as in the rest of the Arab world, Left political parties have not been very effective in Palestine. At times, the Left was able to organize mass popular movements. But, generally, it did not work sufficiently with people on the ground. Now the Left has become an elite group of people removed from the majority of the population. They speak a different language and are not able to deliver. People are less likely to follow them and are turning instead to groups like Hamas that can provide them with resources, with a vision, with hope.

It is important to note that while NGOs get pressure from foundations to shape their political agenda, they also resist foundations. In Palestine, many NGOs have resisted the Ford Foundation's requirement to sign on to their statement on terrorism. Some groups are refusing to take money, and Ford had funded many educational institutes in Palestine. Other groups have created their own statements and said this is what we are willing to sign, and they have done so.

Equally so, operating outside the NGO system does not necessarily mean that a group will be progressive. For instance, I have seen micro-credit groups in Lebanon decide to end their dependence on the foundation system and still end up operating as if they were NGOs. That is, foundations often expect economic development groups to show "growth" without consideration for the larger political and social context. These micro-credit groups, in order to become independent, also ended up focusing on growth; ironically, once they became self-sufficient, theirs became indistinguishable from a foundation agenda. Although established from a social change framework, these organizations now function as mere lending organizations.

Atef Said: In Egypt, the founders of the movement, in solidarity with Palestine, declared from the very beginning that they would not accept any foreign funding (nor would they accept funding from Egyptian businesses involved with business in Israel). Since one of the main goals for this movement is to mobilize Egyptians in solidarity with Palestine, one of the main activities is to involve and to seek donations from ordinary Egyptians. Our sentiment is that one Egyptian pound from a poor Egyptian for Palestine is more honorable and appreciated (for the movement) than one million dollars or pounds from a corrupt Egyptian business or foreign funder.

The Egyptian solidarity movement started as an intellectual or elitist movement focused on sending donations (food and medical supplies) to Palestine; they refused to criticize the Egyptian government. This changed dramatically after the state began cracking down on the movement around the end of 2001. While the US media portrays Mubarak as a moderate leader, social justice activists in Egypt perceive him as a reactionary whose interests are aligned with the US and Israel. The movement began to criticize Mubarak's role in pressuring the Palestinians to acquiesce to US and Israeli policies, recognizing the connection between mobilizing people for Palestine and mobilizing a pro-democracy movement against the Egyptian government. Also, this movement began to be more critical of the exploitative stance of many Egyptian businessmen (who were happy to use the idea of the divestment from Israel for their own businesses, rather than out of solidarity with Palestine), and their donations were rejected.

They also resisted NGOization, since NGOs in Egypt receive their money from foreign sources. Foreign money then controls the agenda of the movement.

There are some cases in which existing human rights NGOs tried to work on the Palestinian struggle through a human rights framework. For example, the Cairo Institute for Human rights (CIHR), a regional NGO focused on the Arab world, and the Cairo-based Arab Organization for Human Rights, both monitor and report on the situation in Palestine. Some NGOs organized conferences about the rights of Palestinian refugees; others organized conferences or seminars that make comparisons between apartheid South Africa and the situation in Palestine. These NGOs and others in Egypt also coordinate with Palestinian human rights organizations, such as the Palestinian Center for Human Rights.

Notably, the CIHR organized around the 2001 UN Conference on Racism in Durban, South Africa, to highlight Israel's apartheid policies directed against Palestinians. Interestingly, however, the broader movement in Egypt was reluctant to work with CIHR because it is an NGO. As a result, very few grassroots activists were able to go to Durban due to lack of funds; as is often the case with international gatherings such as UN conventions or World Social Forums, only people affiliated with NGOs could attend. And in Egypt, few grassroots activists have ties to NGOs.

Without NGO funding, the Palestinian solidarity movement has funded itself with donations from ordinary people. Young children gave their pocket money; poor women in Egyptian villages gave food from their homes. While this form of organizing may be "the hard way," many activists think this approach is better than seeking meetings with government elites in five-star hotels.

Despite this agreement, however, it is important to note that there are different factions within the movement: broadly speaking, nationalists, communists, and liberals. The liberals focus on charity work and do not want to criticize Egypt's role in supporting the US and Israel's suppression of the Palestinian intifada. The nationalists focus their criticism primarily on Israel. Leftists and communists situate their work and analysis on imperialism and the role of Israel in supporting imperialist wars and occupation in the Middle East. The latter group is most invested in mobilizing mass numbers of peoples.

Generally speaking, the NGOs did not want open meetings and did not have democratic leadership. Some of the more elitist leaders in the movement also opposed public open meetings, insisting that it enabled the Egyptian police to infiltrate the meetings. Movement members have countered that the best way to protect the movement was to have open democratic meetings: the more democratic the leadership is, the easier it is tell who the police agents are. And because the movement membership was so strong, they have always been able to prevent elite leadership from shutting down public meetings.

The NGOs also focus on working with government and economic elites. For instance, an elite representative of the Egyptian Committee for the Solidarity with the Palestinian Intifada (ECSPI) said, "One successful press conference is more important than ten demonstrations." However, this approach is a minority opinion. Generally speaking, the movement does not support NGOization.

notes

1 From Bay Area INCITE! Chapter, www.incite-national.org.

2 Apart from a very small number of family reunification cases, Israel continues to refuse to allow any refugees to return to their homes.

3 The UN has repeatedly affirmed the right of self-determination of the Palestinian people in these territories. General Assembly Resolution 3236, adopted in 1974, for example, reaffirmed the inalienable right of the Palestinian people to self-determination and the inalienable right of Palestinian refugees to return to their homes and lands from which they were uprooted.

4 Researcher Rosemary Sayigh describes the scene as the massacre unfolded: "The targeted area was crammed with people recently returned from the places where they had taken refuge during the war, now supposedly over. Schools would soon open, everyone needed to repair their homes, clear the streets and get ready for the winter. There was fear of what the regime of Bashir Gemayel would bring, but there was also determination to rebuild. People felt some security from the fact that they were unarmed, and that all who remained were legal residents. Many of the massacre victims were found clutching their identity cards, as if trying to prove their legitimacy.

One contingent of the [Lebanese] Special Units commanded by Hobeiqa entered the area through the sand-hills overlooking Hayy Orsan, just opposite the IDF [Israel Defense Forces] headquarters. At this stage they were almost certainly accompanied by Israeli soldiers, since the dunes had been fortified by the resistance. Another contingent entered through the southeastern edge of the Hursh, between Akka Hospital and Abu Hassan Salameh Street. Apart from co-planning the operation and introducing the special forces into the area, the IDF provided several kinds of backup: they controlled the perimeters and prevented escape through light shelling and sniping, as well as by blocking the main exits; they also used flares to light up the narrow alleys at night." From Rosemary Sayigh, "How the Sabra/Shatila Massacre Was Buried With the Victims," al-Majdal, no. 9 (March 2001).

5 One prominent coalition of NGOs, United for Peace and Justice (UFPJ), has been active in opposing the US war on terror. However, this NGOization has impacted the way they address Palestine. The following letter from the Free Palestine Alliance (FPA) to UFPJ serves as an example of how NGOization can affect solidarity movements. The purpose is not to so much to scapegoat UPFJ, which continues to struggle with these issues and hear the critiques of FPA, but to provide a case study that can be instructive for all those involved in doing global solidarity work. In addition, as Bazian notes, this issue is endemic to most if not all US NGOs:

> ▷ **UFPJ: The Absence of Moral Character**
>
> As we join people around the world in mobilizing against the unspeakable atrocities being committed by the Israeli military in Lebanon and Palestine, we are forced to turn our attention to attempts by forces within the US justice movement who have made a habit of condemning the popular resistance of the Arab people. We feel that this is important due to the continued and unabated attempts to marginalize the voice of those at the receiving end of war....
>
> *On July 18, 2006, during peak wholesale murders at the hands of the Israeli military, [UFPJ] issued a statement that condemned the popular resistance movement*

in Lebanon, [which] it equated with Israeli actions. This was followed by a call on July 19 in which UFPJ not only completely eliminated Palestine (once again) from the political scene, but also escalated its condemnation of the resistance and declared that it was in violation of International Law. UFPJ went further to echo the US administration's own political constructs, that the Israeli forces should not use a "disproportionate response"—as if a proportionate one exists, and as if the violence of colonists is just a mere "response." UFPJ's statements join the US-proxy regimes of Saudi Arabia, Jordan, and Egypt in holding the popular resistance movement responsible for the savagery of Zionist colonial conquest—a textbook example of blaming the victim. Given that the vast majority of the Arab masses support popular Arab resistance movements, condemning this movement from the vantage point of a privileged people is very troubling. However, when such a practice becomes habitual, with reckless disregard to the concerns of the victims, the practice amounts to bigotry.

This outlook from UFPJ is no surprise. UFPJ has consistently and vehemently opposed the inclusion of Palestine in the anti-war movement (and continues to do so every time it has a chance) and demanded the removal of Palestinian flags from the New York stage on March 20, 2004, because, according to UFPJ leadership, these flags invoked images of "terror." UFPJ's current leadership rejected opposition to the invasion of Lebanon in June 1982 during a major anti-nuke mobilization in New York's Central Park while the invasion was taking place. The UFPJ leadership also raised the slogan "sanctions not war" during the first Gulf War, later back-pedaling from what is now best known as a policy of infanticide against Iraqi children. And, of course, UFPJ continues to reject the Palestinian right of return to their original homes and property—all while always claiming to know what is best for the Arab people, and always charging that the Palestinians just have to wait their turn.

The position taken by UFPJ (an increasingly Democratic Party functionary organization) regarding the current Israeli colonial conquest is the same as that of the various Saudi and Gulf-funded Arab organizations in the United States. The collective goal of these organizations is to contain the justice movement in the various community sectors and to divert them as far from effective goals as possible. Their modus operandi is always typical and transparent: to condemn "both sides" so as to appease their fund-providers and political sponsors; to issue some benign call for "peace" (albeit, false and unjust); and to declare that the only way to that pseudo-peace is through a specific wing of the existing power structure.

The UFPJ leadership also lacks basic moral courage. Only two years ago, in Beirut, Lebanon, UFPJ claimed to support the resistance movement in the Arab world, including that of Lebanon, Iraq, and Palestine, and joined in opposition to Zionism. Yet, while in the US, UFPJ condemns that very same movement and does not dare speak against Zionism, lest they anger UFPJ's political sponsors. We wish to remind the leadership of UFPJ that the Arab people are the architects of their own destiny, and no amount of condemnation by UFPJ will move one solitary grain of sand in the Arab march for justice. It is the Arab people who stand clear against the advance of empire for the benefit of all, as the likes of UFPJ stand on the side hurling condemnations. UFPJ's continuous racist positions toward the Arab people will only enter the history of social movements as a succession of disgrace after disgrace, befitting of a so-called leadership sheltered from the world and alienated from its suffering. The UFPJ leadership must stop peddling the struggle and suffering of our people as an "exciting" commodity to achieve funding and financial support, as that leadership must not think, for a moment, that their manipulations will not be opposed. We call on the member groups of UFPJ and the social justice movement at large to challenge these self-imposed "leaders," who appear to be bent on destroying the moral compass of the anti-war movement, and to deny them the opportunity to brand the US peace movement as racist. Some argue that organizations that stand against US and Israeli policies, such as UFPJ, should be allowed to express a "differing political point of view." We do not think that continuously insulting the aspiration of the Arab people, through denigrating cherished symbolisms and popular social movements, should be acceptable as a "matter of opinion." Racism is never a "matter of opinion."

Furthermore, we believe that we would all be doing the movement a great disservice if we collectively allow the process of normalizing racist concepts to remain unchallenged. The examples of these concepts are many, including a "resisting Arab" is a "terrorist Arab." As if the Arab people can only be supported if and when they are seen as "helpless victims," or, better yet, dead. Since the people of the US suffer from their alienation from the world, the last thing we need is for the movement to also echo that same troubling alienation by mirroring the behavior of empire within. The Arab people have assumed their responsibilities. The people of the US must do the same, at least within the justice movement.

—Free Palestine Alliance, July 20, 2006 (www.freepalestinealliance.org)

▸▸part iii

Rethinking Non-Profits, Reimagining Resistance

▸▸Adjoa Florência Jones de Almeida

radical social change

Searching for a New Foundation

> *Radical: Of or from the root; going to the foundation or source of something; fundamental.*—Webster's New World Dictionary

AS I MOVE INTO MY MID-30S I SOMETIMES WONDER IF I WILL EVER see "revolution." Of course, as I've gotten older, my idea of what true revolution might look like has become increasingly more complex and multilayered. While I'm not sure if I believe that revolution is something we can arrive at—like runners crossing over the finish line at an Olympic race—I do still believe in radical social change. These days I've been drawing most of my inspiration from what I see happening in Latin America—in Mexico, Argentina, Bolivia, Venezuela, and Ecuador, to name a few. When it comes to mass-based social change movements, the US is in dire need of some "aid" from the Third World.[1] Ironically, it is precisely where people have the least access to foundation funding that they've been able to do the most in terms of developing mass-based movements for radical social change.

What do I mean by radical change? If we think of our world as a garden, then radical change is when we are able to pull out the weeds that choke our existence by their roots—preventing them from being born again. Of course, one woman's weed is another one's medicine, so it's important that we seek to fully understand and define the nature of our oppression. What chokes our existence is not *just* about money. It is about the kind of values, culture, and everyday interactions created by capitalism, heterosexism, imperialism, racism, sexism, and other systems of oppression. Recognizing the need to pull up oppressive reality by its roots, Malcolm X stood apart from activists of his day by pushing African Americans toward more radical action. Malcolm advocated our right to bring about freedom, justice, and equality "by any means necessary." Some might argue that social justice groups operating under the current 501(c)(3) system are doing nothing more than accessing needed funds from powerful foundations in order to achieve their ends. But I don't think Malcolm had in mind what is happening to social justice movements in the US today. We as activists are no longer accountable to our constituents or members because we don't depend on them for our existence. Instead, we've become primarily accountable to public and private foundations as we try to prove to them that we are still relevant and efficient and thus worthy of continued funding.

What has happened to the great civil rights and Black power movements of the 1960s and 70s? Where are the mass movements of today within this country? The short answer—they got funded. While it may be overly simplistic to say so, it is important to recognize how limited social justice groups and organizations have become as they've been incorporated into the non-profit model. I remember when the Sista II Sista (SIIS) Collective, which I was a part of for nine years, began researching the possibility of becoming a 501(c)(3). "If there's all this money out there available to groups like ours," we thought, "we should go for it." We knew our vision for radical, transformative personal and social change, led by young women of color would not necessarily be well-received by most foundations. But we convinced ourselves that we would be able to take their money while still holding on to our autonomy. However, after years of doing the 501(c)(3) thing, we began to feel trapped and tried to figure out ways of going back to being an all-volunteer organization.

We began to understand that there is a very thin line between "milking the system" and being milked by the system. During our infinite number of meetings (e.g., Collective, Staff, Squads, Petals),[2] we would ask ourselves, "In the process of working day and night to meet our budgets so that we can guarantee the salaries of those that work within our organization, what has happened to our radical vision for social change?" This radical vision may still be reflected in our mission statements, in the posters and quotes with which we decorate our work spaces; but how are these ideals manifested in our actual day to day lives and in the work we are doing? For example, many of us believe there is a need to do away with the vicious capitalist order that we live under in this country. However, we depend on and report to foundations whose monies are a direct product of the massive profit of global corporations. They give us an insignificant percentage of the profits they make at the expense of millions of people struggling against the same oppression we claim to fight against in our statements of purpose.

In theory, foundation funding provides us with the ability to do the work—it is supposed to facilitate what we do. But funding also shapes and dictates our work by forcing us to conceptualize our communities as victims. We are forced to talk about our members as being "disadvantaged" and "at risk," and to highlight what we are doing to prevent them from getting pregnant or taking drugs—even when this is not, in essence, how we see them or the priority for our work. This is not to say that no one benefits from our work—of course, many do. But if what we want is to bring about a fundamental change to the way our societies are structured, then what are we really achieving? The means we have chosen are deforming our end; if we're not careful, what we create won't be what we had originally envisioned at all.

And what have we envisioned? Perhaps the real problem is that we don't spend enough time imagining what we want and then doing the work to sustain that vision. That is one of the fundamental ways the corporate-capitalist system tames us: by robbing us of our time and flooding us in a sea of bureaucratic red tape, which we are told is a necessary evil for guaranteeing our organization's existence. We don't have time to stop and collectively reflect on the implications of this—why are we so concerned with saving organizations if they are not fully able to truly address the root of the problems we face? Often we know that something feels off, but we feel stuck because we don't have time to imagine how we might do it differently. We are too busy being told to market ourselves by pimping our communities' poverty in proposals, selling "results" in reports and accounting for our finances in financial reviews.

In essence, our organizations have become mini-corporations, because on some level, we have internalized the idea that power—the ability to create change—equals money. The current non-profit structure is based on a corporate model, just as most of us organize our economic lives along corporate structures that are totally integrated within a larger dominant capitalist order: through our bank accounts, consumption patterns, and the taxes we pay. Because of this, it becomes harder and harder to entertain the possibility of restructuring our lives in a radically different way. After all, capitalism is not only around us in the society we live in—it is also within us in terms of what we value, how we live, and what we believe is possible.

It is true that many progressive social justice non-profits are able to hire experienced community organizers as staff and provide important and fulfilling jobs to many low-income, young people of color. While this is incredibly important, if non-profit jobs are the only spaces where our communities are engaged in fighting for social justice and creating alternatives to oppressive systems, than we will never be able to engage in radical social change. Would the Zapatistas in Chiapas or the Landless People's Movement members in Brasil have been able to develop their radical autonomous societies if they had been paid to attend meetings and to occupy land? If these mass movements had been their jobs, it would have been very easy to stop them by merely threatening to pull their paychecks. In this country, our activism is held hostage to our jobs—we are completely dependent on a salary structure, and many of us spend over half of our staff hours struggling to raise salaries instead of creating real threats and alternatives to the institutional oppression faced by our communities. Meanwhile the imaginative and spiritual perspective that would allow us to question the "givens" dictated by neoliberalism begins to erode.

In his brilliant book *Freedom Dreams: The Black Radical Imagination*, Robin D. G. Kelley begins with a wonderful passage in which he talks about his mother and the importance she placed on imagination and inner vision:

> My mother has a tendency to dream out loud. I think it has something to do with her regular morning meditation. In the quiet darkness of her bedroom her third eye opens onto a new world, a beautiful light-filled place as peaceful as her state of mind....Her other two eyes never let her forget where we lived. The cops, drug dealers, social workers, the rusty tap water, roaches and rodents, the urine-scented hallways, and the piles of garbage were constant reminders that our world began and ended in a battered Harlem/Washington Heights tenement apartment....Yet she would not allow us to live as victims. Instead, we were a family of caretakers who inherited this earth....My mother taught us that the Marvelous was free....She simply wanted us to live through our third eyes, to see life as possibility.[3]

Kelley's description of his mother reminds me of my own mother, who has also always used the spiritual realm as fertile ground for the imagination—which, she taught me, allows us to visualize and manifest the kind of world we want.

Among activist circles on the Left, there is often a silent, sometimes condescending disapproval of talk about faith. In part, this is due to the association of religion with fundamentalism, the Christian Right, and the integral role played by Christianity in the colonization of the Americas, Africa, and parts of Asia. It is important to recognize the Catholic Church's role in the devastation and enslavement of African and Indigenous communities. It is important to look at religious fundamentalist movements (whether Christian, Muslim, or Jewish) and their use of religious texts to promote fear, ego, and repression. However, there is a difference between spirituality and religion. I would define spirituality as a feeling or sense of something larger and more powerful than our existence, while most religions have become mere institutions. At the same time, it is important to recognize how the two are often intertwined and the role faith has played in fueling movements of resistance.

Faith and spirituality can provide us with a new foundation for our work, by shifting our perspective of what is possible. Spirituality provides people with an alternative lens to the deterministic vision of reality which equates power to money and which constantly tries to tell us that there is no alternative to the oppressive reality we live in. Most movements that have achieved seemingly impossible revolutionary change (the Haitian revolution, Gandhi's nonviolent revolution in India, the antiapartheid movement in South Africa, the Zapatista uprising in Mexico, the Sandinistas in Nicaragua, to name a few examples) have done so by applying a spiritual understanding of the world to their struggle.

Inspiration and imagination is critical to radical thought. As Kelley reminds us, "Progressive social movements do not simply produce statistics and narratives of oppression; rather, the best ones do what great poetry always does: transport us to another place, compel us to re-live horrors and, more importantly, enable us to imagine a new society."[4]

So I'm constantly in search of inspiration—some spark of brilliance from past and present that can guide me and others in imagining, through spiritual eyes, the kind of future we want to struggle toward. One of SIIS's ongoing sources of inspiration has been Ella Baker, who was among those who pioneered the concept of egoless shared leadership. Baker was one of the most influential organizers of the civil rights movement during the 1950s and 60s, but she is often forgotten because of her style as a "behind-the-scenes organizer." Although she worked alongside some of the movement's "superstars" including Thurgood Marshall, W. E. B. Du Bois, and Dr. Martin Luther King, Jr., she was not interested in making a name for herself. Baker was also deeply influenced by her mother's faith in terms of how she approached her commitment to social justice. Her mother was deeply involved in the Black Baptist women's missionary movement of the early 1900s, and Baker applied the religious fervor and ideals of that faith into her activism. As Barbara Ransby notes, "For Ella Baker the ultimate triumph of a leader was his or her ability to suppress ego and ambition and to embrace humility and a spirit of collectivism."[5]

Another source of inspiration for me has been learning about the her[his]storical legacies of struggle in Brasil, which is my country of birth. Marginalized communities within Brasil (and in most other parts of the Third World) have reinvented (and are reinventing) social reality in the face of unimaginable odds by tapping into the power of spirit. During Brasil's 500 years of slavery, there was tremendous creative resistance fueled by a spiritual understanding of the world. The independent maroon state of Palmares emerged as a parallel society within Brasil, with over 20,000 inhabitants during the height of slavery.[6] It was founded by a group of runaway slaves during the 1600s with everything stacked against them, and survived for almost a century by resisting through armed struggle and by drawing strength from African spiritual traditions. Likewise, in 1835, Muslim African slaves used their Islamic faith as a central organizing tool in planning one of the largest attempted revolts in Brasil's history.

Another powerful example from Bahia, Brasil, is that of Canudos. After the official abolition of slavery in 1888, a popular Christian messianic leader, Antônio Conselheiro, helped to establish Canudos as an autonomous community. Founded in 1893, it was organized as a communal structure with no individual landholders, no "bosses," and no police. At its height, Canudos is said to have had anywhere from 10,000 to 25,000 residents, including many ex-slaves, Indigenous peoples, and landless agrarian workers who left oppressive job conditions working for large landholders to join this new horizontally structured society. This community survived a series of state and federally sponsored attacks until it was completely wiped out in 1897. The attacks on these remarkable, imaginative communities are clear indicators of the radical threat that they posed to the status quo.

Conselheiro's socialist interpretation of the Bible re-emerges within other movements in Latin America through links to liberation theology. This radical strand of the Catholic Church broke rank with the Vatican-based hierarchy during the 1960s and 70s and has been influential in various popular-based movements throughout Latin America. Under this new interpretation of Catholicism, local priests and nuns see their calling as that of serving the local struggles for justice in their communities. The life of Jesus is taken as an example of a man who not only spoke about God's love but, more important, lived in a way that reflected God's love. The sins of humanity are interpreted as the dehumanizing oppression which human beings impose on one another. Jesus is seen as a revolutionary who fought against sin/oppression by rejecting the cult of greed and materialism.

Liberation theology has also been critical to one of Brasil's largest current social movements: the Landless Workers Movement (MST, or Movimento dos Trabalhadores Sem Terra). In the late 1970s, the MST gained momentum during the height of Brasil's military dictatorship and during a period that became known as the "Brasilian Miracle." While the modernization of the nation reached new heights, rural farm workers and sharecroppers increasingly found themselves displaced by the mechanization of agriculture.[7] This led to increased protests and many deaths amongst rural communities across Brasil. In 1979, the MST was formed by landless farmworkers who occupied a piece of land in the Encruzilhada Natalino (in the state of Rio Grande do Sul) with the support of church organizations also based in the liberation theology movement.

During the 1980s and 90s the MST grew tremendously and continues today in advancing a radical, participatory, socialist vision for land reform in Brasil. Today more than 300,000 families have won land titles to over 15 million acres after MST land takeovers. MST communities have spread throughout the country and can be found in 23 of Brasil's 27 states.[8] What is most powerful about this movement is that it has gone beyond the question of land to address the more fundamental question of how to structure the societies that are being created within the settlements and encampments in a manner that reflects their vision of justice. This means that much of their work is about restructuring social relations, including how decisions are made, as they create their own model for schools, community safety, gender equity, economic cooperatives, and other essential frameworks for everyday life.

After attending the Second Latin American Congress of Rural Organizations that took place in Brasil in 1997, US sociologist James Petras reported on some of the lessons and obstacles shared by participants in his article "The New Revolutionary Peasantry."[9] According to Petras, there were close to 350 delegates from every country in Latin America with the exception of Uruguay and El Salvador. At one of the plenary sessions, the Brasilian Catholic priest Fray Beto asked the delegates how many had been influenced by religious teachings. Noting that "over 90 percent raised their hands," Petras suggests that "popular religiosity, the fusion of Biblical lessons, and religious values has had a direct effect in stimulating the new generation of peasant leaders, along with Marxism, traditional communitarian values, and modern feminism and nationalist ideas."[10] Across these movements there is an emphasis on integrity, faith in humans to transform their realities, humility, non-materialism, commitment, and sacrifice. While there are differences in how these elements are understood, these kinds of values are explicitly linked to the idea of divine love, which is seen as holding radical power that can transform any situation, no matter how hopeless it may seem. Love has the power to create miracles for those who believe. Whatever our traditions or beliefs may be, we can be strengthened by recognizing the radical principle of believing and living out our vision. In this way, we might discover ways to more fully integrate our personal and spiritual lives with the social justice work to which we are committed.

During this same conference, the rise of NGOs was cited by many of the movements represented as one of the leading obstacles to their work. One Brasilian activist described the failure of the women of the MST to develop a common strategy at a Latin American Meeting for Peasant Women. According to her, the meeting failed

> because of the manipulative behavior of the NGO professional women, who wanted to control the agenda and limit it exclusively to international cooperation and to confine the struggle to exclusively feminist issues, which meant no support for agrarian reform, anti-imperialism and anti-neo-liberalism....These feminist NGO professionals are authoritarian and with a colonialist mentality; they have nobody behind them except their wealthy outside backers.[11]

This comment holds some important lessons for us in the US. For example, it illustrates how the non-profit sector promotes the separation between feminist discourses from a broader class (and race) analysis. Because non-profits are funded in large part by corporations (with foundations as mere intermediaries), they can't afford to seriously question capitalism, so class issues are always relegated to the background.

An Ecuadorian peasant leader had this to say about NGOs: "I have no objection to overseas NGOs funding our land reform movement if that's what they're willing to do. What is offensive is their setting down their priorities and funding professionals from our country to come in and undermine our struggles."[12] In my experience in New York, I've also witnessed non-profits run by professionals (lawyers, academics, college graduates, and other "experts") who come into a community and completely undermine local struggles that have been led for years by local nonprofessional activists by competing for funding and monopolizing resources. Because they speak the language of corporate non-profits, they get the money—regardless of what their relationship is to those communities.

The struggle for revolutionary change in this country has been derailed not only due to institutionalization of social justice movements, but also because of our inability to quiet our egos. Individual leaders and organizations are constantly playing the "fame game"—reinventing the wheel and promoting their own names instead of focusing on what is truly needed to bring about change. Sometimes what is needed is not so "sexy." Sometimes the most radical thing we can do is to follow the lead of others. Social change is only radical if it promotes struggle and growth at every level—for the society at large, in our intimate and everyday relationships, and internally within ourselves.

It's interesting to note the central role of horizontal, consensus-based, shared leadership in all the emerging revolutionary movements in Latin America. They are expanding the concept of what we traditionally think of as "political work." There, the process of working for change and social justice is intimately linked to how people live their daily lives. That is what I think many of us at Sista II Sista cherish about the collective work that we are trying to do, even while understanding and acknowledging the many contradictions and challenges—it is thorough and integral, and it challenges us to try to model our vision for a different world. So often we are confronted by the lack of integrity and hypocrisy of those who do not practice what they preach. We are so trapped into hierarchical, corporate, non-profit models that we are unable to structure ourselves differently, even when our missions advocate empowerment and self-determination for oppressed communities. When we begin to have the courage to imagine alternatives to the molds we find ourselves in, then we begin to practice what we preach. Our commitment becomes much more about the process we use to engage with our communities than about the work (my outcome, what I'm able to produce)—*this* is truly radical.

After college, I returned to my home country of Brasil for a year and a half to learn more about the social justice education movements emerging from Afro-Brasilian communities in Salvador, Bahia. This was one of the most powerful experiences of my life and truly inspired me to struggle for both personal and a larger collective transformation, *at the same time*. One of the communities I worked with is based in the neighborhood of Massaranduba-Mangueira, which was built over a flooded area used as a dumping ground for the city's garbage. The houses were built on stilts over garbage and water, and the city's government never took responsibility for these conditions. However, over the years most of the streets have been filled in with dirt and concrete because the residents took on the task of doing it themselves through the local residents' association (*associação de moradores*).For communities such as this one, which are totally ignored by the state, social justice is very concretely tied to the struggle for sewage systems, education, water, health care, and housing, to name a few.

In the 1980s, the residents' association—which is completely maintained and supported by community residents—decided to create a school for their children. According to Brasil's constitution, all school-aged children are guaranteed the right to an education. But in practice, this has not applied to poor communities of color, where the only schools available are organized by residents' themselves with no support or funding from government. This community's school, like many others in Brasil, grew out of the residents' association movement. One of the association's founders is a trained Catholic priest who left the church because of his radical interpretation of the Bible and Jesus's life. He, with a group of women from the neighborhood, started a local community school that teaches first through fourth grades. The school's name—Community School: Educate to Liberate—aptly reflects its mission.

One of the teachers and organizers, Ana Rosa da Silva, challenged the school's coordination team (made up of directors, teachers, principal, cleaning lady, and lunch cook, who all receive the same salary) to reflect on issues of race and identity, not only in the classrooms but in their personal, day-to-day lives. The other teachers were not comfortable with their own identity but had reached out to her because the children kept bringing up questions about whether or not they were Black. The teachers asked Ana Rosa to take responsibility for bringing Afro-Brasilian themes into all of their classrooms. There was even the possibility of some extra funding for her to do so. She refused because, in her words, "I refuse to earn [money] to work dealing with the question of Black [people]....For me it's a conflict because I feel that the work I do is a matter of life....It's a question that I work on 24 hours a day inside myself."[13] Instead she proposed that the students, teachers, and coordinators all join a study/discussion group to learn and explore together the significance of an Afro-Brasilian identity within their lives—they all did.

What does it mean for us to be paid to do something that is, for us, a matter of life? Ana Rosa's words have always stayed with me and have inspired me to struggle to find ways of separating my activism from my paid work by trying instead to bring my activism into how I live my life. Ella Baker also saw the importance of separating what was for her a spiritual commitment to the struggle from activism as a professional career. Barbara Ransby, in her essay about the roots of Ella Baker's political passions, recounts that Baker often dreamed of one day writing her autobiography. Although she never did, she knew what she wanted it to be titled: "Making a Life, Not Making a Living."[14]

There is a very rich legacy to remember and study from the religious Left coming out of not only the Christian tradition, but also the Yoruba/Nagô, Muslim, and Indigenous spiritual traditions, among others. Even today, many emerging social movements struggling for radical social change continue to do the impossible because of their faith-based commitment to the practice of spiritual and material liberation. This approach to social justice is reflected throughout Latin America, not only in large-scale revolutions but also in day-to-day cultural and educational practices. If we look at different practices of spiritual development and discipline, there is a direct relationship between them and the power of the political movements that emerged from them. Both faith and political struggle require deep commitment from those involved—it is a way of living, a chosen path and a prayer.

While we can't ignore the pressures and demands of the material world around us, we *can* shift the perspective that dictates our reality. If what we want is a radical transformation of the societies we live in, we must begin to push the boundaries of the material world by allowing our spirit to move us—even when what we see in front of us is a concrete wall. If we approach our work as a spiritual challenge, then we are no longer enslaved by the concept of money and we are fueled instead by our faith and commitment to bring about radical social change; which is actually much more than just "social"—it is also personal and political, *and* about money and privilege, *and* about sexuality, race, and gender, *and* about the relationship between our minds, bodies, and spirit.

notes

1 For more about our need for social movement "aid" from the Third World, see Refugio Collective, "Rethinking Solidarity," *Left Turn,* May/June 2006, 9–11.

2 The SIIS Collective comprises both staff and non-staff members and is responsible for making all major decisions by consensus. All staff members receive the same salary and are responsible for coordinating specific work areas—also known as Petals. In addition, staff members are also asked to volunteer their time as general members. SIIS's young women members who have gone through a cycle of SIIS's Freedom School (one of the main programs for incoming young women) become members of SIIS Squads, which help to coordinate the different Petals within the organization. Squad members are also invited to join the Collective when they feel ready.

3 Robin D. G. Kelley, *Freedom Dreams: The Black Radical Imagination* (Boston: Beacon Press, 2002), 1–2.

4 Ibid., 9.

5 Barbara Ransby, "Behind-the-Scenes View of a Behind-the-Scenes Organizer: The Roots of Ella Baker's Political Passions," in *Sisters in the Struggle: African American Women in the Civil Rights-Black Power Movement,* ed. Bettye Collier-Thomas and V. P. Franklin (New York: New York University Press, 2001), 54.

6 Thomas do Bom-Fim Espíndola, *A Geografia Alagoana ou descrição física, política e histórica da província das Alagoas* (1871; repr., Maceió, Brasil: Edições Catavento, 2001).

7 MST, "Quem somos" [Who we are], http://www.mst.org.br/historico/sumario.html.

8 MST presentation at New York University School of Law, November 2004.

9 James Petras, "The New Revolutionary Peasant: The Growth of Peasant-Led Opposition to Neoliberalism," *Z Magazine*, October 1998, 1–7, http://www.zmag.org/zmag/articles/petrasoct98.htm.

10 Ibid., 4.

11 Ibid., 6.

12 Ibid.

13 Adjoa Florência Jones de Almeida, "Unveiling the Mirror: Afro-Brazilian Identity and the Emergence of a Community School Movement," *Comparative Education Review* 47, no. 1 (February 2003).

14 Ransby, "Behind-the-Scenes View," 55.

>>Paula X. Rojas

are the cops in our heads and hearts?

LIKE MANY OTHER ACTIVISTS ON THE LEFT, I HAVE BEEN STRUG-
gling with the contradictions found in organizing work here in the United States.
I have worked in community-based organizing, both within and outside. My
experiences both in the United States and in Latin America have shaped my analysis of the non-profit system as well as alternatives to it. In the US, I am involved
in grassroots organizing work with a multigenerational community of poor and
working-class women of color in Brooklyn (Sista II Sista and Pachamama). But
what has most pushed my analysis has come from my work and experiences outside of the US, specifically in Latin America. As an adult, I have spent a few years
in Chile, my country of origin, supporting organizing efforts against the military
dictatorship headed by Augusto Pinochet and the neoliberal "democracies" of
the Christian Democratic Party that followed. From Chile, I had the opportunity
to travel to La Paz and El Alto, Bolivia, in 1994, and meet with local activists. In
Mexico, I have worked with women's groups on political and physical self-defense
in rural and urban areas. I also had various opportunities to visit the Zapatistas
in Chiapas, Mexico, first spending three weeks in the autonomous territories in
1999. In 2003, I spent a few days visiting an encampment and a settlement of the
MST (Landless Rural Unemployed Workers Movement) in Brasil and attended a
continental gathering of autonomous movements in Argentina held at an occupied factory in 2005. Through these experiences and many (mostly informal)
conversations over cheap wine and good music, with other *compañer@s*,[1] organizers, friends, and family in both Latin America and the United States, I have
gathered these reflections that I want to share.

lessons from latin america

More than once, *compas* from Latin America have asked me: Why are you getting
a permit from the police to protest police brutality? Why are you being paid to
do organizing? Why are people's movements based in non-profit offices? Behind

these kinds of questions are different assumptions about organizing that might challenge activists in the United States to think outside the non-profit system.

Contemporary Latin America provides a helpful model for reconceptualizing and reimagining organizing strategies in the United States. The relatively recent articulation of powerful new revolutionary movements, as well as the economic connections and geographic closeness to the US makes it an important region for us to watch closely and learn from. In the past 15 years, we have witnessed the rapid development of mass-based movements that have significantly impacted the social, political, and economic structures in Latin America. From the perspective of the establishment Left, the collapse of the Soviet Union and the Sandinista electoral loss in Nicaragua in 1989 seemed to signal the death of revolutionary struggle. But across Latin America, people's movements were quietly but steadily building their base for years before making their work public. Gerardo Rénique notes:

> Today the specter haunting capitalism journeys through Latin America. The region's ongoing social and political upheaval threatens the hegemony of global capital and neo-liberal ideology. In an unprecedented cycle of strikes, mass mobilizations, and popular insurrections extending from the early 90's to the present, the marginalized, exploited, and despised subaltern classes have drawn on deeply rooted traditions of struggle to bring down corrupt and authoritarian regimes closely identified with the IMF [International Monetary Fund], the World Bank and Washington.[2]

Some countries, such as Brasil, Venezuela, Bolivia, and Ecuador, have produced movements aimed directly at resisting US imperialism as a result of people gaining some control over their governments. In other countries, like Mexico, where the government is not in resistance to the US empire, we still see large social movements that are much stronger than current movements in the United States, ones that are able to put significant pressure on their governments.

On January 1, 1994, the day NAFTA was signed into effect, the EZLN (Zapatista National Liberation Army) began an armed uprising by indigenous peasants in Chiapas, Mexico. I have vivid memories of the rebellion and its international impact. I lived in Chile at the time and the uprising made all the mainstream news for days (newspapers, television, and radio). It was major news everywhere along the continent except in the US. Within days, smaller rebellions popped up in various countries. Like the MST, which had been growing in Brasil since 1978, the Zapatistas had been steadily building their base since 1983, before becoming publicly known. This was a powerful moment that reignited hope for movements all across the continent in the possibility of revolutionary transformation from the ground up. It was a 12-day war that succeeded in capturing five municipalities that constitute 25 percent of the state of Chiapas. This defiant action was unprecedented in modern Mexican history. In the next year, 1995, the EZLN held the Consulta Nacional por la Paz y la Democracia, in which 1.3 million people participated in making the decision of what the future structure and scope of the EZLN would be.

This hope grew throughout the late 1990s, and new visions guiding revolutionary struggles emerged. Though there are still a number of traditionally Marxist/Leninist-based armed and/or political party national liberation struggles in Latin America, there are many other examples of revolutionary visions of transformation that are well worth listening to. Instead of a unified line, broad tendencies are developed through critiques of past struggles and organic modes of organization of the most marginalized, and are inspired by movements like the EZLN. These visions embrace principles like *autonomia* (autonomy) and *horizontalidad* (horizontalism); recognize daily life and the creation of liberated communities *as* political work; support collective, nonhierarchical decision-making; and aim, above all, to build a society grounded in justice and peace for all. As Raul Zibechi, a Latin American writer and researcher at the Popular Education Center of the Multiversidad Franciscana de America Latina notes:

> It is revealing that Latin America has seen a whole set of revolts without leadership, without organizational memory or central apparatus. Power relations within the space of the uprising tend to be based on other forms. The mortar which binds and drives those who are in revolt does not correspond to the state-form—vertical and pyramidal—but rather is based on a set of ties that are more horizontal but also more unstable than bureaucratic systems. The best known instance of this rejection of representation is the slogan "que se vayan todos" ("they all should go"—all being the politicians) which emerges in the course of the December 19–20 [2001] events in Argentina. Both in the neighborhood assemblies and among the groups of "piqueteros" (people blocking commercial traffic on major highways) and in the occupied factories, this general slogan has concrete expressions: "entre todos todo" ("among everyone, everything"), which is similar to the Zapatista "entre todos lo sabemos todo" ("among everyone we know everything"). Both statements (which express the daily life of the groups that coined them) are directed simultaneously at non-division of labor and of thought-action, and also at there being no leaders who exist separate from the groups and communities. [3]

Another deep lesson we can learn from these struggles is to question the analysis of power—the difference between taking power and creating power. According to Rodrigo Ruiz, editor of the New Left magazine *Surda* of Santiago, Chile:

> The questioning of the traditional forms of political organization is mixed with the questioning of whether those organizations are necessary. Certainly, what weighs heavily is the combination of popular defeats, in addition to many of the left parties being justly discredited. The new movements, the experiences

of resistance to neoliberal globalization, like Seattle, Quebec, Genoa, movements like the MST...the Bolivarian revolution in Venezuela, or the Zapatista process in Chiapas, has meant a significant shake-up of the old knowledge of parties that were unable to resolve with efficacy the construction of forces. [4]

Historically, both political and revolutionary struggles focus on toppling state power and replacing it with people's power. One problem with this model is that most of these movements re-created oppressive governance structures modeled on the same system they were trying to replace. In addition, this model rested on the notion that power lies mostly in institutions, instead of recognizing and building from the power that people already have. According to Pablo Gonzalez Casanova, for the Zapatistas,

> the project will have succeeded when the struggles for autonomy have evolved into networks of autonomous peoples. Its objective is to create—with, by, and for the communities—organizations of resistance that are at once connected, coordinated and self-governing, which enable them to improve their capacity to make a different world possible. At the same time, as far as possible, the communities and the peoples should immediately put into practice the alternative life that they seek, in order to gain experience. They should not wait until they have more power to do this. It is not built on the logic of "state power" which entrapped previous revolutionary or reformist groups.[5]

Implicit in these models is what could be described as a spiritual framework for understanding power that recognizes and respects the humanity of all peoples. In these newer movements, such as the Zapatistas in Chiapas or the MTD (Unemployed Workers Movement) in Argentina, though each is very different from the other, the emphasis is on the people's struggle for autonomy, not gathering power to topple the state and take it over. Revolution is about the *process* of making power and creating autonomous communities that divest from the state. And as these autonomy movements build, they can become large enough to contest state power. Raul Zibechi, for instance, suggests:

> If we look closely at the more important challenges launched by the popular sectors, we will see that they all emerged from the "new" territories, which are more autonomous and independently controlled than those that existed in previous periods of capitalism: El Alto, in Bolivia; the neighborhoods and settlements of the unemployed in Argentina; the camps and settlements of the landless in Brazil; the popular neighborhoods in Caracas; and the indigenous regions in Chiapas, Bolivia, and Ecuador. [6]

These movements emphasize not just winning a specific political goal, but creating new communities that model the vision for liberation. While direct confrontations with state power are ongoing and necessary, these are actually just one small part of the struggle. As Zibechi observes: "To understand this involves reversing one's perspective: rejecting the negative and state-centered viewpoint—which defines people by what they lack (needy, excluded, marginalized)—and adopting another way of looking which starts with the differences that they have created in order then to visualize other possible paths."[7]

For example, when US activists think about the Zapatista movement, the first image that frequently comes to mind is the popular Left postcard of Zapatista indigenous women fighting with the Mexican military. One of the women is choking a soldier. However, this kind of confrontation, though important, is really a small part of the work being done to build this movement. For over 20 years, the Zapatistas have organized almost 100,000 people to create their own separate communities, their own justice system, their own health care system, their own agriculture, and their own educational system. The day-to-day groundwork of these projects is not the sexy thing that gets the attention of the public like the dramatic confrontation of an unarmed woman with soldiers. But the Zapatistas' global contributions run far deeper. Casanova addresses this directly: :

> Among the rich contributions of the Zapatista movement toward building an alternative is the recent project of the "caracoles" (conches). The project of the "caracoles," according to Comandante Javier, "opens up new possibilities of resistance and autonomy for the indigenous people of Mexico and the world— a resistance which includes all those social sectors that struggle for democracy, for liberty and justice for all." It invites us to build towards community and autonomy with the patience and tranquility of the conch. The idea of creating organizations to be used as tools to achieve certain objectives and values, and to ensure that autonomy and the motto "mandar obedeciendo" ("lead by obeying") do not remain in the sphere of abstract concepts and incoherent words.[8]

This framework is an alternative model for confronting the state and for social transformation. When the Zapatista autonomous communities open their own schools and do not participate in state schools, it challenges state power because there is one less thing that the people need from the state. And the existence of a movement living its vision has deepened the conscience of the people of Mexico as a whole and has inspired many other social movements. All of these are in direct solidarity with the EZLN, like the radical student movements, squatters' movements, teachers' movements, other peasant movements, and more, forming the frontlines of what is now a very advanced mass struggle.

A powerful example of autonomous movements that may speak more directly to current US conditions is that of Argentina. Argentina had long been viewed as a Latin American model of economic growth and development under neoliberalism. But, apparently, this was not the case for the majority of Argentines. Peter Ranis writes,

The rebellion in Argentina [in] December 2001 was a spontaneous outpour-
ing of wrath and a demonstration against the imposition and consequences
of a prescribed neoliberal economic model. But it also included a direct confrontation with the governing institutions and political leadership. Argentines
massively demonstrated in December 2001, beating on pots and pans, directing their opposition to President de la Rúa's establishment of controls over
savings and checking accounts (corralito). The economic turmoil precipi-
tated the sacking of supermarkets by impoverished consumers, which in turn
resulted in a declaration of a state of siege, counter-demonstrations, and the
death of 27 people. De la Rúa resigned, and after a series of interim presidents,
the congress designated the Peronist Eduardo Duhalde as president. The
"cacerolazos" (pots and pans demonstrations) that began in December 2001
represented the mass of Argentine society from all walks of life. Argentina had
never experienced such a spontaneous multiclass uprising.[9]

Even before these mass uprisings, since 1996, groups of unemployed people
had been beginning to organize as MTDs, as autonomous movements (autonomous from political parties and non-profit/NGOs and foundation funding)
throughout the country, mostly concentrated in the marginalized neighborhoods
surrounding the capital of Buenos Aires. Tactics varied and included takeovers
of abandoned factories. These MTDs were also autonomous from each other;
each had its own name, its own political principles and practices, and its own
interpretation of autonomia. After 2001, many began to network and attempt
to coordinate their power while still attempting to maintain horizontalidad; the
goal was not to build a centralized MTD national power. Meanwhile, the mass
rebellions intensified as did the repression of the state.

Many of these movements were thinking beyond the state, and even beyond
an alternative version of current institutions, by politicizing every aspect of daily
life and alternative forms of dealing with them. Specifically, the personal relationships between people also became politicized, with compañer@s looking for just
ways to treat each other in the context of the movement work and beyond.

In Argentina, the *piqueteros* politicize their social differences when, rather
than going back to work for a boss with a miserable wage, they opt to form collectives of autonomous producers without division of labor; when they decide
to take care of their health by trying to break their dependence on medication
and on allopathic medicine; or when they deal with education using their own
criteria and not those of the state.[10]

Though many challenges have emerged along the way, these projects have
demonstrated the possibility of nonhierarchical collective production, self-man-
agement (*autogestión*) on a large scale, in neighborhoods or in large industries
with hundreds of workers.

challenges to the non-profit system

These new organizing models pose some important challenges to the non-profit system. First, they challenge the notion that hierarchy and centralization are required to do mass-based political organizing. In the current non-profit system, organizations, particularly those that have a scope extending beyond the local level, tend to be based on a hierarchical governance model, with an executive director, board of directors, and on down. People often argue that collective and horizontal decision-making structures are inefficient. And to the extent that they do work, many activists insist that they work only for local organizing projects or projects that are small in scope.

However, in some recent Latin American experiences we see horizontal structures for very large groups, groups much larger than any current movements in the United States. Generally these movements hold *asambleas populares* (popular assemblies) to determine political agendas through consensus. They are used by the Zapatistas, the MTD in Argentina, and many others engaged in struggles for autonomía. Grounded in the underlying principle of direct collective power, these practices are used to avoid power cementing in certain people placed in representative roles. People gather locally, in their community or neighborhood, on a street corner or somewhere else public and easily accessible to discuss and reflect on issues that need to be decided. What seems like a facilitator's nightmare—a large, sometimes very large, group of people without a set agenda—becomes a space to practice how we want to live collectively. They may then select rotating representatives who will meet in another popular assembly to share what is going on throughout the movement. These non-permanent representatives take these ideas back to their original popular assembly, where they then report to fellow community members and gather feedback. Popular assemblies are very inclusive—even children can participate if they are interested. Sometimes, the decision-making can be slow: this process went on for a year in order to lay the groundwork of the Chiapas uprising. During the Zapatista negotiations with the Mexican government, they took a pause of several months to consult with their thousands of members before moving forward. However, similar horizontal non-centralized processes have also been used to make almost spontaneous decisions that led to the shutdown of entire countries. These processes were used to make very quick decisions to shut down Argentina in 2001 and to force out the president of Bolivia in October 2003. In other words, horizontal decision-making can be done on a mass scale.[11]

These models demonstrate that everyday life is political and that everyone can participate politically. Political work is not outside the struggle for subsistence or in an organization's office or center, but in life. For example, some of the MTDs in

Argentina set up collective kitchens, whether in joint community spaces or in the homes of MTD members. As Raul Zibichi notes, this kind of shared "domestic" space became one of MTD's most important organizing fronts:

> The tendency was for the non-state orientation of domestic spaces to extend as a form of action into very broad public spaces. The rupture of the "domestic wall" brought with it, to the surprise of the protagonists themselves, the novelty that public space was occupied using the articles and practices associated with domestic space (pots and pans in Buenos Aires; rumor-mongering in El Alto). Thus, in Buenos Aires, neighbors came to the assemblies—in the local squares—with their domestic animals and with chairs from their houses, while in El Alto they watched over their dead in the dusty streets built by the community.[12]

This contrasts strongly with the frequent habit of US non-profits to show their ownership over an issue or a particular campaign: to be considered engaged, community members must go to their office for training or attend their events. But for some movements, political education does not necessarily take place in a building; instead, it is integrated into the organizing itself. For instance, Brasil's MST centers education, including political education, in its work, arguing that one cannot build a movement among people who are not actively engaged in learning. This is in the context of a movement that is 300,000 families strong. Given the instability with which people in the landless movement live, education must take place "on the run," in whatever conditions people are living under. So the MST developed Itinerant Education, an education system available for all children and adults based on Paolo Freire's principles of popular education, which work toward liberation, not indoctrination.

"The Movement of Unemployed Landless Workers of Brazil (MST) that gathers homeless, tenants, rural workers, squatters, and small-scale farmers is without a doubt, the most powerful social movement of Latin America," says Marta Harnecker, a Chilean political writer, analyst, journalist, and researcher who has spent the past 30 years gathering and raising the visibility of popular struggles in Latin America from La Habana, Cuba. Nevertheless, as movement leader Joao Stedile points out, "It's evident that both the right and the left have not been able to correctly interpret the political character of the Movement."[13] But the MST has no intention of becoming a political party, focused instead upon on-the-ground commitments to centering everyone's education, the development of settlements that model the world they are trying to create, and a spiritual grounding that points to unlearning internalized social practices, including an active "gender" sector and monthly rituals called *místicas* (mystics). The "gender" work includes safety patrols of MST members, armed with machetes and trained in gender issues. They intervene in domestic abuse situations and bring offenders to community accountability sessions. This organizing work breaks with the traditional revolutionary mold and centers activities that most non-profits could ever dream of getting away with.

the cop in the head—internalized capitalism

One of the scariest manifestations of modern capitalism is the system's ability to co-opt experiences, practices, even culture, and to then re-create and repackage them within a careerist, profit-driven (even in "non-profits"), and competitive logic. The non-profit system, as other essays in this volume demonstrate, supports the professionalization of activism rather than a model of everyday activism. For many of us, activism has become something that you do as a career. When organizers from other countries see that activists are paid to do work in the United States, it makes them wonder. It took my father (who is very familiar with grassroots struggles) a few years to understand the work that I was doing. "Your job is a community organizer; what does that mean, it's your employment? Who is paying you to do this work? And why?" And since many of us are being paid by foundations allied with corporate interests, my father also said, "Clearly, they are paying you to keep you from really challenging the system, to make sure that you are accounted for." As long as we are doing our social transformation work through a paid job, it is much easier to pressure, relate to, and keep track of what we are doing.

When we focus on organizing as part of everyday life, the process becomes as important as the final product. In many cases, foundation funders and the non-profit culture expect groups to achieve a campaign goal in a relatively short period of time. They are not interested in funding the much slower work of base building, which takes years and years to do. Consequently, non-profits become short-term-goal oriented, even if they did not begin that way. Many also become focused on "smoke and mirrors" organizing, in which you do something that looks good for a photo op but has no real people power behind it. A critique from some organizers in Latin America on this is that there is no one who can do "smoke and mirrors" tricks better than the mainstream corporate right-wing media. They are better at manipulating information to push forward their political agenda. Why would we want to play that game? Our true power is people's power, but that work is slow and does not necessarily catch the attention of the mainstream public and actually challenge the interests of those behind the funders.

When models focus on everyday activism, they have achieved a mass scale that can really push for change. Here in the United States, we are impressed if 100,000 people come to a march on Washington. In Chile, during the Socialist

Popular Unity government, you could expect to see a turnout of almost a million people (out of a population of about 10 million), on a regular basis. At the last mass demonstration a week before the military coup on September 11, 1973, the number reached a million people. If we were to have the same level of participation in the United States, that would be a protest of about 28 million people! This is exactly the kind of large-scale movement building we need to create in the United States. But if the revolution will not be funded, then we have to be ready to stop jet-setting to conferences on airplanes every few months or weeks, and stop staying in hotels and fancy retreat centers with "all you can eat" buffets. We would have to be prepared to do the hard work of long 20-plus hour bus rides, sleeping on the floor in communal halls, and peeling 50 onions to cook one meal. Yet the non-profit system clearly hinders us from building such movements. Through the non-profit industrial complex's institutionalization of our movements, people who are not "professionals" do not have equal access to organizing. Negotiating all these bureaucratic systems requires specialized skills that are unfamiliar to many of us. Rather than challenging state power, the non-profit model actually encourages activists to negotiate, even collaborate with the state—as those police permits for anti–police brutality marches illustrate.

I have known some widely respected organizers in Latin America who were part of land occupations and settlements involving thousands of people. Clearly, activists in the United States could learn so much from these movement builders, particularly those that are now in this country. Instead, their work and efforts have been marginalized because many are not fluent in English or formally educated; nor are they "executive directors" with professionalized organizer skills. Meanwhile, the NPIC has cultivated an "elite class" of non-profit managers skilled at fundraising and formally educated, but often not deeply connected to the communities they are working with, even as people of color. Many of these managers/directors know a lot less about political history, analysis, and movement building that some *autodidacta* (self-taught/organic) political organizers/intellectuals who don't stand a chance at getting a non-profit job.

But this critique of the NPIC is just the tip of the iceberg. Our analysis must examine how we have internalized these dominant ideas of how to live and organize as the only possible way. The most radical non-profit "staff collectives" that have formal hierarchies and titles just "to deal with the outside institutions" don't flinch at having the executive director make $40,000 a year and an organizer make $25,000. These are our deeper contradictions. Within Sista II Sista (SIIS), we tried to address these issues by having no titles of position and a flat salary for everyone, regardless of formal education or years of experience. We did not realize that this flat structure was not actually equitable because paying a single person with no dependents, like myself, the same as a single mother made no sense at all. But even after stripping away the corporate non-profit model at SIIS, we did not realize how much we had internalized capitalism, not knowing how to address the new reality that one ex–staff member was going to work making $8 an hour at a store while another was making $30 an hour as a consultant. We never pushed ourselves to collectivize our income and truly break from the cop in our heads. But trying, risking, and creating new ways of existing and living outside the NPIC is one possible step. Another is to keep looking to our imagination while embracing the inspirational stories of others living their future in the present.

new relationships with non-profits

While it is important to be critical of the non-profit system, we do not necessarily need to get rid of it all together. Revolutionary movements around the world use non-profits (NGOs) as well, but they have a different relationship with them. In the United States, many are attempting to do organizing work *through* non-profits. In other places, the movement building happens outside non-profits. However, these groups will sometimes start an NGO that serves a strategic purpose (such as providing technical assistance), but the non-profit does not have power to determine the movement's direction. Rather it is accountable to the movement.

For instance, the MST works with some NGOs that provide technical assistance for agronomy, sustainable development, and organic agriculture. The Zapatistas worked with an NGO to produce a video documentation project that would train Zapatista community members to document their work as well as abuses from the state. After ten years, each region will have its own video documentation center, and that non-profit will dissolve. The Zapatistas have also partnered with an NGO to help communities create their own education systems. Once this task is accomplished, that non-profit must leave the autonomous territory. Other revolutionary movements in Central America started NGOs as fronts to provide a public face and help advocate for the human rights of its members. However, in all these cases, the membership base does not come from the non-profit. Thus if an NGO loses funding, it does not impact the movement. Nowhere do those non-profits have files of the movement's membership; it is completely separate from the non-profits. NGO "professionals" bring tools and skills but have no decision-making power at all. In many cases (when the NGO is not a front for the political organization), the non-profit workers, though they may work very closely with these movements, are not considered members of these movements—they are supporters or allies and see themselves as such.

In the current US context, it's clear we still have a lot of work to do. I would argue that we need to do more organizing and base building that works outside the non-profit system. Non-profits then could participate in structured relationships of accountability created by the movement and support the work without co-opting the movement itself. The work that is now publicly visible in Latin America did not happen overnight but was the result of much trial and error and invisible work that laid the base for a powerful movement. If we want to build powerful movements here, we need a spectrum of approaches and we need to figure out ways to organize without paid staff and without funding. We need to take risks, and then compare strategies. In addition, we need to think of strategic ways to involve people of all sectors in the movement—be they unwaged mothers, non-profit workers, teachers, or grocery store workers. We need to answer the question of how to strategically involve not just traditional political sectors to effect mass social change.

the cop in the heart—internalized patriarchy

These reflections, lessons, and revolutionary guiding principles are particularly helpful for those of us who are organizing at the crossroads of oppression (on the basis of class, gender, race, sexuality, and so on). Prior to the collapse of the Soviet Union, there were many national revolutionary struggles that did achieve real change in their respective countries. However, these movements generally focused only on overthrowing capitalism and did not address the intersections of capitalism with patriarchy, racism, and other forms of oppression. Class was identified in the classic Marxist analysis as the "primary" contradiction. By the early 1970s, organizers began critiquing this model for marginalizing women, indigenous peoples, and other people from "ethnic minorities." In addition, these older models conceptualized the struggle as happening only at the level of institutional change, either armed or traditional electoral political struggles. Struggle was not something one could participate in through one's everyday life. Rather, true revolutionaries were supposed to leave their home, go to the mountains to be trained to join armed struggle, or work grueling political election campaigns for months away from home and family. This mode of organizing was based on a macho revolutionary standard of struggle in which commitment is measured by how "tough" you are, how much you can sacrifice family and love in order to focus on the revolutionary process. Mostly, this resulted in women being left behind to raise children on their own, many times not knowing if their partners had been murdered or if they had chosen new intimate relationships. Some women were also integrated into these struggles, but only if they "dressed like men," acted in cold blood, left their children and families for years at a time, and followed the order of command and obey.

As economic, military, and ecological devastation continues, to make life in our world ever more violent and dehumanized, there is a clear need to step up our commitment and militancy. But we must be careful not to equate patriarchal, hierarchical militarism with militancy. Some US-based organizers, including feminists of color, seem to romanticize this "old-school" revolutionary model, equating militaristic talk and dress, top-down chains of command, "tight security," long hours at meetings every night, and personal-life sacrifice with being truly revolutionary. This is ironic because many women's groups and queer folks, and ex-cadres and some comandantes of the revolutionary Left in Latin America have spent the past 15 years critiquing the inherently patriarchal, hierarchical, dehumanizing basis of these models of organizing.

But today it still plays out in strange ways. For example, in 2004, SIIS was part of a citywide coalition that coordinated well-organized community contingents for a series of marches against the Republican National Convention (RNC). This coalition was committed to the important work of keeping our people safe and security was stepped up. But somehow this also manifested as security marshals barking orders at people to get in single file without explanations, and as loud and hard commands to the young people holding the banner to "Hold Up the Banner!" whenever they lowered it from being tired. Security persons were not to socially interact with marchers, and talking and smiling were not allowed. When SIIS shared in the debrief session our concerns about what we felt were patriarchal practices and unnecessary levels of hierarchy, others looked at us with blank faces; most of them were other women of color.

This story is not *at all* meant to disrespect those organizers. Rather, it is an opportunity to think about how deeply we have internalized patriarchal dominance, even as women and queer folks. Our critique did not fully register with some people present at that meeting, in large part because we did not know how to clearly and compassionately articulate it, as we were trying to figure it out for the first time. It was only the next year, when a few of us were visiting with the Argentinean autonomous MTD Solano movement, that we learned much from listening to their reflections of how important it is that "security" people at the roadblocks not have any power over others. The political intentionality they put toward not re-creating policing relations between people was eye-opening, especially considering the high-risk conditions of their struggles— people in the past had lost their lives. Learning from these practices and comparing them to our relatively small and peaceful RNC protests was an important lesson.

Many powerful voices have spoken of these conflicts and contradictions of the revolutionary Left. One example comes from the 1979 film by Pastor Vega, *Retrato de Teresa* (Portrait of Teresa), which documents how many women in postrevolutionary Cuba did not end up with easier lives, but, rather, with a triple workload: the work of earning a living, the work of participating in revolutionary politics/culture, and the work of taking care of children and the home. Similarly, Lorena Pena, better known as Comandante Rebeca of the FPL (Fuerzas

Populares de Liberación) in El Salvador, has pointed to her organization's lack of understanding of the extra burdens carried by the women and mothers who are militants and combatants. She shares her own experience of having had to part with her 8-month-old child in order to fulfill her responsibilities as a clandestine organizer working in the *tugurios* (shantytowns): "Separating from a child is like having your arm amputated. I cannot explain the sensation even physically that one feels....I remember that to give myself strength I even read some writings of Lenin aimed at women where he speaks of motherhood in the historical-social sense."[14] Rebeca also critiques her organization's policies toward women combatants who become pregnant; they are subsequently demoted regardless of their technical and political skill level. While she recognizes the need for pregnant women to take on a role with less physical strain, she argues that this should not mean being placed in roles of less political value and recognition within the organization. These experiences eventually led Rebeca to help create the *movimiento de mujeres* (women's movement) Melida Anaya Montes, which began within the FPL and later became an autonomous organization in order to more powerfully challenge the patriarchal, discriminatory practices and culture of political organizations in El Salvador.

One of the most confrontational and beautiful voices belongs to Pedro Lemebel, a gay communist from Chile. In his poem "Punto de Vista Diferente" (A different point of view), Lemebel directly addresses—and critiques—the "revolutionary" Left parties of Latin America with a radical vision of his own.

> But don't talk to me about the proletariat
> Because being poor and gay is worse...
> What will you do with us "compañeros"?
> Will you tie us up by our braids
> Destined for a Cuban "sidario"[15]
> Will you put us on a train to nowhere...
> Are you afraid of the homosexualization of life?
> And I'm not talking about sticking it in and pulling it out
> I'm talking about tenderness "compañero"...
> I'm not going to change for Marxism
> That rejected me so many times
> I don't need to change, I'm more subversive than you.

Still active in the autonomous Chilean Left, Lemebel has found a way as a writer and radio/television personality to make his experience and politics accessible to ordinary Chileans, including older working-class women like his mother and my grandmother. He speaks of everyday struggles of everyday folks as political, reaching many more people than the official Left parties ever could. Like Lemebel, many activists realize that this hierarchical and male-dominated model of being a revolutionary ultimately fails to address the concrete experiences of oppression in everyday life. Committed to building movements that are sustainable in the long term, increasingly activists are focused on creating struggle within the context of one's life. The battleground of the struggle is in how we live, how we survive, and how we sustain our lives. Instead of bringing people to a political world, argues Gerardo Rénique, this model grounds the political in everyday life:

> Confronted by the retrenchment of the state from its most basic social duties, many popular movements organize to address such aspects of everyday life as housing, nutrition, childcare, education, and productive work. One thinks here of the communal kitchens in Peru, squatter organizations in Uruguay, cooperatives of unemployed workers in Argentina, landless peasants in Brasil, and the autonomous municipalities and Juntas de Buen Gobierno (good government councils) in the territories in Mexico controlled by the EZLN. Driven by principles of solidarity, self-respect, collective participation, and communal interest, these popular institutions constitute a powerful challenge to the individualism, self-interest, and exclusion that are the core values of neoliberalism.[16]

In these new movements, much of the political work happens close to home. It's not that mass demonstrations are no longer considered useful. But there is a growing understanding that such tactics, once required on a regular basis to demonstrate your political commitment, are largely, if not entirely, alien to the reality of most people's lives, especially poor people struggling just to survive. When collectively reimagined by movement members, however, mass demonstrations can take on a new and differently gendered character. For the Zapatistas, as Javier Elorriaga, one of the EZLN's main public figures explains,

> it's necessary to build from below, to be constantly consulting; to be looking for new forms of participation, for those who have time [to] participate and those who don't have time; the woman who has children and has, in addition, another job and comes home to feed them; even the mother who can't attend the assemblies, that she, too, have the possibility to participate politically. And all of this on the margins of power.[17]

In other words: What if, as a tired, overworked, and underpaid or unpaid woman I do not have to add going to this march to my list of things to do? What if, instead, I could integrate my political participation into my daily life? What if there were a "space" where I could build and learn politically with others, a space I could go to that was part of how I take care of myself and others? Here again, the Zapatistas' caracoles offer us another visionary model that extends beyond mere protest or demonstration to a long-term and integrative approach to resistance.

It has taken me a long time to truly understand how to apply this theory to my lived experience as a social justice activist. Until recently, I was a full-time organizer type, single with no dependents, who received a paycheck from a non-profit for part-time work (while also teaching self-defense part-time). That non-profit is Sista II Sista, an organization I've been a part of for ten years. For almost the first four years of its life, SIIS was run as a volunteer collective; this all changed in 2000, when we incorporated as a non-profit with paid staff and foundation funders.[18] Ultimately, financial crisis, as well as the reflections of paid and unpaid collective members, led us to decide to return to our roots as a volunteer grassroots organization. This difficult transition, in addition to my becoming a first-time mother, showed me how challenging yet important it is to participate politically. In my view, living a full, difficult, and complicated life, like all the folks we are organizing with, while also being a caretaker for an individual and/ or a volunteer for an organization is *the* political task at hand.

If our commitment to organizing is to build with those who are most marginalized, if we want to prioritize poor and working-class women of color in the US, most of whom are responsible for the care and survival of children and/or other family members, then it is essential that we look for alternative models to movement building. We must also recognize another major challenge observed from outside the US: the dismantling of "community," social connections, and relationships of solidarity and love. If we are faced with these conditions, it seems crucial that we try forms of organizing that center the daily experiences of those caught in the crossfire of all forms of oppression. From Latin America, we can draw from the examples of the gigantic efforts for daily survival by the oppressed, an effort that involves strengthening the communitarian spaces and ties they are constructing and re-creating every day. It is not enough to center poor and working-class women and queer folks of color's experiences in our organizing if the mode of organizing is still very similar to male-dominated labor or US-style community organizing. In this model, only those who have the privilege and/or obligation of being full-time organizers—because they are single without dependents, or fathers who do very little parenting, or people who can afford to pay others to do the caretaking of their families—can actively participate, let alone lead our movements. Ultimately, political involvement that comes at the expense of our relationships with loved ones and the larger community is not truly liberatory.[19]

As the material conditions worsen in the US, it is ever more clear that many people's lives in this country are becoming as precarious as those of the peoples of the Global South, as we have seen with the impact of Hurricane Katrina on the Gulf Coast. Especially during these times, I encourage US activists to keep thinking outside the non-profit box and learn from movements, both past and present, wherever they may be, that have been able to achieve much more by working outside this narrow, even compromising structure. While the contexts are not the same, the principles of the movements in Latin America and elsewhere can help inform our organizing work here. Because they come from people who are not living in the "brain of the monster," the US empire, they can help us identify the cops in our heads and hearts, release us from the US-centric tunnel vision, and expand our dreams of possibility.

acknowledgments

As this is the first time that I have written an article alone (not as a collective process), I feel it is my responsibility to include some of the names of those with whom I have developed these reflections in practice over the last ten years in New York City. The collectives of Sista II Sista, Pachamama, Community Birthing Project, Sisterfire, Center for Immigrant Families, NYC Childcare Collective, Sistas on the Rise, Harm Free Zone, Refugio, INCITE! and Lola's informal childcare crew have been working hard to embody and support these alternative revolutionary visions. Along with all those amazing compañer@s, I have had the incredibly valuable experience of being able to learn, organize, cry, and struggle closely with Nicole, Adjoa, and Ije, powerful mothers or caretakers of family. All of these folks along with my closest *familia,* my mother, Ximena, my grandmother Dolores, my mentor Eugenia, as well as my compañero Eric and my daughter, Xue-Li Dolores, have lovingly taught me more than I could have learned in ten more years of radical organizing as a single "organizer" with no dependents.

notes

The term "cop in the head" comes from an acting exercise in Theatre of the Oppressed to identify the dominant social ideology that becomes internalized through a complex series of cultural, political, historical, and economic processes. Theatre of the Oppressed is a methodology created by Brasilian theater director and activist Augusto Boal in the 1970s.

1 *Compañer@s* or *compas* are warmer terms for the English equivalent, *comrades;* rather than using the letter *a* or *o* to designate a gender, as traditionally required by Spanish grammar, some activists and writers use the @ symbol to make the term both feminine and masculine.

2 Gerardo Rénique, "Introduction, Latin America Today: The Revolt Against Neoliberalism," *Socialism and Democracy* 19, no. 3 (November 2005): 1.

3 Raul Zibechi, "Subterranean Echos: Resistance and Politics 'desde el Sotano,'" *Socialism and Democracy* 19, no. 3 (November 2005): 30.

4 Marta Harnecker, introduction to *America Latina la Izquierda después de Seattle,* by Rodrigo Ruiz (Santiago, Chile: Surda Ediciones, 2002), 10. My translation.

5 Pablo Gonzalez Casanova, "The Zapatista Caracoles: Networks of Resistance and Autonomy," *Socialism and Democracy,* 19, no. 3 (November 2005): 81–82.

6 Zibechi, "Subterranean Echos, 19.

7 Ibid., 18.

8 Casanova, "The Zapatista Caracoles," 79.

9 Peter Ranis, "Argentina's Worker Occupied Factories and Entreprises," *Socialism and Democracy* 19, no. 3 (November 2005): 97–98.

10 "Un Jardín Piquetero en la Matanza," *Página* 12 (May 2004). My translation.

11 In Bolivia, these sectors "were capable of mounting an insurrection without leadership or leaders....when workers formerly left the organization of their work to employers and the management of society to the state, they had to rely for their struggles on hierarchical and centralized structures, and depended on their leaders—union and political—to represent them and make decisions. The autonomy of such persons *vis-à-vis* capital runs in tandem with their autonomy *vis-à-vis* the state. In fact, the most important problems of their daily lives, from the construction and maintenance of their environment (dwelling, water, sewage, and streets) to essential aspects of education and health, have been taken in hand via an impressive network of basic organizations. In El Alto alone there are, according to different sources, between 400 and 550 neighborhood juntas, one for every 1,000 inhabitants over the age of 10." Zibechi, "Subterranean Echos,"23.

12 Zibechi, "Subterranean Echos," 31.

13 Joao Pedro Stedile, *Brava Gente* (Buenos Aires, Argentina: Ediciones Barbarroja, 2000), 42. My translation.

14 Marta Harnecker, *Retos de la Mujer Dirigente* 2 [includes an interview with Comandante Rebeca] (Havana, Cuba: Colección Letra Viva, MEPLA, 1993), 2.

15 *Sidario* is a Cuban quarantine for people living with HIV.

16 Rénique, "Introduction, Latin America Today," 1.

17 Javier Elorriaga, interview, *Viento Sur* 35 (December 1997): 24. My translation.

18 For a fuller history of SIIS's journey through the non-profit system and beyond, see "On Our Own Terms: Ten Years of Radical Community Building With Sista II Sista," which appears in this volume.

19 One project I am currently involved in was inspired by *colectivos de mujeres* (women's collectives) from different Latin American movements, such as the Sandinista struggle in Nicaragua. Prior to the revolution, much work was done through day care centers clandestinely developed by the Sandinistas. No one realized they were revolutionary institutions that provided women and children with an opportunity in their everyday lives to meet for political education, organizing, and mobilizing. We are currently developing a childcare cooperative in Brooklyn, Pachamama, that is attempting to be financially self-sustaining through barter and sliding-scale fees. We opened our first Pachamama cooperative in April 2005 and it has inspired some of the members to break off and begin a separate similar cooperative, Little Maroons, launched in September 2005. We are also connecting with two other working-class women-of-color groups interested in starting similar projects. In our vision these spaces can become a base for doing grassroots political education and organizing work that fits in with the lives of poor women of color in Brooklyn. Is this as a legitimate location from where to organize and participate in movement building? I hope so.

»Eric Tang

non-profits and the autonomous grassroots

ONCE UPON A TIME, THERE COULD BE NO NASTIER INDICTMENT than to be labeled an affiliate of the state. Yet today, some of the movement's best and brightest openly, even self-confidently, claim membership in organizations whose links to the state—through either public funding or through official registration with the government—are unambiguous and well documented. Indeed, there are an impressive number of radical-minded grassroots groups which, while continuing to sincerely abide by the ethos of "our movement," have assumed the form of a non-profit (NP) entity. At times NPs go by their other name, non-governmental organization (NGO)—a term more commonly used in the rest of the world, which ironically underscores its complementary relationship to government. Among grassroots organizers in the United States, there is yet another moniker: 501(c)(3). The grassroots parlance cuts straight to the chase, stripping the NP down to its most essential nature—that of an IRS tax category, an official registration with the US government that allows, among other privileges, the accreditation needed to receive government funding, as well as the majority of funds available through private philanthropic foundations. In exchange, the grassroots NP must adopt legally binding bylaws, form a board of directors modeled after the corporation, and make its board minutes and fiscal accounting accessible to the public. While these practices were once considered anathema to the grassroots Left, they are actually the long-standing rules which have governed many community organizations, particularly religious institutions and some labor unions.

fractured left

"We, the Left, have been described as being weak, fractured, disorganized. I attribute that to three things: COINTELPRO. 501(c)(3). Capitalism," deadpanned Suzanne Pharr, while speaking before an audience of 800 at the historic 2004 conference The Revolution Will Not Be Funded: Beyond the Non-Profit Industrial Complex. Few grassroots organizers can claim a body of work more impressive than that of Pharr. In addition to authoring a number of books, including *Homophobia: A Weapon of Sexism,* Pharr served as a founding member and director of the Arkansas Women's Project for 19 years, followed by her run as the director of the Highlander Research and Education Center for nearly a decade. During her days in Arkansas she participated in the internal struggles that eventually led the Women's Project, an anti–domestic violence organization, to adopt the NP model. After years of effectively organizing its grassroots core, the group had reached an impasse. If their movement to end violence against women was to have broader impact, then perhaps it needed to become palatable to an array of political forces outside the grassroots Left. Becoming an NP would represent one major step in that direction, facilitating the political goals of "credibility...the approval of churches, clubs, and even law enforcement."[1] At the time, it was unclear that the NP model would actually deliver on these goals. Even more uncertain was what it would take away.

Eventually, time would tell. Reflecting on the oversaturation of NP models within today's leftist struggles, Pharr noted, "I've seen the loss of political force and movement building." The most troubling aspect of these losses, however, is that they were not so much based on sharp differences on key political issues, but rather "the dreadful competition among organizations for little pots of money."

As I sat in the audience—which consisted mostly of 20-somethings who were perhaps too young to be familiar with organizational structures other than the NP (let alone the conference's playful shout to Gil Scott-Heron)—Pharr's words seemed to me something akin to tough love: Twenty years ago the Left made a decision to go down a certain road. Yeah, there were some small victories. But also a great number of casualties. When were we going to talk about what we had lost?

Open dialogues on the myriad challenges posed by the NP have repeatedly taken a back seat to the exigencies of simply "getting the work done"—as if the form and content of struggles could somehow be separated. The problem, having gone unchecked for so long, seems now to have metastasized. And those poised to inherit the ever-growing dilemma are a new generation of grassroots leaders.

heavy legacies

Those new to today's community, labor, and justice struggles are soon made aware that they bear heavy legacies. They carry forth movements that ended Jim Crow, that gave rise to the contemporary environmental justice movement, and that inspired the massive student and labor walkouts demanding an end to the US war in Vietnam. Chances are, through some political education course, the young organizer will come across a good read on César Chávez, Dolores Huerta, and the United Farm Workers (UFW). Eventually, she or he will learn that it was demanded of all UFW members—the majority of whom were earning the lowest of wages—to contribute regular membership dues. From the pages of history, the young organizer will hear Chávez insist, "This is the only way the workers will 'own' the organization." Inevitably, the young organizer takes a hard look at how his or her present-day organization does business and questions the deeper strength of an organization that depends on foundation grants for its survival, that hires a development director to raise funds so that others can turn their attention to the "real" work, and that adopts management systems which are foreign, if not alienating, to the values and skill-sets of the base. This self-inventory leads to even more questions:

▷ *"Why do we apply for a police permit to protest the police?"*
　　Because if we break the law, our board is liable.
▷ *"Why can't we lobby?"*
　　Because that would violate our 'c3 status and the conditions of our grant.
▷ *"Why not just take the streets?"*
　　Because insurance doesn't cover it.

non-profit blues

The NP is cast as the straw man against which a multitude of political frustrations can be vented. Indeed, the severe limitations (shackles?) placed on today's Left calls not only for defense against right-wing attack, but also for exorcising those untidy "internal contradictions." And here the NP serves as very effective foil, for few will deny the ways in which it keeps in check the Left's more radical impulses or even, at times, its basic common sense. While we have yet to precisely assess just how far and wide the "trouble with the NP" has spread throughout the Left, my own empirical survey, gleaned from the opportunity I have these days to meet and support numerous grassroots youth groups across the country, indicates that the NP poses as many challenges to organizing as it does solutions. Indeed, the majority of organizational leaders I've sat down with over the past year and a half—whose work ranges from defeating the onset of neoliberal policies in public schools to the ongoing struggle against police violence to defending the rights of immigrant communities—have experienced, to varying degrees, an onset of the NP blues. They are concerned about the ways in which the priorities of philanthropy tamper with the organizing work, or how NP governance makes impossible the principle of unity, which calls for youth and working-class people at the center, or worse, how hiring and promotion policies have led to competition and individualism among the ranks.

Still, despite the seeming ubiquity of the dilemma, a broad and consistent public discussion is absent. Each finds his or her own way to manage the contradictions. In my conversations with participants who attended the Revolution Will Not Be Funded conference, many lefties talked of participating in the NP as a tactic on the "down low," a temporary ride toward a more radical end. Yet candid discussions on just how long we ride this Trojan horse, or how far we've actually traveled, are few and far between. A related but more pragmatic view suggests that NPs provide the only spaces in Right-dominated times to do meaningful work. That's the "take the money and run" and "build what you can now" attitude, according to scholar-activist Ruthie Gilmore.[2] But here, too, there's a silence, as a deeper discussion is missing: What's our ultimate purpose? Where are we running to? For those who have steadfastly refused to go NP, they, too, maintain silence—for the most part. But at times their reticence comes off as gracious condescension: Let the wayward NP reformists and revisionists do their thing. Eventually they'll come 'round.

Perhaps it would be beneficial to examine the historical origin of this conflict, located at the dawn of the Reagan era in the early to mid-1980s. It was the moment in which several forces within the New Left decided to turn down the NP road. What were the internal conditions that led to that turn? At least three interrelated factors influenced this trend: deconsolidation of the party builders and the proliferation of new social movements (NSMs); baby boomers with loot; and the "legitimacy" question.

Deconsolidate and proliferate. Throughout much of the 1970s, there was a strong current within the New Left that sought to harness and consolidate the political energies of the late 1960s into a revolutionary party. The years 1965–1969 saw the rise of numerous liberation struggles led by groups such as the Black Panther Party (and the ensuing "Panther effect": Young Lords, I Wor Kuen, Brown Berets), as well as the more visibly fragmented women's and queer liberation movements (especially along lines of race and class), and, of course, the meteoric rise of the anti-war movement. Max Elbaum, an activist who has chronicled the New Communist Movement, describes the period as being one with "revolution in the air"—it was a feeling, a texture, of multiple resistances, each with its own brilliance and complexity.[3] By the 1970s, many of the self-identified revolutionary forces within this New Left turned their attention to party-building efforts aimed at consolidating the many movements in order to strike a unified revolutionary blow against the establishment. But for some, party building came at the cost of taking away valuable time and attention from community-based struggles. For others, it meant erasing or subordinating the particular character of race, gender, sexual, and class oppression for the sake of a "higher degree" of unity. And for others still, party building would mark the beginning of deep sectarian fighting between different cadres, not to mention the nasty conflicts and abuses of power within parties and revolutionary organizations.

The troubled efforts of the party builders paralleled the rise and proliferation of NSMs, led by those who had either departed from, resisted, or simply ignored the push to consolidate the revolutionary party, and instead continued to organize—on the ground, as it were—throughout the 70s. By the early 1980s, with many party-building efforts in decline, the NSMs continued to grow and proliferate, codifying their struggles under new banners. Among the more popular and lasting issue areas were environmental justice, racial justice, no nukes, housing organizing, youth development, and community economic development. These would, in turn, become the social justice silos that guided the funding strategies of philanthropic foundations.

Baby boomers with loot. Yet who are the people behind these foundations who donate a portion of their excesses to the grassroots? And since when do the wealthy give generously to progressive, let alone radical, causes? The New Left was one part of a broader countercultural movement whose core consisted largely of middle-class youth, along with a few children of the wealthy. By the 1980s, many of the baby boomers born to wealth were inheriting portions of their families' estate. Those still partially faithful to their movement values became reliable individual donors to NSM struggles close to their hearts. And those with *serious* loot established "family foundations"—non-profit institutions that do the work of finding and funding innovative projects. Because the vast majority of these foundations can only give grants to groups with NP status, the past 20 years has seen the rapid proliferation of non-profits among politically progressive to radical sectors. Between 1975 and 1988 the total number of philanthropic foundations in the United States grew from 21,887 to 30,388. By 2000, that number had jumped to 56,582.[4] Many of these were family foundations, signaling a new, albeit small and selective, funding source for the grassroots. This was a much-needed respite for community-based struggles weathering the cutbacks to federally funded antipoverty programs that were originally designed under the Kennedy-Johnson "Great Society" era before being cut down by Reagan.

Legitimacy. During this same period, many activists on the Left began to insist that in order to have impact, the movement needed to take on the sharper image. It needed to get with the times (or the *Times*) and make an impression on institutional power, as opposed to being its incessant pain in the ass. Instead of "mau-mauing" the suits for big promises that amounted to mere bread crumbs, it was suggested that the Left try donning a suit and grabbing a seat at the table to win big. The penultimate examples of this are the former New Lefties who ran for political office during the 1980s and 90s, deciding to work with, instead of against, the Democratic Party. For others, the mission was to start influential non-profit organizations that could press for the incremental gains that would perhaps lead, finally, to those Marxian qualitative leaps.

Of course, there were those who pleaded in vain with their erstwhile comrades not to go the route of "legitimacy"—to hold out just a little longer. For many of them the story abruptly ends here. Their generation simply "sold out," as the crabby expression goes, forever abandoning the good idea of revolution. But sell-out talk does little to guide us through our present-day dilemmas. In many ways, it's a lot like breakup talk—doing the work of suturing hurt feelings, adjudicating quick and easy verdicts, and, above all, obscuring complicated truths.

The "whole sellout theory crowds out the discussion of burn-out," remarks Makani Themba-Nixon, director of the Washington, DC–based Praxis Project.[5] In evoking the "burn-out," she's referring not only to those who failed to pace themselves and in the end ran out of gas, but also to those who, during their days in various revolutionary parties and collectives, were burned by internal political processes and abuses of institutional authority—either individual or collective—that resulted in many members wanting and needing alternative spaces to carry forth their work. According to Themba-Nixon, "Women in particular needed a way to [escape] from the sexism, the exploitation, the rough stuff" that would play out within self-identified revolutionary organizations. At times, these heretofore internal matters were "more the issue behind people leaving than the external politics" of any given group. The emergence of the NP therefore provided the opportunity to continue to "do smart work, practical work, in a way that allowed you to survive. This was especially important after witnessing those who did not survive."

Themba-Nixon offers a crucial rebuttal to those who would reduce the "NP-turn" to the defeatist attitude of a generation that had grown politically soft. Moreover, for those whose frustration with the NP has now reached its limit, prompting the call for the Left's full retreat from this particular industrial complex—something like a moratorium on NPs—her reflections on recent history caution us that the matter is far more complicated. After all, what would today's Left look like had its grassroots never adopted the NP structure, staying faithful to a purist notion of organizational forms unmediated by the government or philanthropic sectors—those lauded for being entirely "by, of, and for the people"? Would it be inoculated from the sharp power imbalances (typified by white, male, heterosexual, and middle-class leadership), competitiveness, and even the internal exploitation of members that is so often the basis criticism against overly professionalized NPs? A dubious claim, at best. One could even infer that it is precisely the New Left's failure to implement and sustain these antihierarchal principles, to care for the long-term development and health of all its members, to promote a movement culture wherein folks from many walks of life could contribute in a variety of ways, that led to the sweeping NP phenomena we're seeing today.

civil society on the horizon

These days, there's a small movement storm brewing in Atlanta, Georgia. From June 27 through July 1, 2007, the city will play host to the first United States Social Forum (USSF), a gathering projected at 20,000 participants from a wide cross-section of the grassroots: labor, environmental justice, immigrant rights, racial justice, anti-war, youth and student, women, queer, and international solidarity, to name but a few. Although the USSF will not take up resolving the NP dilemma as a stated objective or "thematic area" (so far the issue has not surfaced in its initial planning), it may nonetheless shed some much-needed light on the matter. By bringing together the heart and soul of the grassroots Left, the event will explore the promise of its future movements and, consequently, the many obstacles and contradictions that stand in the way of fulfilling that promise. What organizational forms the movement chooses, how it ultimately proposes to structure itself, seems an unavoidable issue. Moreover, there is an ever-advancing global phenomenon propelling this discussion.

The USSF is an official regional forum of the World Social Forum (WSF) which, for the past six years, has coalesced social movements from around the world to discuss an array of locally derived "global strategies" to defeat the agendas of world trade, war, and the new imperialism. The groups that compose this new global movement are not political parties or government representatives of left-leaning nation-states. Rather, they consider themselves part of a new "civil society"—an array of locally based struggles and supporting NGOs that seek varying degrees of political autonomy from the nation-state, the freeing of indigenous lands, and the end to territorial domination by transnational corporations.

On January 1, 1994, the world caught a glimpse of this new civil society in action, as a relatively small band of indigenous Mayan freedom fighters from the state of Chiapas, Mexico, led the once-improbable people's uprising against globalization. Over the next decade, the struggle of the Zapatistas would introduce millions to the notion of a "fourth world war" being waged against the world's poorest communities by the global corporate elite. For example, neoliberal policies such as the North American Free Trade Agreement (NAFTA) have enabled transnational corporations to steal indigenous land and labor, forcing (often at gunpoint) subsistence-based agrarian communities into market-system dependence, largely through the privatization (i.e., theft) of natural resources. Moreover, the Zapatistas would advance the idea that those who were to defend the people in this new war were not the national liberation armies of old—those for whom the goal was to capture state power—but rather a new Mexican civil society comprised of indigenous social movements completely independent of the public and private sectors, as well as non-indigenous Mexican civilian groups who saw their own futures inextricably linked to that of the indigenous struggle against neoliberalism. Among these groups are Mexican NGOs who support the work of these movements in a variety of ways.

No sooner had the Zapatista Army of National Liberation (EZLN) seized several cities in Chiapas during its New Year's Day offensive, than it deferred the position of revolutionary vanguard to civil society. The revolution would not be about a military campaign to capture the nation-state town by town, region by region. Rather it would be a chain of communities across which the notion of civilian autonomy in the face of neoliberalism would spread like wildfire: each community would, through locally derived efforts, resist the conquering of their land. In the words of the Zapatistas, "Indigenize the nation, indigenize the world."

complementary roles

Under the auspices of Mexican civil society, the autonomous social movement and the institutionalized NGO strive for balance—each understands the specific and complementary role it plays in articulating the new social formation. The former shapes the ethos of the struggle, does the work of locating power among those most afflicted by the onset of neoliberalism. The latter, on the other hand, understands that it is not the subject of the social movement for autonomy, but rather the political and technical support for it. From its specific location, the NGO leverages funds to the autonomous movements, helps the movement build connections to those beyond the borders of the nation-state, provides training, education, and infrastructural support—the development of health clinics, schools, alternative media centers—and, at times, serves as liaison between government officials and the autonomous movements.

Yet, before we take heart that the new paradigm of civil society and its WSF provide a solution for our generation, it is worth noting that, here too, contradictions abound. The WSF has been criticized for being overrun by NGOs—most of whom can afford to send large delegations by plane—while the members of their nation's autonomous movements have less access, often arriving to the forum after weeks of traveling over rough terrain. Many have trouble affording the costs of the WSF upon arrival. What's more, the balance of civil society illustrated by the Zapatista's vision for Mexico is not usually the case in many a Global South country, nor is it without contention in Mexico itself. There are indeed NGOs throughout Latin America, Asia, and Africa that have come under fire for at times tipping the balance and eclipsing the autonomous movements. Writer-activist Arundhati Roy, for example, has been a particularly harsh critic of NGOs operating in India, noting the ways in which they often serve neoliberalism's drive toward expropriating land and privatizing national industries in the name of development. At the same time, Roy, though known internationally for her literary achievements, became something of a global movement icon herself when, during the 2003 WSF, she delivered one of the most passionate and memorable speeches the international Left had heard in quite some time.[6]

However, for the US Left, adopting the concept of civil society—wherein the NPs play a specific and complementary role in relation to the autonomous grassroots—may prove valuable to those attempting to navigate their way through today's movement-building dilemmas. Take a moment to imagine yourself, 20 years ago, in a room full of US leftists discussing strategies for moving forward in a country drifting ever rightward. Few of you would conjure the image of lefties sitting around the table, envisaging a vast army of NPs leading the people's revolution. To be sure, the Left's present oversubscription to the NP was never the intended course. Yet today, US-based NPs find themselves awkwardly at the movement's center. There is little to distinguish between autonomous grassroots and the NP. To illustrate the point, if one today were to conduct a peer-to-peer exchange between a US-based grassroots organization and, say, members of Brasil's landless movement, chances are the US representative would belong to the NP group. Here, the goal of striking a balance—of arriving at clear roles to be played by autonomous movements and NGOs, respectively—is an impossibility because the border between the categories has been blurred to the point of irrelevance.

"We never had the 501(c)(3) from the beginning," says Jerome Scott, as he reflects on his organization's 20-year history.[7] The organization is Project South[8] based in Atlanta, and it will play the role of anchor organization for the USSF. An autoworker and shop floor organizer from Detroit, Scott once participated in the famous wildcat strikes of 1973, led in part by the League of Revolutionary Black Workers. In the late 1970s, he relocated to the Southeast, where things were a bit "more raw."

By the early 1980s, the Southeast was experiencing major political backlash against the gains of the civil rights movement. Scott, along with several comrades from Detroit who had also made their way down South, began organizing campaigns to bring attention to the profound poverty, unemployment, and racism that characterized the post–civil rights era. The founding of Project South can be viewed as the continuation of Scott and his comrades' efforts back in Detroit to build independent movements.

During the first ten years of its existence, Project South was not a NP, nor did it receive significant grants from foundations or individual donors. The work was carried out by a collective of volunteer activists, organizers, and visionaries. It was only in 1995, long after the organization had been on the radar of many progressive philanthropy groups eager to fund it, that Project South decided to incorporate as an NP. According to Scott, this decision represented not so much a political shift within the organization but rather exemplified how an organization may respond to, if not capitalize upon, significant shifts within the broader political culture. By the mid-1990s, with the conservative movement in full swing, the attack on "big government" had made a real impact. With less public funds available to support even the most modest programs aimed at social equity, the realm of progressive, private philanthropy expanded. As such, it comes as little surprise that some private foundations sought to support the vision and work of Project South. The challenge for the organization, according to Scott, was in how to become a 501(c)(3) without "losing sight of the mission." "By taking the 501(c)(3) status, we could not be deterred from our vision and how we do our work," Scott said. "We made a conscious decision to keep on doing the work in the way we believe it needs to happen. If this means that we're not following the 501(c)(3) rules, well then they can just come right over and take our status away from us."

Today, despite maintaining a staff of six, a large office within a community space, and the support of several foundations, Project South likes to think of itself as operating outside the NP box. Flying in the face of traditional NP policies and practices, it insists on salary parity for all staff, regardless of work experience; in its public materials the organization boldly (though without bombast) describes the situation facing southern Blacks as a "genocide" while most other NPs would choose the more acceptable if not cautious "structural inequality"; and it feels emboldened to engage in a range of political tactics, some of which are strictly forbidden for 501(c)(3) organizations (e.g., lobbying). Yet for all its unorthodoxies, Project South harbors no illusions of itself as some kind of rarefied movement vehicle—the autonomous grassroots in NP drag. "The 501(c)(3) is not a movement and cannot make the movement," Scott observed. And here, he includes Project South in this crowded field of 501(c)(3)s. When asked where, then, he believes this movement actually resides, Scott offers that it's in a "low stage of development," it's unformed and inarticulate, thus allowing for the seeming dominance of the NPs. "But things are stirring," he adds.

For Scott, the hope is that other forms of autonomous struggle, independent of NPs, will continue to grow and push forward. The role of Project South and other NP institutions would therefore become complementary, supplemental, or supportive to the movement—one of several means of tilting the broader political spectrum toward liberation politics.

In conclusion, perhaps a worthy goal for today's movement-oriented NPs is to somehow self-correct the stark imbalance that presently exists between 501(c)(3)s and the autonomous grassroots, to do the work of ensuring that autonomous struggles become not only visible but the generative force behind a future movement that will bring about tremendous change. There's an ontological question embedded here: Can the NP give life to that which is a precondition of its own existence? The NP can clear a path for revolutionary change by dismantling the policies and practices that prevent autonomous movements taking hold in the US—from the electoral college, to the denial of proportional representation, to the collapse of the social welfare state, to the rollback on civil rights. So too, it can do the work of coalescing grassroots forces at opportune times, a prime example being the US Social Forum. And at the very least it can challenge the Left's discernable shift toward purely elitist strategies—pushing legislative policy, gaining elections in swing states, winning over the commercial media—practices which eclipse the mass strategy of gradually building the base of opposition over time, of truly investing in "change from below."

No, the revolution will not be funded. We would need to find it first.

acknowledgments

A version of this chapter first appeared as a feature-length article in *Left Turn*, no. 18 (Fall 2005). It is reprinted here with the permission of the author and *Left Turn*.

notes

1 Suzanne Pharr (plenary session, The Revolution Will Not Be Funded: Beyond the Non-Profit Industrial Complex, INCITE! Women of Color Against Violence conference, Santa Barbara, CA, spring 2004).

2 Ruth Wilson Gilmore (plenary session, The Revolution Will Not Be Funded conference, see note 1).

3 Max Elbaum, *Revolution in the Air: Sixties Radicals Turn to Lenin, Mao, and Che* (New York and London: Verso, 2002).

4 These statistics are gleaned from the Foundation Center, *Foundation Yearbook: Facts and Figures on Private and Community Foundations* (New York: The Foundation Center, 2004).

5 Makani Themba-Nixon, interview by Eric Tang, August 15, 2005.

6 Arundhati Roy, "Confronting Empire" (speech, World Social Forum, Porto Alegre, Brasil, January 27, 2003). Reprinted in Arundhati Roy, *War Talk* (Cambridge, MA: South End Press, 2003), 103–112.

7 Jerome Scott, interview by Eric Tang, August 20, 2005 (subsequent quotes are also from this interview).

8 For more information about Project South, see their essay "Fundraising Is Not a Dirty Word," which appears in this volume.

>>Nicole Burrowes, Morgan Cousins, Paula X. Rojas, & Ije Ude

on our own terms

Ten Years of Radical Community Building With Sista II Sista

TEN YEARS AGO, A GROUP OF SISTAS AT A LOCAL GATHERING GAVE birth to an idea that would become Sista II Sista (SIIS). Inspired by a conversation about what they felt was missing from the workshops and panels presented, this group of young women in their 20s committed to addressing these and other silences. They envisioned a space for younger women of color that would speak to their complex identities, nourish their holistic development, and be responsive to their needs. Ultimately, this space would support sistas in their efforts to challenge the larger societal structures imposing on their daily lives. This essay is a reflection both of our current vision and some of what we've come to learn along the way about building collective power and justice for our sistas.

vision

Based in the Bushwick section of Brooklyn, New York, SIIS supports young women to develop their personal and collective power. We began as a grassroots, all-volunteer organization in 1996 and remained so until 1999, when we formally incorporated as a non-profit and received our first foundation grant. In our first few years, SIIS's primary program was our Freedom Schools for Young Women of Color. This comprehensive series of workshops and classes reflected our commitment to the holistic development of young women and included popular education workshops on oppression and b-girl dancing. With our first foundation grant, SIIS rented our own space and hired part-time staff to coordinate our programs and collective tasks.

Our work with young women of color is rooted in the principle of self-determination—the idea that all groups are able to identify and work toward solving their own problems. With this liberatory principle as our starting point, SIIS has created an organization in which young women of color take leadership in transforming themselves and their communities. In line with our commitment to modeling our vision for the world we are fighting for, we have a flat, nonhierarchical collective structure that recognizes the value each individual brings to the organization.

Another principle that guides our work is the intersectionality of oppression that young and adult women of color confront. Poor and working-class young women of color face a braid of oppression composed of various strands—racism, sexism, capitalism, ageism, and more—which presents them with multiple and unique challenges. While we have learned from Marxist critiques of capitalism, we don't see class as the only form of oppression or location from where to resist. We choose to work from the braid of oppression because it makes our analyses and strategies stronger; after all, a braid is harder to cut then its individual strands. When we are able the hold the complexities of our identities and work to create justice, we ask ourselves harder questions and are forced to be more creative in our approaches toward the challenges we are facing.

Another aspect of our work that we stress is the personal as political, specifically the relationship between individual healing and larger community empowerment. Personal healing in isolation from a larger community cannot transform the world; neither can social action without personal and emotional development. We view internal transformation as being interconnected with social transformation; thus, creating spaces for emotional support should be viewed as political work. At SIIS, our work goes beyond political education workshops and attending marches. We often use street theater, block parties, videos, dance contests, and hip-hop culture—methods that help us to engage the community in deeper ways than traditional political work allows.

Because many of our members are immigrants or children of immigrants, we feel connected to current revolutionary struggles in Latin America, Africa, and the Caribbean. Living in "the belly of the beast," we recognize that our role is to learn from and support the leadership of women struggling in the Global South—women who are directly confronting the intersection of sexism and racism under capitalist imperialism. (One way we try to make these direct connections and express solidarity is through the exchange and sale of crafts by various women's collectives.) Through these liberation struggles we are reminded that power does not reside only in state institutions; it also resides in communities. Our struggles must go beyond merely seeking to hold those institutions accountable and instead seek to create alternatives and put into practice how we think our communities should address violence, childcare, health care, education, and other pressing social issues. These are the realizations that led us to develop Sistas Liberated Ground, which we will discuss in greater detail later.

foundations

Over the past few years, we have made some tough decisions at Sista II Sista. One of our major decisions was to stop pursuing foundation grants. After 9/11, foundations rapidly started moving in more conservative directions, reflecting the larger national climate. We were doing anti-war and anti–police brutality work, and some foundations found that distasteful in this new political climate. SIIS had been the "flavor of the month" among the foundations, and that time was coming to an end. In the beginning, we were the "new kids on the block" with ideas and approaches that very few other organizations were using. Some foundations even pursued us and "strongly encouraged" us to apply for monies. As the political climate grew more overtly oppressive, our new and innovative ideas came to be seen as threatening and "unfundable."

It was around this time that we started working on Sistas Liberated Ground, a project aimed at creating violence-free zones for women in our community. We wanted the community to stand up against violence as a long-term solution because our dependence on a police system that was inherently sexist, homophobic, racist, and classist did not decrease the ongoing violence against women we were seeing in our neighborhoods. In fact, at times the police themselves were its main perpetrators. While some foundations continued to support us and saw our work as groundbreaking, many did not perceive our work as organizing because we weren't "targeting an institution." Other foundations that funded our Freedom School program found out about the organizing work and would accuse us of "brainwashing little girls." It was one thing for them to support the holistic development and empowerment of young women and quite another when they realized these young women were collectively taking action to challenge the police and other oppressive figures in their lives and community.

Simultaneously, we started feeling ever more constrained by the amount of grant writing, administration, site visits, and reports required by our dependence on foundation funding. We were drained by the rejections, the waiting, and the constant explanations of our work to people who just didn't get it, yet greatly influenced its direction. Our efforts to fit SIIS's work into quantitative outcomes began to drain our energy and morale, and before long, SIIS was transformed from a labor of love to a J-O-B. An impasse was coming.

To determine our next steps, we organized two caucuses: one with "young" women and one with "adult" women (over 21 years old). When the two groups reunited to share their findings, the adult women returned with heavy hearts and tired minds. They had not been able to come to a decision; more, several women had said that although they thought SIIS needed to exist, they couldn't devote much time to it. Even though we were just shy of our tenth birthday, closing was a very real possibility for us. Luckily, the young women presented the results of their discussion first. In their session, there had been no talk of closing SIIS. They talked about what they wanted to see: They wanted more members...a new building...more dancing...a video project...and more organizing campaigns. They wanted Sista II Sista products that we would make and sell to raise money. As for foundations—who was thinking about them?

new directions

After several meetings with SIIS membership, board members, the collective, and staff, we decided to take a leap of faith. We began asking ourselves some hard questions that stirred our minds and our spirits. What if we no longer had to raise $300,000 every year? What if our unrealistic timelines weren't based on promises made to foundations? What if SIIS was not a job, but a passion? How can we ask people who are struggling to survive to join this project in their very little free time, yet think we should get paid to do the work? Why are we building our memberships within structures based on the corporate non-profit model? What if we operated more like grassroots organizations in other countries? Hadn't the movement in the States been stifled by this 501(c)(3) structure? What percentage of our time was spent raising money and writing reports versus doing the work? What happened to our commitment to self-determination?

We felt blessed for several years to be able to receive money from foundations and feel somewhat autonomous. But we realized the revolution would not be funded. So we decided to take a risk and return to our roots—no more massive amounts of time doing foundation fundraising and no more full-time staff. We would return to being a volunteer collective and operate mainly through grassroots fundraising and the support of those who believed in our mission and work.

At SIIS we always ask ourselves: Where are we as a people's social justice movement in the US today? Somehow many of us got sucked in by the notion that the most effective way to build a base for political education and community organizing is by creating non-profit organizations. Part of the problem with this is that it wasn't necessarily a strategic decision, but more just "the way that most people do it." For us at SIIS, finally questioning these ideas came in part through our holistic approach, the cultural work we do, and our connections as immigrants to our extended families and communities, where no one has ever been paid to care for each other and create justice in our world.

a global perspective

In recent decades, the concept of social justice organizing has undergone tremendous change. Today, foundations and nongovernmental organizations (NGOs) are taking over movements in many Third World countries just as they did in the US in the 1960s. In both cases, increased state and foundation involvement—and control—has actually weakened revolutionary social movements. For example, in the late 1960s and early 70s thousands of poor Chileans engaged in organized takeovers of rural and suburban land and factories. Today there are NGOs in those same communities working toward more reformist policies, urging the community to adopt less militant tactics. At one point, it was not uncommon for community leaders with little or no formal education to coordinate huge popular demonstrations; today, leadership is often restricted to paid professional sociologists running NGO-driven projects "in service of" a community to which they often have little or no relationship.

This important critique notwithstanding, SIIS does not intend to oversimplify this often complicated dynamic. Truth be told, the relationships between NGOs and the communities in which they work are not always negative; nor do they all work in the same way. Some are strategically linked, and even directed by the revolutionary movements themselves. Others serve as a mechanism through which resources may be funneled to autonomous organizations of tens of thousands. For example, the Landless People's Movement (LPM) in South Africa has strategically partnered with NGOs working on labor, tenant, and land rights both locally as well as internationally. Both the Zapatistas in Chiapas, Mexico, and the MST (Landless Rural Unemployed Workers Movement) in Brasil have relationships with NGOs. And while many of these NGOs were started at the request of the movements, usually to provide specific skills or resources, ultimately they are not essential. If those NGOs collapsed tomorrow, the movements would remain intact. Their members are connected to each other through participation in the movement, not through NGO trainings.

This is in stark contrast to movements in the US, where many initiatives that came out of past revolutionary movements are now non-profits of various sizes. Many of these organizations are creative and beautiful but bear the mark of both the state and outside funders. That is, they are still clearly non-profits: professionalized and run with a corporate top-down structure, they spend much of their time chasing after foundation money instead of truly creating spaces for organic community participation and collective power. But if self-determination is key, then we need to approach collective organizing in ways that build collective power that is truly autonomous from the state. For SIIS, this has meant returning to our origins as an all-volunteer grassroots organization. We aren't sure if it will work or if SIIS will be around in five years. But we do know that had we continued along the path we'd been traveling, we probably wouldn't have survived. In the end, we think the risk is worth trying to find what does actually work, especially if it might help other activists think differently about what kind of movement building is and is not possible within the non-profit system.

reality check

Recently, a survey of 20 youth organizing groups from around the country indicated that 71 percent of folks felt somewhat secure with their funding base. This comes as a bit of a surprise, considering that 92 percent of folks named foundations as their number-one source of income. This translates into a huge problem for the movement. Ultimately the foundation world will never offer longevity or financial stability to social justice movements or organizations. A recent report by the Greenlining Institute indicates that only 4 percent of grants from independent foundations and 3 percent of grants from community foundations are given to minority-led organizations.[1] Nevertheless, we're caught in the funding chase, endlessly running around, trying to connect with fellow activists and organizers (also caught) who haven't had the time or space to reflect or build politically with others in their community—while we are worried about completing five interim reports that are due the following day.

There is another important piece to the sustainability puzzle. Philanthropy was not created to sustain any organization, movement, or idea that would undermine the goals of that small percentage of the population that controls most of society's wealth in the first place. Most foundations are endowed by the profits made from exploiting people of color through capitalism, and anything that threatens the interests of capitalism or the current social order is ultimately targeted by the foundation industry for obliteration.

Foundations, overall, exert far too much control over organizations and, ultimately, over our movements for social change. Luring social justice activists with the promise of financial support, they also determine the rules of engagement. Meanwhile, we become trapped in the cycle of apply, apply, apply—threatened with proposal rejections or even promised money being pulled if folks do not understand or agree with our vision. This is not to say that foundations cannot be a part of our strategy in raising money for social justice in this country. But for many activists it seems like it is the main one, and for some, the only one.

So what are some concrete ways that the youth movement could become self-sustaining? Most crucially, we must help each other diversify funding. There is a clear need for support in building solid personal donor bases, throwing benefit parties for organizations, and offering one-on-one technical assistance with whatever area of focus folks identify as their priority. When organizations do go a different route, supporting their various grassroots fundraising initiatives continues to be incredibly important—whether it's selling tickets, doing committed outreach for fundraisers, or, better yet, how about buying and selling some of our products?

Overdependence on foundation fundraising weakens our imagination and poses one of the greatest threats to our movements. In reality, we should not expect much from something that was never created with our benefit or interests in mind. That is why there are activists and organizers out there every day, trying to get folks to envision what this world could look like. Every day, as chunks of this huge mockery fall to the ground, another activist begins to ask hard questions about the non-profit model. There is more heart than there is cash for this work. Fighting for freedom has always been, and remains, unpaid work, regardless of what any capitalist system might tell us. Once we connect with that spirit, we will soon realize that we have always been powerful, bestowed with an untouchable wealth—something to which no amount of tracking or monitoring of our organizations will ever give them access.

the morning after

Things move more slowly now. We've lost a few people in the transition. Our lives are crazy. We have more outside requests than we can handle, and there is the pressure to succeed after such a drastic step. On the other hand, young women have stepped up and their leadership is more prominent than ever in SIIS. Although all of the attention is hard at times, it's empowering to know that people are open to finding alternative ways to build and work in this movement.

We are not saying that all foundations are bad. In fact there are program officers who have been like partners to us and who continue to support us however they can. But once the chase for foundation dollars begins to seriously affect your direction and your energy, something has to change.

We are also not of the belief that 501(c)(3)s are bad. In our view, the problem is a lack of balance. The proliferation of 501(c)(3)s in the US has meant a decline in grassroots movement organizations, and this has definitely blunted our edge and willingness to challenge the system. We need more grassroots movements that can partner and collaborate with non-profit organizations to forward their visions.

As a non-profit organization that started as a grassroots organization, we constantly reflect on our work to ensure it remains aligned with our values. At SIIS, we are willing to stumble as we experiment with different ways to create alternatives and model our vision. We want to make sure that we are whole and connected—and doing the *real* work, the work that saves our lives and empowers our communities. With every sista that is a little more powerful and thinks differently because of their encounter with SIIS, we are successful.

We don't know what the most effective strategy is for revolution, but we do know that many different approaches are necessary. It isn't about toppling capitalism in one swift blow, but creating cracks in the system. We are a small crack inspired by larger ones like the MST in Brasil, the EZLN in Chiapas, Autonomista movements in Argentina, the Ogoni people in Nigeria, and many others all over the world. As we build these alternative and autonomous movements we will crack the whole thing. We know capitalism will crack!

notes

The coauthors are all Sista II Sista Collective members. If you want to support SIIS, please contact us at info@sistaiisista.org or visit our website at www.sistaiisista.org.
1 Orson Aguilar et al., *Fairness in Philanthropy, Part I: Foundation Giving to Minority-Led Nonprofits* (Berkeley, CA: The Greenlining Institute, 2005), http://www.greenlining.org/uploads/pdfs/1202122910-Foundation1.pdf.

▸▸about the contributors

Christine E. Ahn is a policy analyst who writes and speaks frequently on human rights, poverty, globalization, militarism, philanthropy, and North Korea. After obtaining her master's degree in public policy from Georgetown University, she was awarded a Ford Foundation New Voices Fellowship to work with Food First. Ahn's work has appeared in the *New York Times, Boston Globe, San Francisco Chronicle, International Herald Tribune*, and other media. She coauthored (with Pablo Eisenberg) the groundbreaking Georgetown University report "Trustee Fees: Use and Abuse." She also edited *Shafted: Free Trade and America's Working Poor* (Food First Books, 2003). Formerly the director of the Peace and International Solidarity Program at the Women of Color Resource Center, in Oakland, California, Ahn now serves on the board of the National Committee for Responsive Philanthropy.

Robert L. Allen is an adjunct professor of African American studies and ethnic studies at the University of California, Berkeley. Allen received his Ph.D. in sociology from the University of California, San Francisco. He is an editor of *The Black Scholar* and the author/editor of several books, including *Black Awakening in Capitalist America; Reluctant Reformers: The Impact of Racism on Social Movements in the US; The Port Chicago Mutiny;* and *Brotherman: The Odyssey of Black Men in America*. Allen has been the recipient of many honors including a Guggenheim Fellowship and an American Book Award (shared with coeditor Herb Boyd for *Brotherman*).

Alisa Bierria is a Communities Against Rape and Abuse (CARA) member and co-founder as well as national steering collective member of INCITE! Women of Color Against Violence.

Communities Against Rape and Abuse (CARA) is a vibrant grassroots project in Seattle, Washington, that promotes a broad agenda for liberation and social justice while prioritizing antirape work as the center of our organizing. Learn more about us at www.cara-seattle.org.

William Cordery is the development director at Project South and works on innovative funding strategies with the National Fundraising Working Group for the US Social Forum.

Stephanie Guilloud is the program director at Project South, coordinates the membership program, and facilitates the Building a Movement workshops with grassroots organizations.

Among the largest feminist organizations in the world, **INCITE! Women of Color Against Violence** is a national activist organization of radical feminists of color advancing a movement to end violence against women of color and their communities through direct action, critical dialogue, and grassroots organizing.

Adjoa Florência Jones de Almeida has been a member of several collectives/ cooperatives, including Nûcleo de Educadoras Afro-Brasileiras (Nucleus of Afro-Brasilian Women Educators), Third World Within, INCITE! Women of Color Against Violence, Soko Underground Network, Rethinking Solidarity Collective, Community Birthing Project, and Little Maroons Day Care Cooperative. Since 1996 she has also helped to build Sista II Sista, a young women's organization dedicated to the personal and political development of young women of color in Bushwick, Brooklyn.

Tiffany Lethabo King is a founding member of Resistahs in Wilmington, Delaware. Resistahs codevelops community education projects and anti-oppression workshops with Black women throughout the city. Resistahs has collaborated with Black women in high schools, community colleges, ABE classes, and tenants groups to create community education projects such as "Breakin' Down bell: The Works of bell hooks" and "Violent Intersections."

Paul Kivel (www.paulkivel.com) is a violence prevention and social justice educator, activist, and writer. He develops and conducts interactive and participatory talks and workshops on such topics as alternatives to violence, racism, class and economics, family violence and sexual assault, and parenting. He is the author of several books, including *Men's Work*, *Boys Will Be Men*, *Uprooting Racism: How White People Can Work for Racial Justice* (winner of the 1996 Gustavus Myers Award), and most recently *You Call This a Democracy? Who Benefits, Who Pays, and Who Really Decides*. He is also coauthor of several widely used curricula, including *Making the Peace*, *Young Men's Work*, and *Helping Teens Stop Violence*.

Ewuare Osayande (www.osayande.org) is a poet, political activist, and author of several books including *Black Anti-Ballistic Missives: Resisting War/Resisting Racism* and *Blood Luxury* (Africa World Press). He is cofounder and director of POWER (People Organized Working to Eradicate Racism). Additionally, he is the creator of ONUS: Redefining Black Manhood, a resisting sexism workshop initiative. Osayande works and resides in the Philadelphia region.

Amara H. Pérez is the executive director of Sisters in Action for Power.

Project South: Institute for the Elimination of Poverty and Genocide (www.projectsouth.org) is a leadership development organization based in the US South creating spaces for movement building. We work with communities pushed forward by the struggle to strengthen leadership and provide popular political and economic education for personal and social transformation. We build relationships with organizations and networks across the US and Global South to inform our local work and to engage in bottom-up movement building for social and economic justice.

Dylan Rodríguez is a Pinoy scholar/activist who is currently employed as an associate professor in the department of ethnic studies at the University of California, Riverside. He has worked with and alongside a variety of progressive and radical organizations and movements, including the founding collective of Critical Resistance: Beyond the Prison Industrial Complex. His first book, *Forced Passages: Imprisoned Radical Intellectuals and the US Prison Regime,* was published in 2006 by the University of Minnesota Press.

Paula X. Rojas is a Chilean community organizer based in Brooklyn, New York. After ten years as part of the Sista II Sista collective, she is now on its advisory board as well as a member of Pachamama, a childcare cooperative and organizing collective for Black and Latina women in Brooklyn. She also works with INCITE!, Community Birthing Project and Sisterfire-NYC, but mostly she's the mother of Xue-li Dolores. After almost a decade of working within the NPIC she has transitioned back to being a volunteer organizer. She currently makes a living as a self-defense teacher, translator, and doula.

Ana Clarissa Rojas Durazo was raised in Mexicali, Baja California; México; and Calexico, California. She has organized in raza and communities of color for over 15 years, working to resist violence and injustices committed against and within these communities. She served on the founding national planning committee of INCITE! and the INCITE! anthology committee. Rojas is completing her doctorate degree at University of California, San Francisco, and has taught in

Raza studies and ethnic studies at San Francisco State University since 1999. Her poetry has appeared in literary journals in the United States and México.

Sista II Sista is a Brooklyn-based collective of working-class young and adult Black and Latina women building together to model a society based on liberation and love. Our organization is dedicated to working with young women to develop personal, spiritual, and collective power. We are committed to fighting for justice and creating alternatives to the systems we live in by making social, cultural, and political changes.

Based in Portland, Oregon, **Sisters in Action for Power** is dedicated to developing the leadership, critical analysis, and community organizing skills of low-income girls and girls of color ages 10 through 18. Over the past ten years the organization has received national recognition for its innovative leadership-development model and youth-led organizing victories.

Andrea Smith (Cherokee) is a co-founder of INCITE! Women of Color Against Violence. She is a coeditor of *Color of Violence: The INCITE! Anthology* (2006) and author of *Conquest: Sexual Violence and American Indian Genocide* (2005).

Born and raised in New York City, **Eric Tang** served as a community organizer in the refugee neighborhoods of the Bronx from 1995–2005. He currently works as a researcher, writer, and trainer for community organizing groups across the country. The author of several articles on race, immigration, and social justice movements, Tang received his doctorate from New York University's American studies program. He teaches in the Workers Education Program of the City University of New York.

Madonna Thunder Hawk is an elder member of the Oohenumpa band, Lakota Nation, and lives on the Cheyenne River Sioux reservation in central South Dakota. A veteran of the Red Power Movement of the 1960s and 70s, she continues to be an activist for Native American rights, environmental protection advocacy, and local community empowerment organizing. She is a very proud grandmother!

Ruth Wilson Gilmore is chair of the American Studies and Ethnicity Program at the University of Southern California. Her book *Golden Gulag: Prisons, Crisis, Surplus, and Opposition in Globalizing California* (UC Press) explores the state's prison expansion since 1980. Author of many articles on race, gender, space, political economy, and justice, Gilmore has provided expert witness testimony on behalf of rural communities seeking alternatives to prisons for local economic development. In 2002–2003 she was a Senior Justice Fellow at the Open Society Institute. She has received numerous honors and awards, including the Ralph Santiago Abascal Award for Environmental and Economic Justice. In 2006 she was named the first winner of the James Blaut Memorial Award. Active with many social justice groups, Gilmore is a founding member of both the California Prison Moratorium Project and Critical Resistance. She is also former president of the Central California Environmental Justice Network.

▶▶index

▶▶about south end press

SOUTH END PRESS IS AN INDEPENDENT, COLLECTIVELY RUN POLIT-ical book publisher with more than 250 titles in print. Since our founding in 1977, we have met the needs of readers who are exploring, or are already committed to, the politics of radical social change. We publish books that encourage critical thinking and constructive action on the key political, cultural, social, economic, and ecological issues shaping life in the United States and in the world. We provide a forum for a wide variety of democratic social movements and an alternative to the products of corporate publishing.

From its inception, South End has organized itself as an egalitarian collective with decision-making arranged to share as equally as possible the rewards and stresses of running the business. Each collective member is responsible for core editorial and administrative tasks, and all collective members earn the same base salary. South End also has made a practice of inverting the pervasive racial and gender hierarchies in traditional publishing houses; our collective has been majority women since the mid-1980s, and at least 50 percent people of color since the mid-1990s.

Our author list—which includes bell hooks, Andrea Smith, Arundhati Roy, Noam Chomsky, Mumia Abu-Jamal, Winona LaDuke, Manning Marable, Cherríe Moraga, and Howard Zinn—reflects South End's commitment to publish on myriad issues from diverse perspectives.

To expand access to information and critical analysis, South End Press has been instrumental to the start of two on-going political media projects—Speak Out and *Z Magazine*. We have worked closely with a number of important media and research institutions including Alternative Radio, Political Research Associates, and the Committee on Women, Population and the Environment.

Read. Write. Revolt.

▶▶community supported publishing

CELEBRATE THE BOUNTY OF THE BOOK HARVEST! COMMUNITY Supported Agriculture (CSA) is helping to make independent, healthy farming sustainable. Now there is *CSP: Community Supported Publishing!* By joining the South End Press CSP, you ensure a steady crop of books guaranteed to change your world. As a member you receive one of the new varieties or a choice heirloom selection free each month and a 10 percent discount on everything else. (That is: every new book we publish as well as selected backlist titles and best-sellers.) Subscriptions start at $20/month.

For more details, please email us at southend@southendpress.org or visit our website at www.southendpress.org.

▶▶related titles from south end press

Color of Violence: The INCITE! Anthology
edited by INCITE! Women of Color Against Violence

Conquest: Sexual Violence and American Indian Genocide
by Andrea Smith

*Disposable Domestics: Immigrant Women Workers
in the Global Economy*
by Grace Chang

Earth Democracy: Justice, Sustainability, and Peace
by Vandana Shiva

Feminist Theory: From Margin to Center
by bell hooks

Keeping Up With the Dow Joneses: Debt, Prison, Workfare
by Vijay Prashad

How Nonviolence Protects the State
by Peter Gelderloos

Ideas for Action: Relevant Theory for Radical Change
by Cynthia Kaufman

An Ordinary Person's Guide to Empire
by Arundhati Roy

Outsiders Within: Writing on Transracial Adoption
edited by Jane Jeong Trenka, Julia Chinyere Oparah,
and Sun Yung Shin